STRENGTHENING HUMAN RIGHTS PROTECTIONS IN GENEVA, ISRAEL, THE WEST BANK AND BEYOND

This collection of essays is written by some of the world's leading experts in international human rights law, and corresponds to the main junctures in the professional life of Professor David Kretzmer, a leading human rights academic and practitioner.

The different essays focus on contemporary human rights protection challenges. They address conceptual problems, legal doctrinal responses to changing realities, the weakness of monitoring institutions, and practical difficulties in applying international human rights law. Collectively, the essays offer a rich picture of the current potential shortcomings of international human rights law in addressing complex problems of law, politics and ethics.

JOSEPH E. DAVID is Professor of Law at Sapir Academic College, Israel, and a Visiting Professor at the Program in Judaic Studies and Law School at Yale University. He is the co-editor of the *Journal of Law and Religion* (Cambridge University Press). His research focuses on Jewish studies, law and religion, legal history and comparative jurisprudence, on which he has published extensively.

YAËL RONEN is Professor of Law at the Academic Center for Science and Law, Hod Hasharon, Israel, and Research Fellow at the Minerva Center for Human Rights at the Hebrew University of Jerusalem. She is the Academic Editor of the *Israel Law Review* (Cambridge University Press). She specialises in issues of territorial status including occupation, international human rights law and international criminal law.

YUVAL SHANY is Professor of Law at the Hebrew University of Jerusalem, Vice-President for Research at the Israel Democracy Institute and a former member and Chair of the UN Human Rights Committee in Geneva. He specialises in international human rights law, international humanitarian law and international courts and tribunals.

J.H.H. WEILER is University Professor at NYU Law School and Senior Fellow at the Center for European Studies at Harvard. Until recently he served as President of the European University Institute, Florence. He is the Co-Editor-in-Chief of the *European Journal of International Law* (*EJIL*) and the *International Journal of Constitutional Law* (*ICON*).

STRENGTHENING HUMAN RIGHTS PROTECTIONS IN GENEVA, ISRAEL, THE WEST BANK AND BEYOND

Edited by

JOSEPH E. DAVID

Sapir Academic College

YAËL RONEN

Academic Center for Science and Law, Hod Hasharon

YUVAL SHANY

Hebrew University of Jerusalem

J.H.H. WEILER

New York University

CAMBRIDGE
UNIVERSITY PRESS

CAMBRIDGE
UNIVERSITY PRESS

University Printing House, Cambridge CB2 8BS, United Kingdom

One Liberty Plaza, 20th Floor, New York, NY 10006, USA

477 Williamstown Road, Port Melbourne, VIC 3207, Australia

314–321, 3rd Floor, Plot 3, Splendor Forum, Jasola District Centre, New Delhi – 110025, India

103 Penang Road, #05–06/07, Visioncrest Commercial, Singapore 238467

Cambridge University Press is part of the University of Cambridge.

It furthers the University's mission by disseminating knowledge in the pursuit of education, learning and research at the highest international levels of excellence.

www.cambridge.org
Information on this title: www.cambridge.org/9781108833127
DOI: 10.1017/9781108973069

First published 2021

A catalogue record for this publication is available from the British Library.

Library of Congress Cataloging-in-Publication Data
Names: David, Joseph E. (Writer on law), editor. | Ronen, Yaël, 1968– editor. | Shany, Yuval, editor. | Weiler, J.H.H. 1951– editor.
Title: Strengthening human rights protections in Geneva, Israel, the West Bank and beyond / edited by Joseph E. David (Sapir Academic College), Yaël Ronen (Academic Center for Science and Law, Hod Hasharon), Yuval Shany (Hebrew University of Jerusalem), J.H.H. Weiler (New York University).
Description: Cambridge, United Kingdom ; New York, NY : Cambridge University Press, 2021. | Includes bibliographical references and index.
Identifiers: LCCN 2020055527 (print) | LCCN 2020055528 (ebook) | ISBN 9781108833127 (hardback) | ISBN 9781108973069 (epub)
Subjects: LCSH: International law and human rights. | Human rights. | Human rights–Israel. | Human rights–Palestine.
Classification: LCC KZ1266 .S77 2021 (print) | LCC KZ1266 (ebook) | DDC 341.4/8–dc23
LC record available at https://lccn.loc.gov/2020055527
LC ebook record available at https://lccn.loc.gov/2020055528

ISBN 978-1-108-83312-7 Hardback

CONTENTS

CONTRIBUTORS

EYAL BENVENISTI is Whewell Professor of International Law at the University of Cambridge, Director of the Lauterpacht Centre for International Law, and C. C. Ng Fellow of Jesus College, Cambridge; Visiting Professor at the Hebrew University of Jerusalem; and Global Professor of Law at New York University.

JOSEPH E. DAVID is Professor of Law at Sapir Academic College, Israel, and Visiting Professor at the Program in Judaic Studies and Law School at Yale University.

RUTH HALPERIN-KADDARI is Professor of Law and Founding Academic Director of the Rackman Center for the Advancement of Women at Bar-Ilan University, Israel, and former member and Vice-Chair of the UN CEDAW Committee in Geneva.

ECKART KLEIN is Professor of Law (Emeritus) and Founding Director of the Human Rights Centre at the University of Potsdam and a former member of the UN Human Rights Committee.

MORDECHAI KREMNITZER is Senior Fellow at the Israel Democracy Institute; Professor Emeritus and former Dean of the Faculty of Law at the Hebrew University of Jerusalem, and President of the Israeli Press Council. He served as chair on several government committees, including the Committee to Examine the Use of Force by the Police and the Committee on Civic Education in Israel. He led the 2019 reform of Israel's Homicide Offenses Law. His areas of expertise include criminal law, public law, military law, and human rights.

PNINA LAHAV is Professor of Law and Law Alumni Scholar, Emerita, and member of the at the Elie Wiesel Center for Jewish Studies, Boston University.

FIONNUALA NÍ AOLÁIN is Regents Professor at the University of Minnesota Law School and Professor of Law at Queen's University, Belfast, Northern Ireland.

GIANLUIGI PALOMBELLA is Professor of Applied Legal Theory, and Director of the PhD program in Law and of the Center for Research on Interlegality at the Sant'Anna School of Advanced Studies in Pisa.

YAËL RONEN is Professor of Law at the Academic Center for Science and Law, Hod Hasharon, Israel, and Research Fellow at the Minerva Center for Human Rights at the Hebrew University of Jerusalem.

ANJA SEIBERT-FOHR is the Hengstberger Professor of Public Law, International Law and Human Rights at the University of Heidelberg, and a judge of the European Court of Human Rights.

YUVAL SHANY is Professor of Law at the Hebrew University of Jerusalem, Vice-President for Research at the Israel Democracy Institute and a former member and Chair of the UN Human Rights Committee in Geneva.

GILA STOPLER is Associate Professor and Dean of the Law School at the College of Law and Business, Israel, and Editor-in-Chief of *Law and Ethics of Human Rights*.

Introduction

JOSEPH E. DAVID

> Human rights are, literally, the rights we have simply because we are human. They are equal rights . . . They are inalienable rights: one . . . cannot lose one's human rights, no matter how horribly one behaves nor how barbarously one is treated. Human rights are also universal rights, held by every human being, everywhere.[1]
>
> Universal human rights have a context-transcending appeal . . .[2]

1 Historical Context and Human Rights

Contemporary philosophers remind us that the conceptual bases of human rights law, human rights movements and human rights discourse are not sufficiently grounded, tend to overlook the distinction between values and rights and engage inadequately with the practice of human rights.[3] Other commentators criticise human rights on practical bases, casting doubts on whether human rights treaties have indeed improved the well-being of people, or even resulted in respect for the rights in those treaties. Such criticisms emphasise the relative weakness of humanitarian impulse that underlay human rights law and the unsystematic strategic and instrumental bases for human rights.[4]

Yet, from a functional perspective the idea of human rights asserts itself as a timeless and self-evident truth, rather than a set of subjective beliefs about human beings. It presents itself as a supra-contextual concept, not a contingent outcome of historical experience and cultural circumstance. Yet to ignore the contextual cultural values and political

[1] Jack Donnelly, 'Human Rights' in John S. Dryzek, Bonnie Honig and Anne Phillips (eds), *The Oxford Handbook of Political Theory* (Oxford University Press 2006) 601.

[2] Seyla Benhabib, *The Rights of Others: Aliens, Residents, and Citizens* (Cambridge University Press 2004) 19.

[3] Joseph Raz, 'Human Rights Without Foundations' in Samantha Besson and John Tasioulas (eds), *The Philosophy of International Law* (Oxford University Press 2010).

[4] Eric A. Posner, *The Twilight of Human Rights Law* (Oxford University Press 2014).

settings in which the idea of human rights emerged and ascended would be something between naïveté and denial. Human rights talk is thus entrapped in ambivalence between rejection of contingency and acknowledgment of historicity. The insistence that human rights rest on fundamental, ahistorical truths is crucial to the argument that the validity of human rights precedes and transcends human actions and decisions. At the same time, the acceptance of human rights in political theory and law is depicted and celebrated as an historical human achievement – a result of heroic battles for recognition of the inherent value of human beings.

Historical context is a central focus of contemporary scholarship on human rights, motivated by the presumption that historical investigation is inseparable from normative and conceptual comprehension of human rights and their implementation. Historical inquiry into the background of the relevant legislation and discourse is crucial to understanding the nature and meaning of these rights: are they the product of centuries-long political struggles for human equality and liberty, or just a political and legal reaction to the exceptionally cruel human evils and humanitarian catastrophes of the World Wars?

The historical framing of human rights serves to characterise different conceptions of human rights and those conceptions' intellectual origins, justifications, goals and achievements. Cultural commentators and historians of ideas disagree about the genesis of the idea of human rights – a controversy that is very much a function of how those rights are defined and claimed. Some view the idea of human rights as the manifestation of the continuous development of the 'universal ethic', which is traceable to ancient times.[5] Others emphasise modern movements – especially the Enlightenment[6] and the Reformation[7] – as engendering the modern formulation of human rights. A common narrative highlights political movements and events of the eighteenth century, notably the American War of Independence and the French Revolution,[8] alongside the secularisation of 'natural rights', as the crucial moments that gave rise to the modern status of human rights. By contrast, there are those who argue that the conception of international human rights that is embedded in

[5] Micheline Ishay, *The History of Human Rights: From Ancient Times to the Globalization Era* (University of California Press 2004).

[6] James Griffin, *On Human Rights* (Oxford University Press 2008).

[7] John Witte, *The Reformation of Rights: Law, Religion and Human Rights in Early Modern Calvinism* (Cambridge University Press 2010).

[8] Lynn Hunt, *Inventing Human Rights: A History* (W. W. Norton 2007); Leo Strauss, *Natural Right and History* (University of Chicago Press 2008).

the post-World War Two era's globalist perspective and is epitomised by the 1948 Universal Declaration of Human Rights and the international politics of the 1970s[9] significantly differs from the earlier conception of the rights of 'man' and of the citizen that developed in the eighteenth century.[10]

This debate highlights how indispensable history is to legal analysis and ethical discussion of human rights. Conceptions of human rights, their justifications and how they are implemented depend on these narratives. Nowadays more than ever before, advocacy of human rights on the basis of conventions and legislation alone seems weak and insufficient.

A corollary to the historical dimension of human rights is the fact that they brandish a progressive vision and global agenda. The progressiveness of human rights is associated with the redemptive ethos shared by the major modern political and philosophical movements that inspired the modern human rights discourse. Thus, human rights are not only presumptive moral truths, but also part of a broader modern project of looking past traditional perceptions of human beings that are informed by status and group identity, and focusing instead of the inherent features shared by all humans. The placement of the human rights project within a progressive historical scheme is strongly reflected by the generally accepted classification of first-generation rights (civil liberties and political rights and freedoms), second-generation rights (economic, social and cultural rights) and third-generation rights (collective rights).[11]

2 New Challenges to Human Rights Protections

The historical framing of human rights also forms the backdrop for claims about the decline of human rights protections. The very possibility of talking about the 'end of human rights'[12] or the 'post human rights

[9] Samuel Moyn, *Human Rights and the Uses of History* (Verso 2014).

[10] Mary Ann Glendon, 'Knowing the Universal Declaration of Human Rights' (1999) 73 Notre Dame Law Review 1153.

[11] The classification of human rights in terms of generations was introduced by Karel Vašák, 'Human Rights: A Thirty-Year Struggle – The Sustained Efforts to Give Force of Law to the Universal Declaration of Human Rights' (1977) 30(11) UNESCO Courier 29. A more recent proposal seeks to add a fourth generation of human rights, viz., those associated with information technology.

[12] David Luban, 'The War on Terrorism and the End of Human Rights' (2002) 22(3) *Philosophy and Public Policy Quarterly* 9.

era'[13] goes hand-in-hand with human rights' historicisation. This is another reason for not ignoring the historical aspects of the idea of human rights. The identification of a point in the middle or end of the 2010s when 'the age of human rights' began to decline discloses internal tensions and disagreements about human rights. It illuminates fissures where human rights were conceived as solid, and above all indicates historical changes in the array of challenges to human rights.

An historical framing of the human rights project helps us better grasp its insurgent agenda, the ideas behind that agenda, the trends that drive its successes and failures. The historical aspect of international human rights enhances our sensitivity to the challenges to this venture and helps human rights activists develop strategies to face them. Furthermore, certain contemporary phenomena raise questions about the completeness of the idea of human rights, on the theoretical and practical levels. Whether these phenomena are causes, symptoms or consequences of the decline of human rights is not always clear. However, they expose the insufficiency, as a functional matter, of the idea of human rights and the need for its updated articulation. They also demonstrate the limitations of human rights as a mobilising social force, given other concerns of the human condition such as identity, the craving for responsibility, duty and power, rather than 'rights'.

2.1 Human Rights and (De)Globalisation

Despite attempts to portray human rights as an uncontested supra-political project, globalism and the decline of the primacy of state sovereignty underlie the entire venture; so mutually dependent are universal human rights and globalism, that it is doubtful whether the former can be implemented without the latter. At the same time, universal human rights and globalism increasingly prove themselves incompatible with the Westphalian model of international relations. One way or another, any resistance to globalism is often perceived as resistance, whether intended or incidental, also to global values, including universal human rights.

Resurgent nationalism and populism, alongside the emergence of authoritarian regimes, pose another challenge to the universal human rights project in our time. Likewise, massive migrations boost nationalist

[13] Ingrid Wuerth, 'International Law in the Post-Human Rights Era' (2017) 96 Texas Law Review 279.

sentiment, hatred and identity politics in which the us–them dichotomy prevails over egalitarian views of humans and their rights. The fact that the world's superpowers (the United States, Russia and China) do not act as guarantors of international human rights is yet another reason for the erosion of the protection of those rights on the global scene.

2.2 Emergencies and Violation of Human Rights

Since ancient times, the idea that necessity prevails over law (*necessitas legem non habet*) has been an accepted part of legal systems and legal orders. Medieval jurists, striving to preserve the integrity of the law, rearticulated the idea in terms of exemption from the law, rather than its suspension or annulment. In modern times, Carl Schmitt used the concept of emergency to revitalise the idea that necessity marks the limits of the law, so that emergency circumstances are both the foundation of the law and the point of departure from it.[14] Following Hobbes, Schmitt argued for a conceptual dependency between emergency and sovereignty, so that the sovereign is revealed and reaffirmed in emergencies. A key question here is whether the definition of emergency should, or can, be defined by the law. Moreover, emergency as an expression of necessity is a vague concept to begin with, potentially encompassing security threats, ecological disasters, financial crises, medical calamities and more, and the distinction between intrinsic, unavoidable, logical necessity and the instrumental necessity of a means to achieve an end is far from clear-cut, in theory or in practice.

Without delving deeply into theories of emergency, it is no profound observation that from the second half of the twentieth century to these very days, emergencies have been used as convenient mechanisms for justifying human rights violations. Ironically, one can analogise the Dworkinian idea of rights as trumps against utilitarian goals[15] with a conception of emergency declarations as trumps against human rights, but with definite potential for abuse.[16]

[14] Carl Schmitt, 'Definition of Sovereignty' in *Political Theology: Four Chapters on the Concept of Sovereignty* (University of Chicago Press 2005).

[15] Ronald Dworkin, 'Rights as Trumps' in Aileen Kavanagh and John Oberdiek (eds), *Arguing about Law* (Routledge 2013) 335.

[16] Nomi Claire Lazar, *States of Emergency in Liberal Democracies* (Cambridge University Press 2009).

2.3 *The Ease of Violating Human Rights*

Information and accelerated technological development continually introduce new challenges to attempts to advance human right norms and the values that underlay them. The ability to monitor through technological means the location of individuals, as well as their movement, behaviour, activities and preferences, confers unprecedented power on organisations that collect and control such information. The use of big data further empowers them to profile individuals, manipulate them, and interfere in their choices and preferences. Processed data can also be used to create market trends and to obstruct democratic processes. As we can bear witness, the use and the abuse of these means are not limited to times of declared emergency, but increasingly constitute part of the new normal, serving political and commercial interests alike.

In this new technological environment, violations of personal autonomy and the right to privacy have become almost trivial. As a result, the traditional mechanisms for protecting these rights have become outdated, requiring new and far more sophisticated regulatory policies and mechanisms.

* * * * *

Since ancient times, equal protection and justice have been perceived as better protected by written legislation than by entrusting human beings as gatekeepers in order to uphold them.[17] Unfortunately, history has also taught us that the entrenchment in statutes of the rule of law cannot guarantee the protection of human rights. Even when constitutionalised, legal norms protecting individual rights and interests may prove a dead letter, an ineffective law on the books. Certainly in the absence of a sense of justice and a commitment to opt for effective implementation, legislating human rights is insufficient to advance the cause of humanity aspired by those holding any specific conception of human rights.

David Kretzmer is, in the eyes of his colleagues and his students, a model for the individual who guards the gates of human rights while critically evaluating the justice of advancing them in specific normative

[17] 'Nothing does more harm to the state than a tyrant; when he rules, equal application of law comes to an end . . . and so perishes justice. But when the laws are written down, rich and poor alike have equal justice, and it is open to the weaker to use the same language to the prosperous when he is reviled by him, and the weaker prevails over the stronger if he has justice on his side.' Euripides (*c*.480–*c*.406 BCE), *The Suppliants*, lines 429–40.

and institutional configurations. His academic studies, teachings and public activism embody the spirit of human rights law. His character and personality bear witness to the living law of human rights – the compulsory complement to the written law of human rights. David's career and activities, in pursuit of deep ideas about the potential value of human rights, to which this collection of articles is dedicated, are an expression of devotion, determination and uncompromising commitment to human rights as a way to improve the human condition. David, his ideas and his work are an ongoing source of guidance and inspiration to each and every one of the contributors to this volume.

3 The Articles

The articles in this collection address principal themes with which David Kretzmer has engaged in his scholarly and advocacy work, and institutions in which he has served. They represent key contemporary challenges for the human rights movement generally, and for human rights activists in Israel/Palestine in particular. They deal with normative and institutional gaps in the existing system of international human rights protection, discuss key institutional challenges and conceptual shortcomings that invite reconsideration, and propose ways to strengthen protections afforded to individuals under human rights law.

The first cluster of chapters deals with the adjustment of human rights law to new geopolitical, technological and sociological developments. It opens with a conceptual piece by Eckart Klein (Professor of Law at the University of Potsdam and former member of the UN Human Rights Committee), which discusses the use and misuse of limits and restrictions under human rights law. The balancing of rights and interests, which is at the heart of contemporary human rights law, introduces flexibility into the law, but also threatens to dilute its contents. Klein argues that distinguishing between limits (scope of the right) and restrictions (exceptional circumstances that would lead to disapplication) plays an important role in the system of human rights protection. Anja Seibert-Fohr (former member of the UN Human Rights Committee and a judge at the European Court of Human Rights) explores the specific challenge presented by mass surveillance technology to the right to privacy under international law. Seibert-Fohr discusses the manner in which the Human Rights Committee has addressed this new challenge, and proposes that its approach may assist in adjusting old rights to new technology. The third chapter in this cluster, by Gianluigi Palombella

(Professor of Legal Theory of the Scuola Sant'Anna in Pisa), deals with the right to access to justice. Palombella points out that its absence in the transnational context constitutes in effect a violation of the Arendtian right to have rights. The final chapter in this cluster, by Ruth Halperin-Kaddari (Professor of Family Law and former Vice-Chair of the Committee on the Elimination of Discrimination against Women), explores the standard-setting role of human rights treaty bodies (including criticism of this role). It focuses on the contribution of CEDAW to the development of a new branch of human rights law, international family law.

The second cluster of chapters deals with some human rights challenges arising in situations of belligerent occupation. Significantly, these challenges also beleaguer international human rights law more broadly. Eyal Benvenisti (Director of the Lauterpacht Centre in Cambridge and Professor of International Law at the Hebrew University) explores the potential international responsibility for international organisations that control territory as part of international administration. General questions of accountability gaps loom large in this regard. Yaël Ronen (Professor of International Law at the Academic Center for Science and Law, Hod Hasharon, and Research Fellow at the Minerva Center for Human Rights at the Hebrew University of Jerusalem) also examines the role of non-state actors in situations of occupation. Ronen discusses the responsibility for violations of international law, and specifically human rights standards, of businesses associated with civilian settlements in occupied territory, using the Israeli settlements in the West Bank as a case study. The third chapter in this cluster, by Fionnuala Ní Aoláin (Professor of International Law and the UN Special Rapporteur for Human Rights and Counter-Terrorism), examines the application of the law of occupation in the Israeli-Palestinian context from a gender perspective. Ní Aoláin underscores the potential contribution of feminist theory to modernise the rather antiquated laws of occupation, and by extension, human rights law. The final chapter in this cluster is by Yuval Shany (Professor of International Law at the Hebrew University of Jerusalem and member of the UN Human Rights Committee). Shany discusses the unique contribution of Judge Meir Shamgar, former President of the Israeli Supreme Court, to the development of jurisprudence on the interpretation and application of the laws of belligerent occupation to the territories occupied by Israel in 1967.

The third and final cluster of chapters deals with the tension between human rights law and alternative ideologies. The first chapter in this cluster, by Gila Stopler (Professor of Constitutional Law and Editor of

Law and Ethics of Human Rights), addresses the theory of political liberalism and its application to a semi-liberal society such as Israel, in which considerable parts of society do not subscribe to tolerance and other basic liberal values. The second chapter by Joseph E. David (Professor of Law at Sapir Academic College and Yale University), explores the constructed tension between law and identity from a jurisprudential perspective. David argues that identity rights claims are not only disjointed from dignitarian constitutionalism and the rule of law, but conceptually problematic and thus deserve reconsiderations.

The annexure cluster focuses on David Kretzmer's work and professional career. It includes an interview conducted with Kretzmer by Pnina Lahav (Professor of Law at Boston University) that portrays Kretzmer's main achievements and contribution to legal scholarship and practice. Mordechai Kremnitzer (Professor Emeritus at the Hebrew University of Jerusalem, co-founder with Kretzmer of the Minerva Center for Human Rights at the Hebrew University) surveys Kretzmer's contribution to the promotion of human rights in Israel and internationally. This collection concludes with a list of David Kretzmer's principal scholarly works.

1

On Limits and Restrictions of Human Rights

A Systematic Attempt

ECKART KLEIN

The chapter tries to establish a systematic framework which allows us to structure the examination of human rights cases by indicating the necessary legal components and putting these elements in their proper place and in context to each other. Substantive human rights guarantees as, e.g., enshrined in the International Covenant on Civil and Political Rights or the European Convention, cannot be fully understood without taking account of their explicit or implicit limitations; only together do they form the basis for their successful invocation. Therefore the legal limits of and restrictions to human rights as well as the limitations drawn to the use of restrictions, as particularly the principle of proportionality, are discussed. Primacy of freedom, (strict) interpretation, balancing of rights, absolute rights, margin of appreciation and derogation from human rights are other issues that have to be dealt with in the given context.

human rights, explicit and implicit limits and restrictions, limitation on restrictions, proportionality principle, abuse of rights, primacy of freedom, International Covenant on Civil and Political Rights, European Human Rights Convention

1 Introduction

It might not be very popular to discuss the limits and restrictions of human rights. In times of swift expansion of human rights[1] and increasing numbers of human rights activists on the one hand and of growing pressure on human rights on the other, limits and restrictions drawn to human rights could be seen as a malicious attempt to undermine the effect of the rights. Still it is necessary to do so, and for different reasons.

[1] Cf Alison Brysk and Michael Stohl (eds), *Expanding Human Rights: Twenty-first Century Norms and Governance* (Edward Elgar 2017).

To distinguish between rights and exceptions is important from the perspective of the right holders and duty bearers alike. Only by taking account of the limits of and possible restrictions on the rights they wish to invoke are the right holders able to recognise the full possibilities of their entitlements. More often than not, they just rely on the designation of the right or even its abridged form as 'freedom of expression' or 'freedom of assembly', ignoring a more specified terminology limiting or restricting the freedom. Naïvely they sometimes infer from (only) morally founded rights the existence of legal rights, not realising that the declaration of a moral value alone is not sufficient to bring a legal title into existence and that only such a title is apt to create legal and enforceable obligations.[2] Further, they often neglect that even the establishment of a legal right by a treaty will favour them only if the state concerned has ratified it and not declared a respective (admissible) reservation. Attitudes like this are often encouraged by NGOs, probably with the intention to improve the human rights situation on the ground. But in most cases this will unavoidably lead to disappointment and loss of trust.[3] Thus, not ignoring the exceptions, but rather viewing the whole picture, will better serve the right holders.

States as the main duty bearers are probably less tempted to neglect the limits and restrictions of the rights, because they open the way for the state to carry out its task of balancing the colliding rights of different right holders and protecting the common good. It cannot be denied that this competence can be, and actually is, very often heavily abused, as is nearly daily illustrated by the news from every part of the world.[4] The fact that states are the usual violators of human rights but at the same time the guarantors of these rights creates a permanent dilemma, which international monitoring mechanisms try to solve or at least to mitigate. Likewise, being aware of the limits and restrictions is a necessary requirement for all the states parties, enabling them to claim from

[2] Eckart Klein, 'The Importance and Challenges of Values-Based Legal Orders' (2015) 10 Intercultural Human Rights Law Review 1, 8.

[3] Yasuaki Onuma, *International Law in a Transcivilizational World* (Cambridge University Press 2017) 417, warning against the 'deification' and 'overevaluation' of NGOs.

[4] Human rights are presently for different reasons under strong pressure. The argument, however, that the state-centred construction of human rights is the main reason for its defects may be theoretically correct, but does not help as long as no other institution than the states can shoulder the task of human rights protection on the ground; for a more pessimistic vision, see Conor Gearty, 'Is the Human Rights Era Drawing to a Close?'(2017) 22 European Human Rights Law Review 425ff.

the other parties the faithful fulfilment of their obligations and to react to violations.[5]

It is therefore fair to say that the limits and restrictions together with the substantive guarantee constitute the right (and corresponding obligation). In fact, liberty and freedom without borders cannot exist in any community, irrespective of the underlying anthropology.[6] This is quite evident in systems where the individuals are primarily seen as members of their community, but it is also true for societies where a much more individualistic approach to human rights is predominant, because real freedom can only be understood as freedom equally shared with other individuals. Thus freedom can only exist and evolve in a framework of legal order,[7] but the respective order decisively influences the factual degree of respect and protection of human rights. Of course, this merely underscores the general necessity of limits and restrictions of human rights. An example from the German Basic Law (BL) might be instructive[8]. Different from other national and all the international human rights catalogues, Article 2, paragraph 1, BL provides for the right of any individual to choose between what are, in principle, unlimited ways of conduct ('Every person shall have the right to free development of his personality . . .'), but this comprehensive statement is immediately in the same provision followed up by the limitation 'insofar as he does not violate the rights of others or offend against the constitutional order or the moral law'. Thus, the broader the rights are framed, the more generally the limitations will be drawn.

[5] The different construction of reciprocity in human rights treaties compared with other treaties does not exclude a formal reciprocity among the parties to such treaties; see Michel Virally, 'Le principe de réprocité dans le droit international contemporain' (1967-III) 122 Recueil des Cours 1, 26: 'chaque partie à un tel traité a le droit d'exiger des autres parties qu'elles respectent ses engagements, pris envers lui-même'. This is affirmed by International Covenant on Civil and Political Rights (entered into force 23 March 1976) 999 UNTS 171 (ICCPR) art 41 and explained by HRC, General Comment No. 31: The Nature of General Legal Obligation Imposed on States Parties to the Covenant, 29 March 2004, UN Doc. CCPR/C/21/Rev. 1/Add. 13, para. 2.

[6] Mark Goodale, 'Anthropology and the Grounds of Human Rights' in Dinah Shelton (ed), *The Oxford Handbook of International Human Rights Law* (Oxford University Press 2017) 144ff.

[7] Friedhelm Hase, 'Freiheit ohne Grenzen?' in Otto Depenheuer et al. (eds), *Staat im Wort: Festschrift für Josef Isensee* (CF Müller 2007) 549, 558. In this sense also Aharon Barak, 'Proportionality and Principled Balancing' (2010) 4 Law & Ethics of Human Rights 2, 6: 'the constitutional right and its limitations are flip sides of the same constitutional concept'.

[8] Basic Law for the Federal Republic of Germany, 1949.

Certainly, the limits of human rights should not be explained only by general considerations. A closer look at the constitutive elements of the rights is necessary. They consist of different factors which circumscribe the scope of a right in a personal (right holders, duty bearers), substantive (protected value) and temporal manner as well as through admissible modes of protection. Together they define the material requirements that must be met in order to apply the right, and to effectively (not necessarily successfully) claim it. Beyond these limiting requirements the underlying value is not protected, at least not by the human right norm itself. The constitutive requirements are founding the right but limiting it by the same token. I shall use for them the term 'limits'. An international human right does not legally (though perhaps morally) exist outside the limits drawn. It has to be seen whether only explicit or also implicit or inherent limits can be found.

'Restrictions', on the other hand, are normative additions which open the way for the state to intrude in or interfere with the right in order to pursue appropriate goals as far as the added rules permit. Logically, restrictions only come into play if the scope of a right has been curtailed or is about to be curtailed. Then, it must be examined whether the intrusion can be justified. The requirements allowing for an encroachment on the rights, among them particularly the need to have a legal basis, must be strictly defined and respected. The principle of freedom, recognised on the international level by the ratification of human rights treaties and the existence of relevant customary law or general principles, has reversed the relationship between individual rights and restricting laws as it had existed in times of unlimited state sovereignty.[9] Unlike resort to the right, any restriction has today to be explained and justified.

In the following parts of this contribution I shall try to systematise what can be said on limits and restrictions of international human rights and, because of the limited space, to lay down only some very preliminary foundations on which then a general system or doctrine may be built, that would most certainly deserve to be further extended and refined elsewhere. The materials on which my studies are based are mainly taken from the International Covenant on Civil and Political Rights (ICCPR)[10] and the relevant work of the UN Human Rights Committee (HRC or

[9] Detlef Merten, 'Grundrechtlicher Schutzbereich' in Detlef Merten and Hans-Jürgen Papier (eds), *Handbuch der Grundrechte in Deutschland und Europa Vol III* (CF Müller 2009) 3, 38–40.

[10] ICCPR (n 5).

Committee) where David Kretzmer, to whom this chapter is dedicated in admiration and friendship, and I had the privilege to serve as members from 1995 to 2002. Partly also the European Convention on Human Rights and Fundamental Freedoms (ECHR) and the jurisprudence of the European Court of Human Rights (ECtHR) will be taken into account.[11] Of the Committee's work, its review of the state reports[12] and its views and decisions on individual communications will be used, particularly as they have been summarised and assessed by its General Comments (GC).[13] The aim of this chapter is, to quote Pierre d'Argent, 'to put some order within the abundance of rules'.[14] This may help to create a more profound understanding of the functioning of human rights *legal* norms and facilitate their application.[15]

2 Limits

The limits define the scope of a human right; they determine whose spheres of liberty and freedom are protected and to what extent. It is useful to distinguish between express and inherent or immanent limits.

2.1 Express Limits

(a) Usually the protected value is determined by a generally well-known term that still, for the purpose of application, has to be interpreted. In

[11] European Convention for the Protection of Human Rights and Fundamental Freedoms (entered into force 3 September 1953) 213 UNTS 222 (ECHR). It is true that a much broader approach would be necessary to exhaust the total treasure of human rights law. But this work, based on a holistic perception of human rights law, cannot be performed by the present chapter. On the other hand one should not neglect the traps which are set on the way to such a broad research; see Eckart Klein, 'Some Remarks on the Interpretation of Human Rights Treaties between Text and "Unlimited Dynamic Interpretation"' in Óscar Parra Vera, Romina I. Sijniensky and Gabriela Pacheco Arias (eds), *La lucha por los derechos humanos hoy: Estudios en homenaje a Cecilia Medina Quiroga* (Tyrant Lo Blanch 2017).

[12] David Kretzmer and Eckart Klein, 'The Human Rights Committee: Monitoring States Parties Reports' (2015) 45 *Israel Yearbook on Human Rights* 133.

[13] Eckart Klein and David Kretzmer, 'The UN Human Rights Committee: The General Comments – The Evolution of an Autonomous Monitoring Instrument' (2015) 58 German Yearbook of International Law 189. Up to now (June 2019), 36 GCs have been adopted.

[14] Pierre d'Argent, 'Teachers of International Law' in Jean d'Aspremont et al. (eds), *International Law as a Profession* (Cambridge University Press 2017) 423.

[15] Very deliberately, because of the advanced development of the dogmatics of fundamental rights in Germany, German literature and jurisprudence have largely been used as a source of inspiration for the present attempt at a coherent systematisation.

some cases the text itself will give hints about the correct understanding. The protected value 'life' (Article 6, paragraph 1, ICCPR) has obtained specifications with regard to the admissibility of the death penalty (Article 6, paragraphs 2, 4–6); 'liberty of movement' has been typically described by the freedom to choose one's residence, to leave any country and the right to enter one's own country (Article 12, paragraphs 1, 2 and 4, ICCPR). In many other cases the interpreter has to find his own path. This, for example, is true with the interpretation of the term 'family' (Article 23, paragraph 1, ICCPR), whose understanding, according to the Committee, may vary 'from State to State, and even from region to region'[16], or 'religion' and 'belief' (Article 18, paragraph 1, ICCPR), which 'are to be broadly construed', not only encompassing traditional forms but also newly established kinds of religion and belief,[17] or 'discrimination', prohibited by Article 26 ICCPR, but which does not include every differentiation of treatment 'if the criteria for such differentiation are reasonable and objective and if the aim is to achieve a purpose which is legitimate under the Covenant'.[18]

(b) It is not always easy to find out whether a certain clause should be understood as a limit or restriction. An example presents itself in Article 9, paragraph 1, ICCPR, guaranteeing everybody's right not to 'be subjected to arbitrary arrest or detention'. Should one argue that a non-arbitrary arrest *a limine* does not interfere with 'the right to liberty and security of person', or would it be more reasonable to deal with the possibility of a non-arbitrary arrest as a restriction to the right to liberty?[19] Taking the first alternative would mean that an affirmative assessment of a governmental act as not being arbitrary

[16] HRC, General Comment No. 19: Protection of the Family, 27 July 1990, UN Doc HRI/GEN/1/Rev.6 (2003) 149, para. 2. See also HRC, General Comment No. 16: Article 17 (The Right to Respect of Privacy, Family, Home and Correspondence and protection of Honour and Reputation), 8 April 1988, UN Doc HRI/GEN/1/Rev.9 (Vol. 1), para 5, where the HRC argues that the term family should receive a 'broad interpretation'. The state should not have an 'exclusive jurisdiction over the definition' as Sarah Joseph and Melissa Castan, *The International Covenant on Civil and Political Rights: Cases, Materials, and Commentary* (3rd edn, Oxford University Press 2013) 668, have rightly put it.

[17] HRC, General Comment No. 22: Article 18 (Freedom of Thought, Conscience and Religion), 30 July 1993, CCPR/C/21/Rev.1/Add. 4, para. 2.

[18] HRC, General Comment No. 18 (Non-discrimination), 10 November 1989, HRI/GEN/1/Rev.9, para 13.

[19] A parallel issue arises concerning ICCPR (n 5) art 12, para 4.

would directly lead to the result that the right has not even been interfered with. However, if we take the second alternative, the intrusion in the right would be evident, and the question of a violation of the right would depend on whether all the requirements of a restriction are given, for example, respect for the proportionality principle.[20] Thus from the perspective of the individual the qualification as a restriction (compared with a limit) has clear advantages. As has been mentioned before, all interferences with rights must be scrupulously justified.

The characterisation of Article 20 ICCPR is more difficult. According to this rule, any propaganda for war, and furthermore any advocacy of national, racial or religious hatred that constitutes incitement to discrimination, hostility or violence, shall be prohibited by law. If a state applying this provision curtails freedom of the press, expression or the right to receive and impart information (Article 19 ICCPR), could this be featured as making use of a limit to those rights or rather a restriction that had to meet all the requirements provided for in Article 19, paragraph 3, ICCPR? Should one argue that propaganda for war, racial hatred and so on are so fundamentally bad that those attitudes should be excluded from the protective scope of freedom of expression from the outset? One may be reminded in this context of the US reservation against Article 20 ICCPR, pointing to its incompatibility with the First Amendment to the US Constitution dealing with the freedom of speech.[21] In fact, the HRC in its GC No. 34 (2011) on freedoms of opinion and expression clearly stated that the 'acts that are addressed in Article 20 are all subject to restriction pursuant to Article 19, paragraph 3. As such, a limitation that is justified on the basis of Article 20 must also comply with Article 19, paragraph 3.'[22]

No less complicated to answer is the question of whether Article 21 ICCPR covers according to its text only the 'right of *peaceful* assembly',[23]

[20] This seems to be also the opinion of General Comment No. 35: Article 9 (Liberty and Security of Person), 16 December 2014, UN Doc CCPR/C/GC/35, paras 11 and 12.

[21] For the text of the reservation see HRC, Reservations, Declarations, Notifications and Objections Relating to the International Covenant on Civil and Political Rights and the Optional Protocols Thereto, 24 August 1994, UN Doc CCPR/C/2/Rev.4, 40.

[22] HRC, General Comment No. 34: Article 19 (Freedoms of Opinion and Expression), 12 September 2011, UN Doc CCPR/C/GC/34, para 50.

[23] Emphasis by the author.

meaning that other forms of assembly are excluded from the protection of this provision (limit), or does the term 'peaceful' merely set out a legal basis for the state to interfere with the right, if it is not peacefully exercised? In view of the fundamental importance of peacefulness not only for the society as a whole but also for the enjoyment of human rights by individuals, one may well conclude that the freedom is confined or limited to peaceful assemblies. Violent assemblies are therefore not protected.[24] This view is shared by the ECtHR with regard to Article 11, paragraph 1, ECHR.[25]

Lastly, Article 5 ICCPR creates intricate problems. According to its paragraph 1, no 'State, group or person has any right to engage in any activity or perform any act aimed at the destruction of any of the rights and freedoms' recognised in the Covenant.[26] The provision is equally directed against the possible abuse of rights by persons or groups and abuses by states. In our context here, it is interesting to consider whether abuse of rights by individuals in the sense of Article 5 deprives them of the right concerned, thus excluding any abusive use of the right from the scope of protection, or just opens the door for the state to restrict the exercise of the relevant right on the basis of the respective rules providing for restriction. The few relevant cases decided by the HRC and the ECtHR suggest that these bodies favour the *a limine* exclusion of rights' abuses from the guarantee.[27] However, in order to submit the abuse argument, which is valid for all Covenant rights, to a stricter examination it would be preferable to say that this provision should be treated as a restriction.[28]

[24] See also Joseph and Castan (n 16) 646. Now also HRC, GC No. 37 (Right of peaceful assembly), UN Doc. CCPR/C/GC/37, 17 September 2020, para 9.

[25] ECtHR, *Stankov and others* v. *Bulgaria*, App no 29221/95, 2 October 2001, para 77.

[26] For parallel rules see Universal Declaration of Human Rights (UDHR), A/Res 217A (III), UN Doc A/810 (1948) art 30; ECHR (n 11) art 17; American Convention on Human Rights, Pact of San José (entered into force 18 July 1978) 1144 UNTS 123 art 29(a); Charter of Fundamental Rights of the European Union (EU Charter) 2007 O.J. C 326, art 54.

[27] HRC, *M A* v. *Italy*, Communication No 117/1981, 10 April 1984, UN Doc CCPR/C/OP/2, 31; European Commission of Human Rights, *Glimmerveen and Hagenbeek* v. *Netherlands*, App Nos 8348/78, 8406/78, 11 October 1979, 18 DR, 187, 207 (1980); ECtHR, *Garaudy* V. *France*, App No 65831/01, 24 June 2003, RJD 2003-IX, 333, 396–7. The opinion of the HRC might have changed: it notes art 5 ICCPR in its GC No. 34 on Article 19 (n 22) para 21, while discussing restrictions. Still the meaning is not absolutely clear.

[28] Eckart Klein, 'Reflections on Article 5 of the International Covenant on Civil and Political Rights' in Nisuke Ando (ed), *Towards Implementing Universal Human Rights: Festschrift for the Twenty-Fifth Anniversary of the Human Rights Committee* (Martinus Nijhoff 2004) 136ff.

2.2 *Inherent Limits*

In the German literature, it is seriously discussed whether peacefulness, explicitly only mentioned in Article 8 BL as well as in Article 21 ICCPR, is a general requirement for the exercise of all human rights even if not distinctly articulated.[29] One may well argue that human rights, whatever they purport to protect, can unfold only under peaceful circumstances and therefore can be claimed only if used in a peaceful way, too. Another important argument in favour of this view is the principle of the monopoly of (physical) force held by the state being the historical requisite for the abolishment of feud and club-law, and thus laying the ground for the peaceful association of human beings.[30] I personally agree with this approach, although here again one could point to the fact that characterising the use of force as a possible reason to restrict the right would grant probably more intensive (judicial) review, which might become necessary if potential individual acts of self-defence have to be assessed. Actually, the issue is not easy to decide. I do not intend to discuss here whether and, if so, under what circumstances individuals may have a right to forceful resistance against state actions;[31] moral norms and positive law, for example on tyrannicide, will usually diverge on this point.

Quite similarly one will have to judge the case that the exercise of a human right is interfering with the human dignity of another person. Human dignity is not protected as a right of its own in the ICCPR or the ECHR, in contrast to Article 1 of the Charter of Fundamental Rights of the European Union (EU Charter)[32] and Article 1 BL, but it is acknowledged as a 'foundational value' as expressed by the preamble and Article 10, paragraph 1, and further inherently by articles 6, 7 and 8 ICCPR.[33] Human dignity therefore draws an immanent limit to the exercise of any

[29] Christian Hillgruber,'§200 Grundrechtlicher Schutzbereich, Grundrechtsausgestaltung und Grundrechtseingriff' in Josef Isensee and Paul Kirchhof (eds), *Handbuch des Staatsrechts der Bundesrepublik Deutschland Vol. IX* (3rd edn, CF Müller 2011) 995; Detlef Merten, '§60 Immanente Grenzen und verfassungsunmittelbare Schranken' in Detlef Merten and Hans-Jürgen Papier (eds), *Handbuch der Grundrechte in Deutschland und Europa Vol. III* (CF Müller 2009) 218.

[30] Eckart Klein, 'Staatliches Gewaltmonopol' in Otto Depenheuer and Christoph Grabenwarter (eds), *Verfassungstheorie* (Mohr Siebeck 2010) 638–41.

[31] For an example of a codified right to resistance, see BL (n 8) art 20, para 4.

[32] EU Charter (n 26).

[33] Arthur Chaskalson, 'Human Dignity as a Constitutional Value' in David Kretzmer and Eckart Klein (eds), *The Concept of Human Dignity in Human Rights Discourse* (Kluwer Law International 2002) 133, 135.

human right,[34] for example the freedom of religion; it is not just a restriction that might be justified under certain conditions.

Finally, human rights, as every right, can only be enjoyed within the bounds of possibility. If persons are in an area where internet cannot be made available, they cannot claim a right to impart or receive information through this medium. In this sense availability forms an immanent limit of the right. Of course, one has carefully to see whether the state has performed its duties to ensure the right in question. This is particularly important where economic, social and cultural rights are at stake, but can also be true for civil and political rights.[35] An example would be the argument of a state that an adequate number of prison cells is not available to detain all prisoners 'with respect for the inherent dignity of the human person' (Article 10, paragraph 1, ICCPR). Such incapacity, and even more certainly the unwillingness of the state to develop the required capacity, will generally not be sufficient to draw a limit to the scope of a human right.

3 Restrictions

3.1 General Remarks

Restrictions entitle the state to interfere with human rights to achieve generally acknowledged legal ends,[36] mainly to delimit the spheres of individual rights in order to avoid or solve collisions with rights of others and to protect and further the common welfare.[37] In many cases restrictions are expressly provided for in the human rights provisions themselves,

[34] This statement does not contradict the fact that human dignity may likewise serve as a source of expanding the scope of protection by redefining the protected value and supporting specific attendant obligations; see, e.g., HRC, General Comment No. 36 on Article 6 of the International Covenant on Civil and Political Rights, on the right to life, 30 October 2018, UN Doc CCPR/C/GC/36, para. 26.

[35] See ICCPR (n 5) art 2, para 1.

[36] These ends are usually called 'legitimate aims', but in fact they have to be 'legal aims', the term legal not only covering the aspect of domestic legality, but also the compliance with the requirements of the international obligations.

[37] The concrete forms of interference with human rights can have many modalities and will vary with the rights to be restricted; see art 12, HRC, General Comment No. 27: Article 12 (Freedom of Movement), 2 November 1999, UN Doc CCPR/C/21/Rev. 1/Add.9, para 17, and for art 19 (freedom of expression), see GC No. 34 (n 22) paras 30 and 31. In this context some issues have not yet found a definitive answer, among others the problem whether an intrusion in a right has actually happened or is merely a legally irrelevant inconvenience.

for example in Articles 12, paragraph 3; 18, paragraph 3; and 19, paragraph 3, ICCPR, thus underscoring the requirement to take all the aspects of the right into consideration. Other provisions protecting rights do not contain an explicit restriction clause, raising the question whether such rights may still be restricted on the basis of immanent restrictions, for example Articles 7, 8, 9 or 25 ICCPR. At any rate, according to the primacy of freedom, every restriction has to be reasoned and must fulfil the relevant legal premises; the restriction clauses should be interpreted in the light of the legal guarantee.[38] In this sense, GC No. 31(2004) on 'The Nature of the General Legal Obligation Imposed on States Parties to the Covenant' also holds that 'any restrictions on any of those rights must be permissible under the relevant provisions of the Covenant'.[39] Restriction clauses must be 'strictly interpreted', though in some cases, if public morals are a possible ground for restriction, a more cautious approach to interpretation is required.[40] If the legal conditions of a permissible intrusion in a right are not met, the State concerned has violated the right and breached its international commitments.

3.2 Legal Basis Requirement

Governmental actions restricting human rights must rest on a domestic legal basis; they must be 'provided by law' as Article 19, paragraph 3, ICCPR puts it.[41] Likewise, if Article 17, paragraph 1, ICCPR prohibits any 'unlawful interference' with privacy, family, etc., this 'means that no interference can take place except in cases envisaged by the law'.[42] This is a commonly recognised prerequisite for all rights' restrictions since the days of the French Declaration on Human Rights in 1789.[43] It is founded on democratic reasons: the law as expression of the will of the people, and on the rule of law: the need for a clear formulation of the law creates

38 GC No. 22 (n 17) para 8: 'In interpreting the scope of permissible limitation clauses, States parties should proceed from the need to protect the rights guaranteed under the Covenant . . .'.

39 GC No. 31 (n 5) para 6.

40 GC No. 22 (n 17) para 8. See also GC No. 34 (n 22), para 32.

41 GC No. 34 (n 22) para 22.

42 GC No. 16 (n 16) para 3.

43 See The French Declaration of the Rights of Man and Citizen, 26 August 1789, arts 4, 5 and 6.

the opportunity to know beforehand the limitations which the state may set to the enjoyment of the rights.[44] Thus '[t]he laws authorizing the applications of restrictions should use precise criteria and may not confer unfettered discretion on those charged with their execution.'[45]

While the notion 'law' in national legal orders, at least in this context, may be confined to written laws or statutes enacted by parliaments,[46] in international human rights treaties it usually has a broader meaning taking account of other traditions as, for example, common law.[47] Therefore, customary law and even judge-made law may also provide the necessary legal basis as far as they are general norms and perceptible for the individuals.[48] Usually a law providing for restrictions will contain specified prescriptions identifying its underlying reasons or purposes. Thus Article 18, paragraph 3, ICCPR mentions as reasons for an admissible restriction of the freedom to manifest one's religion the protection of 'public safety, order, health, or morals or the fundamental rights and freedoms of others'. The application of the law has then to respect these specifications.[49] Further, the law must comply not only with higher-ranking domestic law such as the constitution, but also 'with the provisions, aims and objectives of the Covenant'.[50]

[44] For the context of both ideas, see Christian Tomuschat, 'Democracy and the Rule of Law' in Dinah Shelton (ed), *The Oxford Handbook of International Human Rights Law* (Oxford University Press 2013) 469ff.

[45] GC No. 27 (n 37)) para 13; GC No. 34 (n 22) para 25.

[46] E.g., in Germany, Christian Hillgruber, '§201 Grundrechtsschranken' in Josef Isensee and Paul Kirchhof (eds), *Handbuch des Staatsrechts der Bundesrepublik Deutschland Vol IX* (3rd edn, CF Müller 2011) 1047.

[47] GC No. 34 (n 22) para 24 can hardly be understood as generally departing from this view, as it maintains: 'Since any restriction on freedom of expression constitutes a serious curtailment of human rights, it is not compatible with the Covenant for a restriction to be enshrined in traditional, religious or other such customary law.' But see also Dimitris Triantafyllou, 'The European Charter of Fundamental Rights and the "Rule of Law": Restricting Fundamental Rights by Reference' (2002) 39 Common Market Law Review 53, 60.

[48] See for the ECHR Jochen Abr Frowein and Wolfgang Peukert, *Europäische MenschenRechtsKonvention EMRK-Kommentar* (3rd edn, NP Engel Verlag 2009) 279; William A. Schabas, *The European Convention on Human Rights: A Commentary* (Oxford University Press 2015) 336. For art 52, para 1, EU Charter see Meinhard Hilf, '§164 Die Schranken der EU-Grundrechte' in Detlef Merten and Hans-Jürgen Papier (eds) *Handbuch der Grundrechte in Deutschland und Europa Vol VI/1* (CF Müller 2010) 1186.

[49] GC No. 34 (n 22) para 22; see also ECHR (n 11) art 18.

[50] GC No. 34 (n 22) para 26.

3.3 *Grounds for Restriction*

The most important reasons to restrict human rights are based on the protection of the rights of others and the public welfare.[51] Some restriction clauses contain specifications of these two main grounds, explaining in more detail the appropriate goals to be achieved.[52] In this sense Article 19, paragraph 3 lit. a, ICCPR qualifies the rights of others by adding the word 'reputation', while lit. b identifies relevant elements of the general welfare by relating to the 'protection of national security or of public order (*ordre public*), or of public health or morals'.[53] The same provision (Article 19, paragraph 3) also contains an interesting addition by stating that the exercise of the right to freedom of expression 'carries with it special duties and responsibilities'. Actually, this phrase does not itself establish a limitation; rather it purports to explain the need for the following restriction clauses ('therefore').[54] I think that this reference to duties and responsibilities, certainly appropriate in relation to the freedom of expression, would also fit other human rights provisions.[55]

'Rights' of others are rights having at least the same legal value as the right to be restricted. This includes primarily the Covenant rights themselves, but also other fundamental rights protected under international human rights law.[56] As international human rights law intends merely to guarantee a minimum protection,[57] more far-reaching fundamental rights in national law may also serve as a basis for restriction, if reliance on them does not contravene international human rights obligations. However, one has to consider that, in a horizontal perspective, the expansion of a right for one (freedom of expression) will usually curtail the right for the other (right to privacy, reputation). Restrictions based on

[51] See UDHR (n 26) art 29, para 2; Federal Constitution of Swiss Confederation (Systematische Rechtssammlung (SR) 101), 1999, art 36, para 2: 'Any limitation of a fundamental right must be justified by public interest, or serve for the protection of fundamental rights of other persons' (translated by Pierre A. Karrer).

[52] Barak (n 7) 6 nicely characterises the 'appropriate goals' as 'threshold requirement(s)'.

[53] See also the wording of ICCPR (n 5) art 14, para 1 cl 3.

[54] Cf the nearly identical text of ECHR (n 11) art 10, para 2.

[55] Apart from the reference in UDHR (n 26) art 29, para 1, only the African Charter on Human and Peoples' Rights enumerates general duties of individuals in arts 27–9: see African Charter on Human and Peoples' Rights (entered into force 21 October 1986) 21 ILM 58. An attempt of elder statesmen to make the UN General Assembly adopt a Universal Declaration on Human Responsibilities (1 September 1997) has failed. See www.interactioncouncil.org/sites/default/files/udhr.pdf.

[56] GC No. 34 (n 22) para 28.

[57] ICCPR (n 5) art 5, para 2; ECHR (n 11) art 53.

the rights of others explain themselves by the underlying recognition of the equal worth of every human person. Those restrictions do not concern the private use of a right (*forum internum*), but become relevant only if the manifestation of the right involves the social sphere (*forum externum*).[58] The term 'others' relates to other persons in their capacity as individuals or members of a community, for example of a religious or ethnic community. The HRC has adopted this definition in the context of Article 19 (freedom of expression), but it can well be generalised.[59]

'Public welfare' as a ground for restriction of human rights is reasoned by the more or less strong affiliation of any person to and dependence on a public community whose interests deserve protection as far as they serve the common good and by this the welfare of the individual, too. The quite common definitions of relevant aspects of public welfare may permit rather broad interpretations which might endanger the right as such. Therefore GC No. 34 (2011) on freedom of expression reminds the states parties that provisions relating to national security, such as treason or sedition laws, must not be used to silence critical journalists, environmental activists or human rights defenders. Similarly, contempt of court proceedings must not, on the basis of the maintenance of 'public order (*ordre public*)', 'restrict the legitimate exercise of defence rights'.[60] This reference already leads to the principle of proportionality, which will be discussed later.

The (potential) collision of rights between individuals or between rights of individuals and community interests will usually necessitate the balancing of the opposing normative values.[61] Only in a very few constellations will the result of the balancing process be predecided by the hierarchy of norms, because generally no such hierarchy between human rights norms exists.[62] The only exceptions are norms impeding

58 ICCPR (n 5) art 19 (freedom of expression) presents a clear example. Other rights develop their substance only in the social sphere, e.g. ibid, arts 21, 22 and 27.

59 GC No. 34 (n 22) para 28.

60 GC No. 34 (n 22) paras 30, 31.

61 Critically, Ronald Dworkin, *Taking Rights Seriously – New Impression with a Reply to Critics* (Duckworth 1977, 1994) 199, as far as the balancing of individual rights with public interests is concerned.

62 HRC, General Comment No. 24: Issues Relating to Reservations Made Upon Ratification or Accession to the Covenant or the Optional Protocol thereto, or in Relation to Declarations under Article 41 of the Covenant, 4 November 1994, UN Doc CCPR/C/21/Rev.1/Add.6, para 10; see on this, Eckart Klein, 'Establishing a Hierarchy of Human Rights: Ideal Solution or Fallacy?' (2008) 41 Israel Law Review 477, 480ff.

any restriction, thus granting absolute protection.[63] The most prominent example is the prohibition of torture (Article 7 ICCPR) being closely related to human dignity, the foundational value of human rights.[64] Apart from this specific situation, the balancing process is open and must be decided in each single case on the basis of the specific facts. In one case, the right to freedom of expression may prevail, in the next the reputation of another person or a national security aspect. The consequence that an increase of (quasi-)judicial power is directly connected with this process of balancing should not be ignored, but this result has to be accepted in view of the alternative that international monitoring of human rights obligations would lose its meaning.[65]

3.4 *Rights without Explicit Restrictions*

It is not always clear at first sight whether a human rights guarantee is provided with a restriction possibility. Sometimes, in contrast to articles where the term 'restriction' is explicitly mentioned (for example Articles 21 and 22 ICCPR), less clear wording is used, for example where it is said that '[i]t should not be the general rule that persons awaiting trial shall be detained in custody'[66] or that '[n]o one shall be arbitrarily deprived of the right to enter his own country.'[67] Those texts give some leeway to the state for restriction, but, on the other hand, the Committee has understood the concept of arbitrariness in a way that gives the chance to monitor the state's behaviour rather closely.[68]

63 Most of those norms will be *jus cogens* rules.

64 See also text referred to by n 33.

65 Actually the balancing power has been vividly discussed in the basic rights literature; see e.g. Barak (n 7) 2ff. One of the proposals made in Germany distinguishes between the human rights norm ('Normbereich') and the core of the right as the normatively protected part of the right ('Gewährleistungsgehalt'): if the latter is concerned, no balancing can be performed. This is not identical with the idea that restrictions must not interfere with human rights if they impair the essence of the right; for the whole discussion see e.g. Jochen von Bernstorff, 'Kerngehaltsschutz durch den UN-Menschenrechtsausschuss und den EGMR: Vom Wert kategorialer Argumentationsformen' in (2011) 50 Der Staat 165ff.

66 ICCPR (n 5) art 9, para 3 cl 2; GC No. 35 (n 20) para 38: 'the exception, rather than the rule'.

67 ICCPR (n 5) art 12, para 4; GC No. 27 (n 37) para 21.

68 GC No. 35 (n 20) para 12: 'The notion of "arbitrariness" is not to be equated with "against the law", but must be interpreted more broadly to include elements of inappropriateness, injustice, lack of predictability and due process of law, as well as elements of reasonableness, necessity and proportionality.' Further see GC No. 16 (n 16) para 4 and GC No. 27 (n 37) para 21.

However, some rights are guaranteed without expressly providing for the possibility of restriction. Examples are Articles 7, 8, 10, paragraph 1, Article 14, paragraph 1 cls 1 and 2, Articles 15, 16, 23, 24 and 27 ICCPR. In these cases, the question arises whether, despite the lack of explicit limitation clauses, the exercise of the rights may still be restricted. Here a distinction has to be made. Evidently, all those rights that cannot be restricted under any circumstances, the so-called 'absolute rights', must be excluded from the list. The existence of such rights is acknowledged in some national legal orders, such as the German Basic Law regarding human dignity (Article 1, para 1) and likewise in Article 1 of the EU Charter.[69] Also in international law some human rights norms have been identified as being 'absolute'. This is particularly true for the prohibition of torture,[70] but the HRC has also strictly excluded any restriction to Article 14, paragraph 1, ICCPR as far as the 'requirement of competence, independence and impartiality of a tribunal' is concerned,[71] as well as restrictions to Articles 10, paragraph 1 (respect for human dignity in detention),[72] 18 ('freedom from coercion to have or to adopt a religion or belief'),[73] and 19, paragraph 1 ('right to hold opinions').[74] All these findings can be explained by the very close connection of these rights with human dignity. For the same reason also, the prohibition of slavery and servitude (Article 8, paragraphs 1 and 2) and the 'right to recognition everywhere as a person before the law' (Article 16) must be treated as absolute rights, though the Committee has not expressly stated so.[75] If

[69] Hilf (n 48) 1182.

[70] HRC, General Comment No. 20: Article 7 (Prohibition of Torture, or Other Cruel, Inhuman, or Degrading Treatment or Punishment), 10 March 1992, UN Doc HRI/GEN/1/Rev.6 (2003) 151, para 3. See also ECtHR (Grand Chamber), *Gäfgen* v. *Germany*, App no 22978/05, 1 June 2010, para 87.

[71] HRC, General Comment No. 32: Article 14 (Right to Equality before Courts and Tribunals and to a Fair Trial), 23 August 2007, UN Doc CCPR/C/GC/32 (2007) para 19; see also para 6: 'Deviating from fundamental principles of fair trial, including the presumption of innocence, is prohibited at all times.'

[72] HRC, General Comment No. 21: Article 10 (Humane Treatment of Persons Deprived of their Liberty), 10 April 1992, UN Doc HRI/GEN/1/Rev.6 (2003), 153, para 4.

[73] GC No. 22 (n 17) para 8.

[74] GC No. 34 (n 22) para 9.

[75] From a moral point of view, other rights might become successful candidates for absolute rights, especially the right to life, but in our context only the legal aspect is decisive. In this respect one may point to the development regarding the prohibition of the death penalty according to Protocol No. 13 to the ECHR: the right not to be condemned to death or executed has become absolute for all the states having ratified the Protocol; see Protocol No. 13 to the Convention for the Protection of Human Rights and Fundamental Freedoms,

absolute rights are at stake, they will always prevail if they collide with rights of others and general interests.[76] Thus torture will not be legal, even if it is used to save the lives of others.[77] This view has been criticised by various authors, but is today firmly rooted in international law.[78]

For rights not provided with restriction clauses and not being absolute, the question still has to be answered whether immanent restrictions exist. In Marxism-Leninism for example all societal interests were defined as inherent restrictions; sometimes even a complete concordance between individual and public interests was proclaimed.[79] Very similarly, according to the ideology of National Socialism, the individual disappeared nearly totally behind membership in the people's community defined by blood and race ('Volksgemeinschaft'), and thus in practice public interests could always confine individual fundamental rights as far as those rights were still recognised at all.[80] In Germany, under the Basic Law and according to the jurisprudence of the Federal Constitutional Court, immanent restrictions are recognised to a certain degree. They must be based on colliding fundamental rights of others or other constitutional values.[81] For example, the Basic Law guarantees indoor peaceful assemblies without restrictions (Article 8). However, the police could prohibit an assembly if the house is not sufficiently equipped with means of fire prevention thus presenting threats to the life of the participants. As neither the ICCPR (Article 21) nor the European Convention (Article 11)

Concerning the Abolition of the Death Penalty in all Circumstances (entered into force 1 July 2003) ETS 187.

76 One should consider that an extension of the number of absolute rights is dangerous, because then the opportunity to balance contradicting rights or interests will be too much reduced. This might result in a narrower interpretation of the content of the right itself.

77 Cf. the *Gäfgen case* (n 70).

78 See Dominik Steiger, *Das völkerrechtliche Folterverbot und der 'Krieg gegen den Terror'* (Springer 2013) 240–5 with many references to jurisprudence and literature. For criticism of absolute rights in general see among others Onuma (n 3) 421; Rolf Gröschner and Oliver Lembcke (eds), *: Eine Auseinandersetzung mit dem Absolutheitsanspruch der Würde* (Mohr Siebeck 2009).

79 Georg Brunner, '§13 Grundrechtstheorie im Marxismus-Leninismus' in Detlef Merten and Hans-Jürgen Papier (eds), *Handbuch der Grundrechte in Deutschland und Europa Vol I* (CF Müller 2004) 552.

80 Ernst Rudolf Huber, *Verfassungsrecht des Großdeutschen Reiches* (2nd edn, Hanseatische Verlagsanstalt 1937/1939) 361: abolition of all freedom rights.

81 Hans-Jürgen Papier, '§64 Vorbehaltlos gewährleistete Grundrechte' in Detlef Merten and Hans-Jürgen Papier (eds), *Handbuch der Grundrechte in Deutschland und Europa Vol III* (CF Müller 2009) 372: need for balancing the rights or interests, if no absolute right is involved.

distinguishes between indoor and outdoor assemblies, the general restriction clause of the respective provision can be applied, and therefore no need to discuss immanent restrictions would arise. Actually, it is not easy to find an example of the resort to immanent restrictions. Perhaps one could point to Article 27 ICCPR enshrining the right of minorities 'to enjoy their own culture, to profess and practice their own religion'. Probably the practising of the culture or religion could be impeded if it would endanger the life or physical integrity of a person. Here the immanent restriction could and should be reasoned by the basic rights of others.[82] It is in this sense that the Committee in GC No. 23 (1994) has found 'that none of the rights protected under article 27 of the Covenant may be legitimately exercised in a manner or to an extent inconsistent with the other provisions of the Covenant'.[83] The statement points to the idea of the prohibition of abuse of rights expressed by Article 5, paragraph 1, ICCPR.[84] In its GC No. 25 (1996) on Article 25, the Committee underlines this aspect, too.[85] It is therefore sound to conclude that this provision generally opens the way for states parties to restrict the exercise of the right concerned in order to prevent rights of others being destructed.[86] States taking this path will of course have to respect all the applicable limitations on restrictions. The lack of explicit restrictions should at any rate admonish states to be particularly careful in invoking immanent restrictions.

The jurisprudence of the ECtHR has also affirmed the existence of implicit restrictions. Thus, it has held that the right of access to court[87] is not absolute, but may be restricted for legitimate reasons, for example to protect the immunity of states or international organisations; however,

[82] One could also directly refer to ICCPR (n 5) art 18, para 3, but this would possibly not take account of the speciality of art 27: practising 'in community with the others members'.

[83] HRC, General Comment No. 23: Article 27 (Right of Minorities), 8 April 1994, UN Doc CCPR/C/21/Rev.1/Add.5, para 8.

[84] See also UDHR (n 26) art 29, para 3 and EU Charter (n 26) art 54. For fundamental duties of individuals (cf. UDHR art 29, para 1) as a possible basis for restriction, see n 55.

[85] HRC, General Comment No. 25: Article 25 (Participation in Public Affairs and the Right to Vote – The Right to Participate in Public Affairs, Voting Rights and the Right of Equal Access to Public Service), 12 July 1996, UN Doc CCPR/C/21/Rev.1/Add.7, para 27.

[86] See nn 27 and 28. ICCPR (n 5) art 5 may also be applied to rights which can explicitly be restricted.

[87] ECHR (n 11) art 6, para 1, does not provide for (explicit) restrictions. For references see Eckart Klein, 'Wesensgehalt von Menschenrechten: Eine Studie zur Judikatur des Europäischen Gerichtshofs für Menschenrechte' in Klaus Dicke et al. (eds), *Weltinnenrecht: Liber amicorum Jost Delbrück* (Duncker & Humblot 2005) 387ff.

the restrictions must comply with the proportionality principle and not impair the essence of the right.[88]

3.5 *Limitations on Restrictions*

States restricting human rights have not only to abide by the prerequisites of the respective restriction clauses or of the immanent restrictions, but are likewise bound by the proportionality principle and the prohibition on impairing the very essence of the right at issue. No arbitrary restriction is permitted.[89] It should be underlined that the said limitations on restrictions[90] are only directed at the state and cannot be used as an instrument to define the limits of human rights and their exercise by individuals. Likewise, where human rights cannot be restricted because of their absolute character, the problem dealt with here does not arise.

3.5.1 Principle of Proportionality

The proportionality principle is probably the most effective legal instrument to control the restriction power of states.[91] Today it is acknowledged as a general principle of international human rights law.[92] It is founded on the principle of freedom itself as recognised by human rights and the general precedence of freedom over restriction. In the relation of human right and restriction, this leads to a norm-exception relationship, which must not be reversed.[93] In respect of the European Convention, the principle of proportionality evolved from terms such as 'necessary in a democratic society',[94] interpreted by the ECtHR in the sense of existing 'pressing social needs', which in their turn are now understood as an

[88] ECtHR, *Al-Adsani* v. *UK*, App no 35763/97, 21 November 2001, para 53; ECtHR, *Waite and Kennedy* v. *Germany*, App no 26083/94, 18 February 1999, para 59.

[89] See n 68.

[90] In German constitutional law, the terminology 'Schranken-Schranke' (restriction of restriction) is used for this phenomenon. The judicial practice usually examines the 'Schranken-Schranke' only after it has found that the restriction clause would apply. As far as I can see, no such clear separation of the several steps of legal examination is made in the international jurisprudence of human rights. Expressly on the practice of the EU Courts, see Hilf (n 48) 1158.

[91] The concept of proportionality should be confined to restrictions and not to the determination of the limits of a right: 'The clash between conflicting interests or values should not be expressed in the scope of the right', as was rightly said by Barak (n 7) 5.

[92] Yutaka Arai-Takahashi, 'Proportionality' in Dinah Shelton (ed), *The Oxford Handbook of International Human Rights Law* (Oxford University Press 2013) 448ff.

[93] GC No. 27 (n 37) para 13; GC No. 34 (n 22) para 21.

[94] See ECHR (n 11) arts 8–11.

emanation of the said principle.[95] The same idea has entered EU human rights law through the European Convention and the common constitutional traditions of the member states, both recognised in their turn as general principles of the EU law (Article 6, paragraph 3, TEU)[96], and finally through Article 52, paragraph 1, of the EU Charter.[97]

The principle of proportionality plays an important role in the work of the Committee, too.[98] The text of the Covenant clearly hints at the principle in Articles 21 (right of peaceful assembly) and 22 (freedom of association), using the same terminology as the European Convention in Articles 9, 10 and 11 ('necessary in a democratic society'). Article 19 ICCPR (freedom of expression) admits only those restrictions which 'are necessary' for the respect of others or for the protection of national security, public order, etc. In their concurring opinion in *Faurisson* v. *France,* three Committee members expressed their view that '[t]his requirement of necessity implies an element of proportionality. The scope of the restriction imposed on freedom of expression must be proportional to the value which the restriction serves to protect.'[99] Later on, the Committee step by step consolidated its perception of the proportionality principle as being valid for any restriction of any human right. In its GC No. 22 (1993) on Article 18 (freedom of conscience and religion) the Committee held that limitations 'must be directly related and proportionate to the specific need on which they are predicated'.[100] GC No. 27 (1999) on freedom of movement elaborated on this approach: 'Restrictive measures must conform to the principle of proportionality; they must be appropriate to achieve their protective function; they must be the least intrusive instrument amongst those which might achieve the desired result; and they must be proportionate to the interest to be protected.'[101] 'It continued:' 'The principle of proportionality has to be respected not only in the law that frames the restrictions, but also by the

95 John Joseph Cremona, 'The Proportionality Principle in the Jurisprudence of the European Court of Human Rights' in Ulrich Beyerlin et al. (eds), *Recht zwischen Umbruch und Bewahrung: Festschrift für Rudolf Bernhardt* (Springer 1995) 324ff.

96 Treaty on the European Union [2009] OJ C 290/1.

97 Hilf (n 48) 1188.

98 Arai-Takahashi (n 92) 459–61.

99 HRC, *Faurisson* v. *France*, Communication No. 550/1993, views of 8 November 1996, UN Doc CCPR/C/58/D/550/1993, individual opinion by Evatt, Kretzmer and Klein (co-signed) para 8.

100 GC No. 22 (n 17) para 8.

101 GC No. 27 (n 37) para 14.

administrative and judicial authorities applying the law.'[102] Some years later, GC No. 34 (2011) on freedom of expression completely underlined these findings.[103] Thus, any restrictive measure has to pass three steps of the proportionality test: it must be suitable for the purpose, the least restrictive measure of all the suitable alternatives and proportionate *stricto sensu*.[104]

A particular problem arises when the state does not take a restrictive measure but fails to protect or to ensure a right in question. As the Committee, in accordance with Article 2, paragraph 1, ICCPR has often found, the member states have not only to respect the rights by abstaining from unlawful interferences, but also has to ensure those rights by the enactment of the necessary laws, or by taking protective measures.[105] If the state in such situations neglects to act, or does not act sufficiently, the question, the question is not whether this conduct would be excessive but rather whether the omission fails to achieve the necessary degree of protection.[106] The issue is not about doing too much but about doing too little. The principle of proportionality can be applied also in this context with only a few variations and according to the three steps mentioned above: the measure to be taken must be generally suitable to protect, it must be able to grant at least the minimum of necessary protection, and the measure must be in adequate relation to the value to be protected and to the extent of the threat posed to it.[107]

[102] Ibid, para 15.

[103] GC No. 34 (n 22) paras 34 and 35.

[104] Clearly seen by Arai-Takahashi (n 92) 461; and Barak (n 7) 6ff. It is discussed, with different conclusions, how strongly the rather sophisticated German understanding of the proportionality principle has influenced its evolution on the international plane; see Jonas Christofferson, *Fair Balance: Proportionality, Subsidiarity and Primarity in the European Convention on Human Rights* (Martinus Nijhoff 2009) 34ff; Johannes Saurer, 'Die Globalisierung des Verhältnismäßigkeitsgrundsatzes' in (2012) 51 Der Staat 3ff; Evelyn Ellis (ed), *The Principle of Proportionality in the Laws of Europe* (Hart 1999).

[105] See GC No. 16 (n 16) paras 1, 9 and 11; GC No. 19 para 2; GC No. 23 (n 83) paras 6.1. and 9; GC No. 31 (n 5) para 8.

[106] GC No. 19 (n 16) paras 2 and 3.

[107] In the German literature and jurisprudence, this phenomenon is discussed under the topic of 'Untermaßverbot' in contrast to the 'Übermaßverbot' for cases where possibly excessive state acts have to be assessed. See generally Detlef Merten, '§68 Verhältnismäßigkeitsgrundsatz' in Detlef Merten and Hans-Jürgen Papier (eds) *Handbuch der Grundrechte in Deutschland und Europa Vol III* (CF Müller 2009) 564–5.

3.5.2 Essence of the Right

That 'restrictions must not impair the essence of the right' has been generally acknowledged in human rights law. In many national constitutions respective clauses exist, among them the German Basic Law (Article 19, paragraph 2) and the Swiss Constitution (Article 36, paragraph 4).[108] Article 52, paragraph 1, EU Charter also contains an express provision to this effect. The HRC bases the prohibition on undermining the essence of the right explicitly on Article 5, paragraph 1, ICCPR ('aimed at the destruction of any of the rights').[109] The European Convention includes a parallel provision, but the ECtHR does not use it for this purpose, at least not openly.[110] To determine the essence of a right is not an easy task. One could ask whether it is more important to secure the preservation of the right as an objective element of a democratic society or to focus on its subjective protective function. Both approaches should be taken into account, but the latter should be decisively preferred, since human rights have to serve primarily the individual.[111]

The Human Rights Committee applies the essence argument principally in all cases where human rights are restricted.[112] The only exception would be made, already for logical reasons, with regard to absolute rights, because they cannot be restricted at all.[113] The ECtHR, however, uses the said argument mostly in cases where the application of immanent restrictions is the issue at stake in order to control the application of restrictions not explicitly provided for. Where interferences with human rights by express restrictions have to be assessed, usually the Court is satisfied with applying the proportionality principle.[114]

[108] Federal Constitution of Swiss Confederation (n 51).

[109] GC No. 27 (n 37) para 13; GC No. 31 (n 5) para 6. Other formulations read: 'must not undermine the essence of the right', GC No. 32 (n 71) para 18; 'must not put in jeopardy the right itself', GC No. 34 (n 22) para 21; 'must not be destructive of the right', GC No. 35 (n 20) para 14.

[110] Von Bernstorff (n 65) 171. See also EU Charter (n 26) art 54.

[111] This opinion is widely shared in German basic rights literature; see Hillgruber (n 46) 1071; Juliane Kokott, '§22 Grundrechtliche Schranken und Schrankenschranken' in Detlef Merten and Hans-Jürgen Papier (eds), *Handbuch der Grundrechte für Deutschland und Europa Vol I* (CF Müller 2004) 890. The essence of a right is certainly always involved if human dignity is impaired.

[112] See GC No. 27 (n 37) para 13.

[113] See Entscheidungen des Bundesverfassungsgerichts (Decisions of the German Federal Constitutional Court) BVerfGE 119, 1, 30 and 34 (2007). In such a case a margin of appreciation cannot be granted; see von Bernstorff (n 65) 180.

[114] Klein (n 87) 391ff.

The proportionality principle and the essence argument are closely interrelated.[115] Regularly the question whether the measure at issue is proportionate will be treated first; if the measure is found to be excessive, the question of whether the essence of the right has been undermined has not to be answered any more. But one may well think of cases where the restriction, under the specific circumstances of the situation,[116] might be found to be proportionate, but still impairs the essence of the right.

3.5.3 Article 5, paragraphs 1 and 2, ICCPR

Article 5, paragraph 1, ICCPR is not only the basis for the state-addressed prohibition on impairing the essence of the right ('destruction'), but shall also prevent any restrictions aiming at the limitation of rights 'to a greater extent than is provided for in the present Covenant'. The clause reflects the proportionality principle to a certain extent, but goes further. If a state restricts a right by literally applying the relevant limitation clause, but does not intend to pursue the legitimate aims of that clause, rather using this power for other illegitimate aims, that would be an abuse of the restricting competence of the state, a 'détournement de pouvoir' in the French terminology, and would violate Article 5, paragraph 1.[117]

Likewise Article 5, paragraph 2, ICCPR has to be understood as a limitation to any restriction of a human right. The fact that the Covenant does not at all, or to a lesser extent, recognise a right than it is recognised or exists in a state party 'pursuant to law, conventions, regulations or custom' cannot serve as pretext for restricting this right. The Covenant, as all other international human rights instruments, purports to grant a minimum protection for human rights and must therefore not be used for reducing the level of domestic protection. In doing so the state would violate its Covenant commitments.[118]

[115] Generally hereto Manfred Stelzer, *Das Wesensgehaltsargument und der Grundsatz der Verhältnismäßigkeit* (Springer 1991).

[116] E.g., in cases of emergency.

[117] Thomas Buergenthal, 'To Respect and to Ensure: State Obligations and Permissible Derogations' in Louis Henkin (ed), *The International Bill of Rights: The Covenant on Civil and Political Rights* (Columbia University Press 1981) 87. See also GC No. 27 (n 37) para 13 and GC No. 34 (n 22) para 21.

[118] For the problems connected with art 5, para 2, ICCPR regarding the HRC's examination of the legal sources referred to by this rule, see Klein (n 28) 138ff.

3.6 *Margin of Appreciation*

The term *margin of appreciation* designates a method to grant national authorities a certain degree of deference regarding their decisions on compliance with their international obligations. It is a tool to define the relations between domestic and international supervising authorities.[119] Thus the doctrine cannot itself be viewed as a restriction of a right, but it may influence the practical use of restrictions possibly leading to less protection and should therefore be mentioned here.[120] Many different proposals have been made to clarify the underlying idea, ranging from state sovereignty and the principle of subsidiarity of international supervision, to states' authorities' better knowledge of the facts on the ground and a decision's effects thereon, up to a superior democratic legitimacy of national authorities.[121]

Although the margin of appreciation doctrine has been applied by many international authorities or at least traces of its application can be found,[122] the most prominent and in our context most important example is certainly the jurisprudence of the ECtHR.[123] The numerous

[119] Yuval Shany, 'Toward a General Margin of Appreciation Doctrine in International Law?' (2005) 16(5) European Journal of International Law 907, 909–10; Christian Tomuschat, *Human Rights: Between Idealism and Realism* (3rd edn, Oxford University Press 2014), 107.

[120] Recently this method was called an 'underenforcement doctrine' by Dimitrios Tsarapatsanis, 'The Margin of Appreciation as an Underenforcement Doctrine' in Petr Agha (ed), *Human Rights between Law and Politics: The Margin of Appreciation in Post-National Contexts* (Bloomsbury 2017) 71, or an 'Appeasement Approach in the European Court of Human Rights' by Helen Fenwick, quoted from Martin Kuijer, 'The Margin-of-Appreciation Doctrine and the Strengthening of the Principle of Subsidiarity in the Recent Reform Negotiations' (2016) 36 Human Rights Law Journal 339, 342 fn 28.

[121] For a good overview on the different reasons, see Shany (n 119) 909ff. More recently Andrew Legg, *The Margin of Appreciation in International Human Rights Law: Deference and Proportionality* (Oxford University Press 2012) 69ff, and Josephine Asche, *Die Margin of Appreciation: Entwurf einer Dogmatik monokausaler richterlicher Zurückhaltung für den europäischen Menschenrechtsschutz* (Springer 2018) 179ff; both authors are favouring the democratic legitimacy approach. Stijn Smet, 'When Human Rights Clash in "the Age of Subsidiarity": What Role for the Margin of Appreciation?' in Petr Agha (ed), *Human Rights between Law and Poltics: The Margin of Appreciation in Post-National Contexts* (Bloomsbury 2017) 58, 65ff prefers the subsidiarity approach.

[122] See Shany (n 119) 931ff, particularly for the case law of the ICJ.

[123] Eyal Benevisti, 'Margin of Appreciation, Consensus, and Universal Standards' (1999) 31 NYU Journal of International Law and Politics 843; Yutaka Arai-Takahashi, *The Margin of Appreciation Doctrine and the Principle of Proportionality in the Jurisprudence of the ECtHR* (Intersentia 2002).

applications of the doctrine there are well known and need not be rehearsed again in detail. It should be mentioned, however, the Court's practice does not disclose a clear system, reflecting. Usually, the Court grants a margin of appreciation if legal terms as 'public security', 'morals' or 'necessary in a democratic society' are at stake, providing requirements for restrictions. Also, when the Court has had to decide on cases of clashes between competing individual human rights, it has referred, not always coherently, to a 'wide' or a 'certain' margin of appreciation.[124] The Court also uses the doctrine in the context of examinations of emergency laws and declarations of derogation according to Article 15 ECHR.[125] However, where a 'European consensus' on the understanding of a notion has evolved[126] or the essence of the right would be impaired, the Court rejects the application of the doctrine.[127]

Despite the harsh criticism of the margin of appreciation doctrine levelled from many sides and for different reasons,[128] the Court has adhered to its jurisprudence. This attitude has been supported, even strengthened, by the states parties. By their Brighton Declaration of 2012[129] and adoption of Protocol No. 15 to the Convention in 2013 they have agreed that the states parties 'in accordance with the principle of

[124] See, e.g., ECtHR, *Eweida and others* v. *UK*, App nos 48420/10, 59842/10 and 36516/10, 15 January 2013, para 84; ECtHR, *Odièvre* v. *France*, App no 42326/98, 13 February 2002, paras 45–9.

[125] ECtHR, *A and others* v. *UK*, App no 3455/05, 19 February 2009, para 180; critically Oren Gross and Fionnuala Ní Aoláin, 'From Discretion to Scrutiny: Revisiting the Application of the Margin of Appreciation Doctrine in the Context of Article 15 of the European Convention on Human Rights' (2001) 23 Human Rights Law Quarterly 625.

[126] See ECtHR, *Bayev and others* v. *Russia*, App no 67667/09 and others, 20 June 2017, para 66: 'The Court would generally accept a wider margin of appreciation in the absence of consensus among member States where the subject matter may be linked to sensitive moral or ethical issues. In the instant case, however, the Court notes that there is a clear European consensus about the recognition of individuals' right to openly identify themselves as gay, lesbian or any other sexual minority, and to promote their own rights and freedoms.'

[127] ECtHR, *Muñoz Díaz* v. *Spain*, App no 49151/07, 8 December 2009, para 78.

[128] E.g., Lord Lester of Herne Hill, 'The European Convention on Human Rights in the New Architecture of Europe: General Report' in Council of Europe (ed), *Proceedings of the 8th International Colloquy on the European Convention on Human Rights* (Martinus Nijhoff 1995), 236–7: 'slippery and elusive as an eel'; Jeffry A. Brauch, 'The Margin of Appreciation and the Jurisprudence of the European Court of Human Rights: Threat to the Rule of Law'(2005) 11 Columbia Journal of European Law 113.

[129] Council of Europe (ed), *High Level Conference on the Future of the European Court of Human Rights – Brighton Declaration* (2012) paras 11–12, available at www.echr.coe.int/Documents/2012_Brighton_FinalDeclaration_ENG.pdf.

subsidiarity, have the primary responsibility to secure the rights and freedoms defined in this Convention and the Protocols thereto, and *in doing so* they enjoy a margin of appreciation, subject to the supervisory jurisdiction of the European Court of Human Rights'.[130] Thus the margin of appreciation has been directly derived from the principle of subsidiarity, while the final say remains with the Court.[131]

By contrast, the HRC has generally refused to acknowledge the doctrine. There is only one clear example to the contrary. In its Views on the communication of *Hertzberg and others* v. *Finland* (1982) the Committee held: 'It has to be noted ... that public morals differ widely. There is no universally applicable common standard. Consequently, in this respect, a certain margin of discretion must be accorded to the responsible national authorities.'[132] In a much later case it again indirectly referred to the doctrine,[133] but this is certainly not enough for a positive conclusion.[134] Additionally, at least in the context of Article 19 ICCPR, the Committee clearly underscores the view that 'the scope of this freedom is not to be assessed by reference to a "margin of appreciation"'.[135]

The negative attitude of the Committee is surprising, because the Committee is in a very parallel situation to the European Court. Both bodies have to supervise the compliance of the respective states parties with their international commitments, consisting of the obligation to respect, ensure and protect the various liberty and freedom rights. Many guarantees, their scopes and restrictions, are framed in a very similar, sometimes nearly identical manner. All the ideas discussed as a possible basis of the margin of appreciation doctrine, not least the subsidiarity argument, could be applicable here, too. It seems that the Committee, more than the Court, is afraid of the 'threat to the rule of law' that the doctrine brings along.[136] This is certainly a valid objection,

130 Protocol No. 15 (Amending the Convention for the Protection of Human Rights and Fundamental Freedoms, 2013 (not yet entered into force), CETS No 213, art 1, amends the Convention's Preamble to the effect quoted above. Emphasis by the author.

131 Kuijer (n 120) 341ff.

132 HRC, *Hertzberg and others* v. *Finland*, Communication No. 61/1979, 2 April 1982, UN Doc CCPR/15/D/61/1979, para 10.3.

133 HRC, *Borzov* v. *Estonia*, Communication No 1136/2002, 25 August 2004, UN Doc CCPR/C/D/1136/2002, para 7.3.

134 Tomuschat (n 119) 109.

135 GC No. 34 (n 22) para 36. Differently, ECtHR, *Vo* v. *France*, App no 53924/00, 8 July 2004, paras 81–5.

136 Cf. Brauch (n 128) 113.

particularly if one agrees that a proposition of the doctrine is 'the proper functioning of democratic processes at national level'.[137] In fact, this requirement cannot be taken for granted with regard to all parties to the Covenant (and probably today not regarding all parties to the ECHR, too). On the other hand it cannot be denied that 'widely differing' perceptions of morals exist among these parties. It would be an illusion to think that the same problems are less grave on the universal than regional level. Actually, the Committee uses 'a margin of appreciation type methodology',[138] when it indicates 'that the concept of morals derives from many social, philosophical and religious traditions' and thereby recognises the difficulty of coming to an evident result.[139] In the *Joslin* case, the Committee did not see a violation of the right to marry by New Zealand's prohibition of the marriage of a homosexual couple, but left open the opportunity for states to allow such a marriage. It is true that the Committee found that Article 23, paragraph 2, ICCPR can only be understood in the sense that marriage means only 'the union between a man and a woman'.[140] But it is very clear that another decision would have been completely unacceptable for many states parties. Lastly and in view of swiftly changing moral attitudes, it is necessary to take account of the different perceptions. Thus the Committee will have to adhere to the narrow definition of marriage in spite of the legal and moral changes in many countries of the world. This restrictive interpretation is just another way to respect the different opinions. The idea is the same. The HRC should therefore consider taking a new approach. The margin of appreciation doctrine, if prudently applied, could just by its flexibility be a tool to enable the Committee to gradually extend and consolidate human rights standards even in sensitive areas.[141]

3.7 Derogations

According to important human rights treaties such as the ICCPR (Article 4), the ECHR (Article 15) and the American Convention on Human Rights (ACHR) (Article 27), a state party may in certain serious

137 Kuijer (n 120) 342.
138 Shany (n 119) 938.
139 GC No. 22 (n 17) para 8.
140 HRC, *Joslin* v. *New Zealand*, Communication No 902/1999, views of 17 July 2002, UN Doc CCPR/C/75/D/902/1999, para 8.2.
141 On this general idea see Janneke Gerards, 'Pluralism, Deference and the Margin of Appreciation Doctrine' (2011) 17(1) European Law Journal 80, 114ff.

situations threatening the life of the nation (CCPR, ECHR) or the independence or security of the state (ACHR) proclaim a state of emergency and take measures derogating from its obligations under the treaty. Derogation does not mean abrogation of a right, rather its whole or partial 'suspension' (Article 27 ACHR), meaning a temporary deviation from the accepted legal obligations, but only as long as the reasons for which it was imposed exist.[142] Derogations cannot be equated with restrictions, but they are measures seriously affecting the enjoyment of a right, therefore akin to restrictions and to be mentioned here, too. While derogating measures can only be taken under extraordinary conditions, restrictions are part of the normal application of the human rights guarantees.[143]

Measures derogating from the rights are only admissible 'to the extent strictly required by the exigencies of the situation'.[144] This terminology directly refers to the proportionality principle, being a combining element between derogations and restrictions and operating in two ways. First, the derogation from a right as such must not exceed the extent strictly required. Second, the specific measures adopted under the circumstances must also be proportionate, satisfying the three steps test already described above.[145] For example, states would have to clarify why they do not always apply possible restrictions rather than suspending the right.

In all the relevant emergency provisions some rights, though not completely coinciding across treaties, are excluded from derogation.[146] However, the legal possibility to restrict such rights remains untouched, as far as the right in question provides for the possibility of a restriction. While this is not the case regarding the prohibition of torture (Article 7 ICCPR), which must neither be derogated from nor, as an absolute right, be restricted, the right to manifest one's religion must not be derogated

[142] HRC, General Comment No. 29: Article 4 (Derogations during a State of Emergency), 31 August 2001, UN Doc CCPR/C/21/Rev.1/Add.11, para 4; David Kretzmer, 'Emergency, State of' in Rüdiger Wolfrum (ed), *Max Planck Encyclopedia on Public International Law* (Oxford University Press 2008), para 22, available at https://opil.ouplaw.com/view/10.1093/law:epil/9780199231690/law-9780199231690-e786.

[143] GC No. 29 (n 142) para 4.

[144] ICCPR (n 5) art 4, para 1, and very similarly the parallel provisions of the other treaties.

[145] See texts referred to by n 104 and Kretzmer (n 142) paras 19–20.

[146] Some rights, though not expressly mentioned in the relevant clauses, are assessed, at least to some respect, as non-derogable; see GC No. 29 (n 142) paras 13–16; GC No. 32 (n 71) para 6; GC No. 35 (n 20) paras 65–7.

from (Article 4, paragraph 2, ICCPR), but may be restricted according to Article 18, paragraph 3, ICCPR. These cases illustrate the difference and interplay between derogation and restriction quite well.

It should briefly be noted that the HRC, following its general line, has never referred to the margin of appreciation in this context. By contrast, the ECtHR has applied, perhaps even invented this argument in interpreting Article 15 ECHR, even granting a wide margin of appreciation to the determination of the existence of a threat to the life of the nation and also to the necessity assessment regarding the specific measures. The Court, however, has always reserved the final say for itself.[147]

Article 5, paragraph 2, ICCPR is a limitation to the power of the states parties to derogate from as well as restrict human rights.[148] States are impeded to derogate from a right if it is prohibited under their national law or international commitments, even if the Covenant would permit it.

Finally, the requirement of notification, which the states have accepted under Article 4, paragraph 3, ICCPR, distinguishes the concept of derogation from restriction, reflecting the possibly far-reaching effects of derogation. A derogation affects not only the established human rights protection as far as it temporarily absolves a state party at least partly from its commitments, but affects also the other states parties bound together by the treaty and called upon to uphold its regime. Here the mostly neglected watchdog position of the states parties, reflected in Article 41 ICCPR, is underscored.

4 Conclusion

Dogmatic deliberations have a disciplinary effect: they help to structure the examination of human rights cases by indicating the necessary legal components and putting these elements in their proper place and in context to each other. Thus, a systematic framework can be established that allows one to proceed step by step and to reach conclusive assessments. Conclusiveness cannot be equated with having found the correct or 'true' result, but it is necessary for the attempt to convince all parties to a case to accept the decision.

Two remarks should be added. The picture presented here is not complete. For example, the question of whether and when an interference

[147] Kretzmer (n 142) paras 14–15.

[148] See Klein (n 28). ECHR (n 11) art 53 is not as clear as ICCPR (n 5) art 5, para 2, but should be read as taking the same line.

with a right has happened or not is not always easy to decide, but cannot be discussed here further.[149] Neither can the consequences of a violation (or non-violation) of an international human right be treated here. The issue of reservations cannot be dealt with either. All these and many other issues would belong to a comprehensive discussion of a general theory concerning the examination of alleged violations of human rights.

Finally, any occupation with human rights swiftly shows that law is not everything. Human rights concern all of us and deserve always our support and empathy. Still, when the allegation of a human rights violation has to be assessed, the competent legal authority has to abide by the given law and must not follow its compassionate impressions. Law may be not sufficient, but is in many cases the only way at least to try to bring justice.

[149] See, e.g., ECtHR, *Eweida* (n 124), para 83: 'if a person is able to take steps to circumvent a limitation placed on his or her freedom to manifest religion or belief, there is no interference with the right under Article 9 §1 and the limitation does not therefore require to be justified under Article 9 §2.'

2

Digital Surveillance, Meta Data and Foreign Intelligence Cooperation

Unpacking the International Right to Privacy

ANJA SEIBERT-FOHR*

When a few years ago the discussion of how to deal with the increasing digital interception of private communications started, the call for a new legal instrument quickly erupted. However, this is not a blind spot of international law. The Human Rights Committee has used cyber-related developments as an opportunity to unpack the right to privacy in the context of its state reporting procedure. The chapter describes and systemises the Committee's interpretation of Article 17 with respect to digital surveillance, meta data retention and foreign intelligence cooperation. It demonstrates that the Covenant provides the necessary legal ground to confront new technological challenges without ignoring the exigencies of the altering security situation. The Committee, having identified various shortcomings in national legal frameworks, has specified the necessary safeguards to effectively protect the right to privacy against arbitrary interference. It has also clarified the territorial scope of protection, which is not limited to domestic measures but extends to transnational surveillance and digital intelligence-sharing. The chapter concludes by describing new issues which the Committee will need to consider in the future, and makes recommendations for the conceptualisation of the right to privacy in the digital age more generally.

right to privacy, Human Rights Committee, digital surveillance, meta data retention, extra-territoriality, intelligence-sharing

David Kretzmer, to whom this *liber amicorum* is dedicated, has devoted a substantial part of his life to the protection of human rights, not only academically but also as a former member of the UN Human Rights

* I am grateful to Kirsten Leube and Maggie Van Dop for their research assistance and to Charlotte Währisch for her help with citations.

Committee. While his work has influenced generations of students and practitioners alike, his engagement with the ideas of young academics and his open mind to innovation, including new technologies, have kept him young over time. Though the International Covenant on Civil and Political Rights (ICCPR)[1] is younger in age, having entered into force only a little more than four decades ago, it is equally confronted with advances in modern life requiring innovation and adjustments in its interpretation. One example is the digital revolution, which has opened new spaces of communication, not only domestically but also transnationally.[2] While we can hardly imagine life without these technical innovations any more, it has also given rise to new challenges for the protection of human rights,[3] most notably for the right to privacy and the protection against unlawful interference with correspondence under Article 17 of the Covenant.[4]

[1] International Covenant on Civil and Political Rights (entered into force 23 March 1976) 999 UNTS 171 (ICCPR).

[2] For human rights protection in cyberspace more generally, see Kriangsak Kittichaisaree, 'Regulation of Cyberspace and Human Rights' in Kriangsak Kittichaisaree (ed), *Public International Law of Cyberspace* (Vol. 32, Springer 2017); Joana Kulesza and Roy Balleste (eds), *Cybersecurity and Human Rights in the Age of Cyberveillance* (Rowman & Littlefield 2015); Kubo Mačák, 'From Cyber Norms to Cyber Rules: Re-engaging States as Law-makers' (2017) 30 Leiden Journal of International Law 877; Dinah PoKempner, 'Cyberspace and State Obligations in the Area of Human Rights' in Katharina Ziolkowski (ed), *Peacetime Regime for State Activities in Cyberspace – International Law, International Relations and Diplomacy* (NATO CCD COE Publications 2013); Gabor Rona and Lauren Aarons, 'State Responsibility to Respect, Protect and Fulfill Human Rights Obligations in Cyberspace' (2016) 8 Journal of National Security Law and Policy 503.

[3] See, e.g., Martin Scheinin, Report of the Special Rapporteur on the Promotion and Protection of Human Rights and Fundamental Freedoms while Countering Terrorism, 17 May 2010, UN Doc A/HRC/14/46; David P. Fidler, 'Cyberspace and Human Rights' in Nicholas Tsagourias and Russell Buchan (eds), *Research Handbook on International Law and Cyberspace* (Edward Elgar 2015).

[4] Other rights which are also relevant for the protection of the individual in cyberspace are freedom of expression and association, freedom of information, non-discrimination, the right to equal political participation and the right to enjoy the benefits of scientific progress. For the protection of journalists and opposition politicians against interception see HRC, Concluding Observations on the Third Periodic Report of the former Yugoslav Republic of Macedonia, 17 August 2015, UN Doc CCPR/C/MKD/CO/3, para 23; HRC, Concluding Observations on the Seventh Periodic Report of Colombia, 17 November 2016, UN Doc CCPR/C/COL/CO/7, para 32; HRC, Concluding Observations on the Sixth Periodic Report of Morocco, 1 December 2016, UN Doc CCPR/C/MAR/CO/6, para 37. See also Daniel Joyce, 'Internet Freedom and Human Rights' (2015) 26 European Journal of International Law 493; Emily Laidlaw, *Regulating Speech in Cyberspace: Gatekeepers, Human Rights and Corporate Responsibility* (Cambridge University Press 2015).

The most prevalent cyber-related issue on the docket of the Human Rights Committee in past years has been the protection of privacy against digital surveillance and data collection.[5] Anti-terrorism measures have led to increasing digital interception of private communications and to mass surveillance, the extent of which has been unprecedented. Technological advances and our growing dependence thereon facilitated this development. On the other hand, when terrorists are hiding within society and taking advantage of new technology and social media for their perfidious purposes, the risk scenario has changed to an extent that civil society has become not only the victim of terrorist attacks but also the object of ever more intelligence activities. The dangers of this growing oversight for individual freedom and self-development should not be underestimated and require adequate safeguards of protection.

This has prompted the Committee in the past years to unpack the right to privacy under the ICCPR in terms of cyber rights protection. Its evolving interpretation allows me to give an overview of the Committee's recent interpretation of this important right. The survey demonstrates that the Covenant provides the necessary legal grounds to cope with such changing circumstances without ignoring the exigencies of the altering security situation.[6] The Committee is thus able to confront new challenges and keep human rights protection alive and effective on the basis of the existing legal framework.

1 Digital Surveillance, Meta Data and Foreign Intelligence

Though the threats to the right to privacy in cyberspace are qualitatively and quantitatively new, this is not an unregulated area of human rights protection. The Committee's General Comment No. 16 from 1988 already laid the groundwork for the protection of privacy rights.

[5] See also Yuval Shany, 'On-Line Surveillance in the Case-Law of the UN Human Rights Committee', *Federmann Cyber Security Research Center, Hebrew University of Jerusalem*, 13 July 2017, http://csrcl.huji.ac.il/people/line-surveillance-case-law-un-human-rights-committee.

[6] For the evolving interpretation of human rights more generally see Anja Seibert-Fohr, 'The Effect of Subsequent Practice on the European Convention on Human Rights: Considerations from a General International Law Perspective' in Anne van Aaken and Iulia Motoc (eds), *The European Court of Human Rights and General International Law* (Oxford University Press 2018).

It provides that electronic surveillance, interception of telephonic and other forms of communication and wire-tapping should be prohibited.[7] It also provides that the gathering and holding of personal information by public authorities and private individuals must be regulated by law[8] and that the purpose and content of the personal data must be transparent to the individual concerned.[9]

With these general requirements, the General Comment already provided a solid legal foundation for the issue of digital surveillance. But given the increase in surveillance worldwide, it does not come as a surprise that there has been a considerable increase of the instances in which the Committee has had to deal with abuses over the past five years.[10] Since 2014, the Committee has been able to address various issues concerning cyber rights protection.[11] Most of the pronouncements were related to anti-terrorism measures. Not only has the Committee considered surveillance when reviewing the fourth periodic report of the United States in 2014,[12] but also with respect to a number of other American, European, Asian, African and Oceanian countries.[13] The variety of states' surveillance laws and policies reviewed demonstrates that this is a universal issue requiring global attention.

[7] HRC, General Comment No. 16: Article 17 (Right to Privacy), The Right to Respect of Privacy, Family, Home and Correspondence, and Protection of Honour and Reputation, 8 April 1988, UN Doc HRI/GEN/1/Rev 9 (Vol 1), para 8.

[8] ibid para 10.

[9] ibid.

[10] According to Shany (n 5), the Committee has raised the issue of surveillance with respect to more than 25 per cent of State reports reviewed from 2014–17.

[11] For an earlier instance in which the Human Rights Committee dealt with cyber rights protection, see HRC, Consideration of Reports Submitted by States Parties Under Article 40 of the Covenant: Concluding Observations of the Human Rights Committee, Sweden, 7 May 2009, UN Doc CCPR/C/SWE/CO/6.

[12] HRC, Concluding Observations on the Fourth Periodic Report of the United States of America, 23 April 2014, Un Doc CCPR/C/USA/CO/4.

[13] See, e.g., HRC, Concluding Observations on the Sixth Periodic Report of Canada, 13 August 2015, UN Doc CCPR/C/CAN/CO/6, para 10; HRC, Concluding Observations on the Seventh Periodic Report of the United Kingdom of Great Britain and Northern Ireland, 17 August 2015, UN Doc CCPR/C/GBR/CO/7, para 24; HRC, Concluding Observations on the Second Periodic Report of Turkmenistan, 20 April 2017, UN Doc CCPR/C/TKM/CO/2, paras 36–7; HRC, Concluding Observations on the Second Report of Namibia, 22 April 2016, UN Doc CCPR/C/NAM/CO/2, para 38; HRC, Concluding Observations on the Sixth Periodic Report of New Zealand, 28 April 2016, UN Doc CCPR/C/NZL/CO/6, paras 15–16.

In its recommendations, the Committee departs from the premise that security measures may aim to prevent violence and terrorism.[14] If a state party adopts such measures, it is bound online by the same standard of protection as offline.[15] Thus any anti-terrorism measure needs to comply with the requirements set out in Article 17. The Committee has criticised mass surveillance programs[16] and the exercise of wide surveillance powers in respect of electronic communications without necessary safeguards to protect the right to privacy and correspondence.[17] Amongst the most prominent issues was the question of whether states parties can require private parties to retain data indefinitely, under what circumstances authorities can get access to such data and to what extent communication received from or sent to a correspondent outside the country is protected against interception.[18] When the Committee answered these questions it was led by the following legal considerations.

[14] For the recognition of wire and telephone tapping as an investigative tool see, e.g., HRC, Consideration of Reports Submitted by States Parties Under Article 40 of the Covenant, Concluding Observations of the Human Rights Committee, Netherlands, 25 August 2009, UN Doc CCPR/C/NLD/CO/4, para 14.

[15] Human Rights Council, The Promotion, Protection and Enjoyment of Human Rights on the Internet, 29 June 2012, UN Doc A/HRC/20/L.13, para 1. See also Rona and Aarons (n 2).

[16] HRC, Concluding Observations on the Sixth Periodic Report of Canada, 13 August 2015, UN Doc CCPR/C/CAN/CO/6, para 10.

[17] UN Doc CCPR/C/SWE/CO/6 (n 11) para 18.

[18] See Section 5 below for discussion on extraterritorial application, and see, e.g., Marko Milanovic, 'Human Rights Treaties and Foreign Surveillance: Privacy in the Digital Age' (2015) 56(1) Harvard International Law Journal 81; Anne Peters, 'Privacy, "Rechtsstaatlichkeit", and the Legal Limits on Extraterritorial Surveillance' in Russel Miller (ed), *Privacy and Power – A Transatlantic Dialogue in the Shadow of the NSA-Affair* (Cambridge University Press 2017) 150–6; Francesca Bignami and Giorgio Resta, 'Human Rights Extraterritoriality: The Right to Privacy and National Security Surveillance' in Eyal Benvenisti and Georg Nolte (eds), *Human Rights Extraterritoriality: The Right to Privacy and National Security Surveillance in Community Interests across International Law* (Oxford University Press 2018); Mireille Hildebrandt, 'Extraterritorial Jurisdiction to Enforce in Cyberspace: Bodin, Schmitt, Grotius in Cyberspace' (2013) 63(2) University of Toronto Law Journal 196; Ilina Georgieva, 'The Right to Privacy under Fire – Foreign Surveillance under the NSA and the GCHQ and Its Compatibility with Art. 17 ICCPR and Art. 8 ECHR' (2015) 31(80) Utrecht Journal of International and European Law 104; Manfred Nowak, 'What Does Extraterritorial Application of Human Rights Treaties Mean in Practice?', *Just Security*, 11 march 2014, www.justsecurity.org/8087/letter-editor-manfred-nowak-extraterritorial-application-human-rights-treaties-practice; Peter Margulies, 'The NSA in Global Perspective: Surveillance, Human Rights, and International Counterterrorism' (2014) 82 Fordham Law Review 2137; Rona and Aarons (n 2) 506–9.

2 Scope of Protection

The scope of protection under Article 17 ICCPR is broad. Not only does it protect the substantive information contained in any communication, but also meta data, that is, data that provides information about other data. Meta data, as part of the communication process, can provide sensitive information about the private life of an individual, allowing the construction of a comprehensive personal profile. It thus deserves protection too.[19] Furthermore, even non-confidential communication and data is protected, because the public sharing of data and information does not render its substance unprotected. If such data is accumulated it can be used for generating personal profiles and this enables the data holder to familiarise itself with the private life of the data subject. Therefore, the protection under Article 17 also extents to information, which is shared in public areas, including social media, for example Facebook. This is why the Committee criticised Colombia for excluding the public domain from the legal protection of privacy just because of its free accessibility.[20]

Any interference with personal data that is relevant for the privacy of an individual needs to be tested against the standards of Article 17.[21] Interference includes any digital surveillance, including, for example, online surveillance,[22] interception of digital communication, wire-tapping, hacking, database mining, computer network exploitation, meta data collection, processing, storing and sharing, mandatory data retention and access thereto. Such digital surveillance may take the form of targeted surveillance with concrete targets based on an individualised suspicion or general (or bulk) surveillance.

3 Key Standards of Protection

The key standards of protection that the Committee has recognised so far are substantive and procedural in nature.

[19] Human Rights Council, Report of the Office of the United Nations High Commissioner for Human Rights, The Right to Privacy in the Digital Age, 30 June 2014, UN Doc A/HRC/27/37, para 19. See also Joined Cases C-293/12 and C-594/12 *Digital Rights Ireland* v. *Seitlinger and Others* [2014] ECR paras 26, 29; Peters (n 18) 149.

[20] UN Doc CCPR/C/COL/CO/7 (n 4) para 32.

[21] The same applies for Art 8 ECHR. For a summary of the European Court of Human Right's case law on cyber-related privacy protection see ECtHR, *Roman Zakharov* v. *Russia*, App no 47143/06, 4 December 2015, paras 227ff.

[22] HRC, Concluding Observations on the Second Periodic Report of Turkmenistan, 20 April 2017, UN Doc CCPR/C/TKM/CO/2, paras 36–7.

3.1 *Substantive Safeguards*

First and foremost, interference must not be arbitrary in nature.[23] Thus any unlimited interception is prohibited under the Covenant. In most of its pronouncements the Committee has expressed concerns about overly broad or vague[24] powers held by state authorities[25] leading to mass interception[26] and about the absence of independent oversight mechanisms.[27] For example, in its Concluding Observations on the fourth report by the United states, the Committee criticised the bulk phone meta data surveillance programme under the US Patriot Act and the foreign surveillance through PRISM, which provided for the collection of communications from US-based Internet companies, as Google and Facebook, and the UPSTREAM program, which collected communication from the Internet backbone (from major cables and switches).[28]

According to the Committee's General Comment No. 16, an interference with the right to privacy must be 'in accordance with the provisions, aims and objectives of the Covenant and should be, in any event, reasonable in the particular circumstances'.[29] In other words, interception of communication requires a specific and legitimate objective.[30] In Switzerland's case the Committee considered the reference to 'national interest' as overly broad.[31] Any interference must be in

[23] According to the Committee, the term arbitrary includes elements of reasonableness, necessity and proportionality: see HRC, General Comment No. 35: Article 9 (Liberty and Security of Person), 16 December 2014, UN Doc CCPR/C/GC/35.

[24] UN Doc CCPR/C/NZL/CO/6 (n 13) paras 15–16.

[25] HRC, Concluding Observations on the Fifth Periodic Report of France, 17 August 2015, UN Doc CCPR/C/FRA/CO/5, para 12.

[26] HRC, Concluding Observations on the Initial Report of South Africa, 27 April 2016, UN Doc CCPR/C/ZAF/CO/1, paras 42–3; HRC, Concluding Observations on the Seventh Periodic Report of the United Kingdom of Great Britain and Northern Ireland, 17 August 2015, UN Doc CCPR/C/GBR/CO/7, para 24; HRC, Concluding Observations on the Sixth Periodic Report of Denmark, 15 August 2016, UN Doc CCPR/C/DNK/CO/6, para 27; UN Doc CCPR/C/MKD/CO/3 (n 4) paras 27–8.

[27] See, e.g., HRC, Concluding Observations on the Initial Report of Pakistan, 23 August 2017, UN Doc CCPR/C/PAK/CO/1, para 35.

[28] Un Doc CCPR/C/USA/CO/4 (n 12) para 22.

[29] General Comment No. 16 (n 7) para 4.

[30] UN Doc CCPR/C/FRA/CO/5 (n 25) para 12; HRC, Concluding Observations on the Fourth Periodic Report of Rwanda, 2 May 2016, UN Doc CCPR/C/RWA/CO/4, para 36.

[31] HRC, Concluding Observations on the Fourth Periodic Report of Switzerland, 22 August 2017, UN Doc CCPR/C/CHE/CO/4, para 46.

line with the principles of legality, necessity and proportionality[32] and non-discriminatory in nature.[33] Privileged information, such as information that applies to journalistic sources and to other professions requiring confidentiality, such as client–attorney correspondence and medical records, requires heightened standards of protection.[34] Furthermore, the same safeguards shall apply irrespective of the nationality of the individual affected by the surveillance measure. The Committee therefore criticised Poland for applying different criteria for the interception of foreign nationals.[35] In the same vein it called upon New Zealand to implement sufficient judicial safeguards 'regardless of the nationality' of the affected person.[36]

3.2 *Procedural Safeguards*

Most pronouncements of the Committee so far have dealt with procedural safeguards. Since *ex ante* individual remedies against oversight measures are limited when it comes to surveillance, the protection of privacy is essentially a matter of regulation, procedural protection – most notably independent authorisation[37] – and adequate independent oversight. The secrecy of intelligence services requires a detailed procedural framework in order to protect individuals from arbitrary interference with their privacy rights, irrespective of whether they are aware of the oversight.[38] Accordingly the Committee in its concluding observations

32 UN Doc CCPR/C/FRA/CO/5 (n 25) para 12. See also ECtHR, *Roman Zakharov v Russia* (n 21). For the standards applied to test necessity under Art 17, see also Milanovic (n 18) 133.

33 HRC, Concluding Observations on the Seventh Periodic Report of Poland, 23 November 2016, UN Doc CCPR/C/POL/CO/7, para 39; UN Doc CCPR/C/NZL/CO/6 (n 24) para 15.

34 The Committee asked, for example, the Netherlands to ensure the exclusion from tapping of communications protected by the privilege of confidentiality. See UN Doc CCPR/C/NLD/CO/4 (n 14) para 14. For necessary exceptions see also HRC, *Van Hulst* v. *The Netherlands*, Communication No 903/1999, 15 November 2004, UN Doc CCPR/C/82/D/903/1999.

35 UN Doc CCPR/C/POL/CO/7 (n 33) para 39.

36 UN Doc CCPR/C/NZL/CO/6 (n 13) para 16.

37 UN Doc CCPR/C/RWA/CO/4 (n 30) para 36.

38 For a comprehensive overview of the necessary legal safeguards, see UN Doc CCPR/C/USA/CO/4 (n 12) para 22: 'any interference with the right to privacy or with correspondence should be authorized by laws which are publicly accessible, contain provisions that ensure that collection of, access to and use of communications data are tailored to specific legitimate aims, are sufficiently precise and specify in detail the precise circumstances in

on Namibia explained that the state party should ensure that the interception of telecommunications may only be justified under limited circumstances authorised by law, with the necessary procedural and judicial safeguards against abuse.[39]

3.2.1 Specific and Transparent Legal Basis

First and foremost, any surveillance, interception, access, gathering, retention and dissemination of personal information requires a statutory basis.[40] When the Committee dealt with Italy's sixth report, the Committee critically observed that the state party's intelligence agencies were intercepting personal communications and employing hacking techniques without statutory authorisation.[41] General Comment No. 16 stipulates that legislation authorising interference with private communications 'must specify in detail the precise circumstances in which such interferences may be permitted'.[42] The Committee thus has asked several states to adopt a comprehensive law regulating surveillance activities.[43]

Such legislation needs to specify in detail the reach of the interception possibilities, including the circumstances in which interference may be authorised.[44] The objectives of surveillance powers must not be overly broad.[45] The statutory basis must be precise and clearly define the mandate and the powers of the competent intelligence agency,

which any such interference may be permitted, the procedures for authorization, the categories of persons who may be placed under the surveillance, the limit on the duration of surveillance, and procedures for the use and storage of data collected and for effective safeguards against abuse'. See also (almost verbatim) UN Doc CCPR/C/GBR/CO/7 (n 26) para 24.

39 UN Doc CCPR/C/NAM/CO/2 (n 13) para 38.

40 GC No. 16 (n 7) para 10.

41 HRC, Concluding Observations on the Sixth Periodic Report of Italy, 1 May 2017, UN Doc CCPR/C/ITA/CO/6, para 36.

42 GC No. 16 (n 7) para 8; HRC, Consideration of Reports Submitted by States Parties under Article 40 of the Covenant, Concluding Observations of the Human Rights Committee, Jamaica, 19 November 1997, UN Doc CCPR/C/79/Add. 83, para 20; HRC, Consideration of Reports Submitted by States Parties under Article 40 of the Covenant, Concluding Observations of the Human Rights Committee, Russian Federation, 26 July 1995, UN Doc CCPR/C/79/Add. 54, para 19. See also ECtHR, *Liberty & Others* v. *the United Kingdom*, App No 58243/00, 1 July 2008.

43 UN Doc CCPR/C/PAK/CO/1 (n 27) para 36; UN Doc CCPR/C/TKM/CO/2 (n 22) para 37; see also UN Doc CCPR/C/GBR/CO/7 (n 26) para 2; UN Doc CCPR/C/NAM/CO/2 (n 13) para 37; HRC, Concluding Observations on the Fourth Periodic Report of the Republic of Korea, 3 December 2015, CCPR/C/KOR/CO/4, para 43.

44 Also ibid. See also UN Doc CCPR/C/FRA/CO/5 (n 25) para 12.

45 See UN Doc CCPR/C/CHE/CO/4 (n 31) para 46.

including the surveillance measures.[46] Vague language needs to be avoided to prevent overly broad interference and abuse. Accordingly, the Committee criticised the absence of a clear definition of the terms national security and private communications when it considered New Zealand's sixth report in 2016.[47] Furthermore, the powers must be tailored to a specific legitimate aim. The law should therefore contain provisions that ensure that the collection of, access to and use of communications data are tailored to specific security needs and used exclusively for this purpose.[48]

The statutory basis also needs to specify the duration of surveillance[49] and the institutions which have access to communication data. Furthermore, the regulation must set out the grounds (permissible objectives) and evidence needed to obtain judicial authorisation for surveillance by specifying the nature of the offence that may lead to interception orders, the categories of persons who may be placed under surveillance[50] or those whose communications are likely to be intercepted,[51] and the safeguards against arbitrary interference with the right to privacy, including safeguards for privileged information.[52] The authorisation procedure, and the procedures for the access, use, communication, storage and destruction of intercepted data[53] must be specified in law.[54]

Since digital surveillance and interception are undertaken in secret without the individual's knowledge, it is imperative that the laws authorising such measures are transparent, in order to enhance their legitimacy and to enable anyone potentially affected to know the legal framework and the conditions under which public authorities are empowered to resort to secret surveillance measures so that the measures are

[46] UN Doc CCPR/C/GBR/CO/7 (n 26) para 24. See also ECtHR, *Roman Zakharov* v. *Russia* (n 21).

[47] UN Doc CCPR/C/NZL/CO/6 (n 13) para 15.

[48] UN Doc CCPR/C/GBR/CO/7 (n 26) para 24.

[49] ibid. See also ECtHR, *Roman Zakharov* v. *Russia* (n 21).

[50] UN Doc CCPR/C/GBR/CO/7 (n 26) para 24.

[51] UN Doc CCPR/C/RWA/CO/4 (n 30) para 36; see also ECtHR, *Roman Zakharov v Russia* (n 21).

[52] UN Doc CCPR/C/NAM/CO/2 (n 13) para 37; UN Doc CCPR/C/ITA/CO/6 (n 41) para 36; HRC, Concluding Observations on the Seventh Periodic Report of Sweden, 28 April 2016, UN Doc CCPR/C/SWE/CO/7, para 36.

[53] UN Doc CCPR/C/GBR/CO/7 (n 26) para 24.

[54] See also ECtHR, *Roman Zakharov v. Russia* (n 21); UN Doc A/HRC/14/46 (n 3) Practice 21, paras 34, 36–7.

foreseeable.[55] This is also important for accountability purposes. The Committee thus regularly demands that the rules regulating the scope of surveillance powers and the safeguards on their application[56] shall be publicly accessible.[57] It has also asked states parties to increase the transparency of surveillance powers and the respective safeguards by considering making the policy guidelines and decisions of institutions involved in intelligence public - subject to national security considerations and the privacy interests of individuals concerned in those decisions.[58] Transparency is not only relevant with respect to the regulatory framework but also in regard to judicial practice. The Committee therefore criticised that the interpretation of the Foreign Intelligence Surveillance Act (FISA) in the US and rulings by the Foreign Intelligence Surveillance Court were largely kept secret, thus not allowing affected persons to know the law with sufficient precision.[59]

3.2.2 Authorisation, Independent Monitoring, Notification and Redress

In order to verify the existence of a reasonable suspicion against a person and to ascertain whether the surveillance measure applied is proportionate to the legitimate aims pursued, any such measure requires authorisation by an institution that is independent of the intelligence service.[60] The Committee has indicated a preference for judicial involvement in the authorisation[61] but has not ruled out per se an independent quasi-judicial body that is also politically accountable.[62]

[55] See ECtHR, *Roman Zakharov v. Russia* (n 21).

[56] UN Doc CCPR/C/SWE/CO/7 (n 52) para 36; UN Doc CCPR/C/ZAF/CO/1 (n 26) para 43.

[57] UN Doc CCPR/C/GBR/CO/7 (n 26) para 24. See also ECtHR, *Shimovolos* v. *Russia*, App no 30194/09, 21 June 2011, paras 67–71.

[58] UN Doc CCPR/C/SWE/CO/7 (n 52) para 37.

[59] UN Doc CCPR/C/USA/CO/4 (n 12) para 22.

[60] For independent authorisation, see also ECtHR, *Roman Zakharov* v. *Russia* (n 21); UN Doc A/HRC/14/46 (n 3), paras 34–5.

[61] UN Doc CCPR/C/USA/CO/4 (n 12) para 22; UN Doc CCPR/C/GBR/CO/7 (n 26) para 24: The Committee asked for judicial involvement in the authorisation of surveillance, interception and intelligence-sharing; UN Doc CCPR/C/ITA/CO/6 (n 41) para 37: The Committee asked the judiciary be involved in the authorisation of such measures; UN Doc CCPR/C/CAN/CO/6 (n 16) para 10: the State party should provide for judicial involvement in the authorisation of surveillance measures; UN Doc CCPR/C/FRA/CO/5 (n 25) para 12; UN Doc CCPR/C/ZAF/CO/1 (n 26) para 43; UN Doc CCPR/C/NAM/CO/2 (n 13) para 38; UN Doc CCPR/C/RWA/CO/4 (n 30) para 36: the judiciary should take part in the authorisation and monitoring of the interception.

[62] ECtHR, *Weber and Saravia* v. *Germany*, App no 54934/00, 29 June 2006.

Furthermore, in order to prevent abuse,[63] the application of the law allowing surveillance measures of private communication shall be subject to continuous and appropriate, effective and independent overall *ex post* monitoring[64] through an independent and robust external oversight mechanism that is adequate to the powers and capacities of the intelligence service.[65] Like authorisation, independent oversight is necessary to protect the rights of the individuals affected by intelligence measures and thus operates as a surrogate for, and as a form of trade-off against, the secrecy of intelligence measures, which prevents those affected from protecting their privacy against such measures.[66]

The Committee therefore asks for a robust, independent oversight system regarding surveillance, interception and hacking.[67] States should guarantee that the processing and gathering of information be subject to review and supervision by an independent body with the necessary guarantees of impartiality and effectiveness.[68] For example, the Committee asked Canada to establish oversight mechanisms over the security and intelligence agencies that are effective and adequate, and to provide these mechanisms with appropriate powers as well as sufficient resources to carry out their mandate.[69]

Finally, the Committee asks that persons who are unlawfully monitored are systematically informed thereof and thus have access to adequate legal remedies in order to challenge the legality of the surveillance measure.[70] Where possible, *ex post* notification should also be made to all other

[63] UN Doc CCPR/C/PAK/CO/1 (n 27) para 36 asked for an independent oversight mechanism (including judicial review of surveillance activities) to prevent abuses; See also UN Doc CCPR/C/ZAF/CO/1 (n 26) para 43; UN Doc CCPR/C/GBR/CO/7 (n 26) para 24: including by providing for judicial involvement in the authorisation.

[64] UN Doc CCPR/C/RWA/CO/4 (n 30) para 36.

[65] HRC, Concluding Observations on the Second Periodic Report of Honduras, 22 August 2017, UN Doc CCPR/C/HND/CO/2, para 39. See also UN Doc CCPR/C/USA/CO/4 (n 12) para 22; UN Doc CCPR/C/GBR/CO/7 (n 26) para 24: 'ensure that robust oversight systems over surveillance, interception and intelligence-sharing of personal communications activities are in place, including ... by considering the establishment of strong and independent oversight mandates with a view to preventing abuses'.

[66] See ECtHR, *Roman Zakharov* v. *Russia* (n 21); UN Doc A/HRC/14/46 (n 3) para 36.

[67] UN Doc CCPR/C/ITA/CO/6 (n 41) para 37.

[68] UN Doc CCPR/C/SWE/CO/6 (n 11); UN Doc CCPR/C/PAK/CO/1 (n 27) para 36; UN Doc CCPR/C/ITA/CO/6 (n 41) para 37.

[69] UN Doc CCPR/C/CAN/CO/6 (n 16) para 10.

[70] UN Doc CCPR/C/MKD/CO/3 (n 4) para 23; UN Doc CCPR/C/HND/CO/2 (n 65) paras 38–9; UN Doc CCPR/C/TKM/CO/2 (n 22) para 37; UN Doc CCPR/C/SWE/CO/7 (n 52) para 37. See also UN Doc CCPR/C/GBR/CO/7 (n 26) para 24; UN Doc CCPR/C/USA/CO/4 (n 12) para 22; UN Doc CCPR/C/ZAF/CO/1 (n 26) para 43.

persons who were placed under surveillance.[71] Such remedies are an important safeguard against the improper use of secret surveillance measures.[72] Therefore, if notification does not jeopardise the purpose of the measure, information about the surveillance should be provided to the individuals concerned.[73]

4 Data Retention

A prominent issue apart from digital surveillance involves the permissibility of data retention.[74] This is not a new issue. Already in General Comment No. 16 the Committee explained that, in order to have the most effective protection of his private life, every individual should have the right to ascertain in an intelligible form, whether, and if so, what personal data is stored in automatic data files, and for what purposes.[75] The protection also applies to data retained by private companies. Accordingly, the Committee has asked states parties in recent years to limit mandatory retention by third parties.[76] In the case of South Africa it criticised the wide scope of the data retention regime.[77]

Access to retained communication data, that is, data about phone calls, emails, website visits and so on, shall be subject to strict safeguards and standards in line with the principles of legality, necessity and proportionality.[78] In order to determine whether access is necessary and proportionate, regard shall be taken to the categories of data retained, the means of communication affected and the persons concerned.[79] State authorities may only access retained data to the extent strictly necessary for prosecution of the most serious crimes or, in particular situations, where

[71] UN Doc CCPR/C/ITA/CO/6 (n 41) para 37: the Committee asked the state party to review its law with a view to 'affording persons affected with effective remedies in cases of abuse, including, where possible, an ex post notification that they were placed under surveillance'.

[72] See also ECtHR, *Roman Zakharov* v. *Russia* (n 21).

[73] ibid.

[74] See, e.g., Joined Cases C-293/12 and C-594/12 (n 19).

[75] GC No. 16 (n 7) para 10.

[76] UN Doc CCPR/C/ZAF/CO/1 (n 26) para 43: the Committee called on the state party to 'consider revoking or limiting the requirement for mandatory retention of data by third parties'. See also UN Doc CCPR/C/USA/CO/4 (n 12) para 22.

[77] UN Doc CCPR/C/ZAF/CO/1 (n 26) para 42.

[78] For the principle of legality, necessity and proportionality, see UN Doc CCPR/C/FRA/CO/5 (n 25) para 12.

[79] Joined Cases C-203/15 and C-698/15 *Tele2 Sverige AB* v. *Post- och telestyrelsen* and *Secretary of State for the Home Department* v. *Tomas Watson, Peter Brice, Geoffrey Lewis* [2016] ECR I-970.

public security is threatened by terrorist activities, where there is objective evidence that the data might, in a specific case, make an effective contribution to combating such activities.[80] Access to data retained by service providers requires authorisation by a judicial authority[81] and it should be subject to effective and independent oversight mechanisms.[82] Australia, for example, was asked to introduce judicial control over access to meta data.[83]

Furthermore, a time limit for data retention must be appropriately fixed in regulation, which, in turn, needs to be observed.[84] Accordingly, Italy was criticised for retaining data beyond the period allowed by the applicable statute.[85] A ten-year mandatory retention by service providers and network operators was considered excessive in the case of Cameroon, and the state party was asked to ensure that the length of time for which data are to be retained be reduced to the extent necessary.[86]

5 Foreign Intelligence, Intelligence Cooperation and Protection of Transboundary Data Flow

While there have been some advances in the enactment of national laws protecting individuals from domestic surveillance in recent years, national safeguards for international intelligence cooperations remain significantly lower. The Committee has therefore dealt with the question whether the right to privacy needs to be respected when persons outside the territory of a state party are subjected to interception or surveillance. The issue of transnational application is particularly relevant for social media such as Facebook, and for search engines such as Google, because the communication data is usually sent via, and received from, outside the country. The Committee extends protection also to such transnational communication. For example, the Committee took issue with the US PRISM programme, which provided for the collection of communications from US-based

[80] UN Doc CCPR/C/GBR/CO/7 (n 26) para 24. According to the ECJ, access to such communication data should be limited to the most serious crimes, ibid.

[81] Italy was criticised for the access of authorities to data retained by service providers without authorisation by a judicial authority; see UN Doc CCPR/C/ITA/CO/6 (n 41) para 37.

[82] UN Doc CCPR/C/TKM/CO/2 (n 22) para 37.

[83] HRC, Concluding Observations on the Sixth Periodic Report of Australia, 1 December 2017, UN Doc CCPR/C/AUS/CO/6, para 46.

[84] UN Doc CCPR/C/CHE/CO/4 (n 31) para 47.

[85] UN Doc CCPR/C/ITA/CO/6 (n 41) para 36.

[86] HRC, Concluding Observations on the Fifth Periodic Report of Cameroon, 30 November 2017, UN Doc CCPR/C/CMR/CO/5, paras 39–40.

Internet companies.[87] With respect to the United Kingdom the Committee criticised the distinction between internal and external communications and the untargeted warrants for the interception of external private communications and communication data that are sent or received outside the UK without the same safeguards as those that apply for internal communication.[88]

Furthermore, if a state party extends its jurisdiction beyond its borders, it is bound by the ICCPR. This means that the same safeguards need to be in place for the interception of external and internal communications. In accordance with its traditional approach,[89] the Human Rights Committee has rejected arguments raised against the extraterritorial application of the Covenant when it comes to surveillance abroad. The Committee clarified this in its Concluding Observations on the United Kingdom, where it explained that any interference with the right to privacy needs to comply with the principles of legality, proportionality and necessity, regardless of the location or nationality of the individuals whose communications are under direct surveillance.[90] The Committee took the same approach when it considered the reports by France,[91] New Zealand[92] and the United States.[93]

[87] UN Doc CCPR/C/USA/CO/4 (n 12) para 22.

[88] UN Doc CCPR/C/GBR/CO/7 (n 26) para 24.

[89] HRC, *Lopez Burgos* v. *Uruguay* Communication No 52/1979, Views of 29 July 1981, UN Doc CCPR/C/13/D/52/1979, para 12.3; HRC, General Comment No. 31, The Nature of the General Legal Obligation Imposed on States Parties to the Covenant, 26 May 2004, UN Doc CCPR/C/21/Rev.1/Add.13, para 10. This approach was later affirmed by the ICJ. According to the ICJ, states parties to the Covenant are bound to comply with its provisions if they exercise jurisdiction outside their national territory. *Legal Consequences of the Construction of a Wall in the Occupied Palestinian Territory*, Advisory Opinion [2004] ICJ Rep 136, [107]–[111]. See also *Application of the International Convention on the Elimination of All Forms of Racial Discrimination Georgia* v. *Russia*, Provisional Measures, Order [2008] ICJ Rep 397, para 109. For the interpretation of Art 2 (1) ICCPR that reads the term 'and' interchangeably, see also Thomas Buergenthal, 'To Respect and to Ensure: State Obligations and Permissible Derogations' in Louis Henkin (ed), *The International Bill of Rights: The Covenant on Civil and Political Rights* (Columbia University Press 1981).

[90] UN Doc CCPR/C/GBR/CO/7 (n 26) para 24.

[91] UN Doc CCPR/C/FRA/CO/5 (n 25) para 12: 'The State party should take all necessary steps to guarantee that its surveillance activities within and outside its territory are in conformity with its obligations under the Covenant, in particular article 17.'

[92] UN Doc CCPR/C/NZL/CO/6 (n 13) para 16: the Committee asked the state party to ensure that 'sufficient judicial safeguards are implemented, regardless of the nationality or location of affected persons, in terms of interception of communication and metadata collection, processing and sharing'.

[93] UN Doc CCPR/C/USA/CO/4 (n 12) paras 22–3.

In its concluding observations on the United States, the Committee asked the government to ensure that surveillance activities, both within and outside the US, conform to its obligations under the Covenant, including Article 17, 'regardless of the nationality or location of the individuals whose communications are under direct surveillance'.[94] Accordingly in its concluding observations on New Zealand the Committee asked for sufficient judicial safeguards regardless of the location of the affected persons in terms of interception of communication and meta data collection, processing and sharing.[95] These observations are based on the understanding that states parties exercise jurisdiction pursuant to Article 2 (1) of the Covenant whenever they are exercising authority over a person's communication. Under such circumstances, jurisdiction is based on the virtual control over the data or the person that generated the data.[96] In other words, the meaning of the term jurisdiction depends on the right at stake. While the right to liberty under Article 9 involves physical control over an individual, physical control is not decisive when it comes to the protection of privacy and communication.[97] It is rather the factual authority that is exercised over the communication or other data that is decisive.

Closely linked to the issue of extraterritorial surveillance is the issue of digital intelligence-sharing with foreign governments.[98] The safeguards of Article 17 apply also to such forms of cooperation. Therefore, Pakistan was criticised in July 2017 for sharing information and cooperating with foreign governments without judicial authorisation or oversight.[99] With respect to the United Kingdom the Committee deplored the lack of sufficient safeguards in regard to obtaining private communications

94 ibid.

95 UN Doc CCPR/C/NZL/CO/6 (n 13) para 16.

96 The Office of the United Nations High Commissioner for Human Rights took a slightly different approach in its report 'The Right to Privacy in the Digital Age', relying on a state party's control over the communications *infrastructure*. It explained that a State's human rights obligations may be engaged if digital surveillance 'involves the State's exercise of power or effective control in relation to digital communications infrastructure, wherever found, for example, through direct tapping or penetration of that infrastructure'; if 'the State exercises regulatory jurisdiction over a third party that physically controls the data'; and 'if a country seeks to assert jurisdiction over the data of private companies as a result of the incorporation of those companies in that country'. UN Doc A/HRC/27/37 (n 19) para 34. For a critique, see Milanovic (n 18) 145.

97 See also Milanovic (n 18) 129, who considers that human rights treaties apply to most, if not all, foreign surveillance activities.

98 UN Doc A/HRC/14/46 (n 3) para 45.

99 UN Doc CCPR/C/PAK/CO/1 (n 27) para 35.

from foreign security agencies and sharing of communications data with such agencies.[100] Similar concerns were expressed in the dialogue with Sweden.[101] The Committee therefore asked for effective and independent oversight mechanisms over intelligence-sharing of personal data.[102]

6 Prospects

When a few years ago the discussion started about how to deal with digital surveillance and international intelligence cooperation, the call for a new legal instrument quickly erupted.[103] However, the above analysis of the Human Rights Committee's interpretation of Article 17 of the Covenant demonstrates that this is not a blind spot of international law, but an area subject to specific legal standards.[104] Any interference with this right needs to be in line with the principles of legality, necessity and proportionality. Mass surveillance cannot be reconciled with the right to privacy absent the necessary safeguards required by these principles.[105] Safeguard procedures play a central role in order to balance security interests against individual protection.

The major challenge thus is not the development of new international rules but the application and implementation of existing law.[106] Most needed is the development of national legal safeguards including effective oversight mechanisms. The Committee has clarified in various

[100] UN Doc CCPR/C/GBR/CO/7 (n 26) para 24.

[101] UN Doc CCPR/C/SWE/CO/7 (n 52) para 36: 'lack of sufficient safeguards against arbitrary interference with the right to privacy with regard to the sharing of raw data with other intelligence agencies'.

[102] ibid.

[103] Fidler (n 3); Laidlaw (n 4); Andreas Zimmermann, 'International Law and "Cyber Space"' (2014) 3(1) European Society of International Law Reflections 1; Ashley Deeks, 'An International Legal Framework for Surveillance' (2015) 55 Virginia Journal of International Law 291.

[104] UN Doc A/HRC/27/37 (n 19) para 47. See also Milanovic (n 18) 137–8; Tim Maurer, 'Cyber Norm Emergence at the United Nations – An Analysis of the Activities at the UN Regarding Cybersecurity', Science, Technology, and Public Policy Program, Belfer Center for Science and International Affairs, Harvard Kennedy School, September 2011.

[105] See also Report of the Special Rapporteur on the Promotion and Protection of Human Rights and Fundamental Freedoms while Countering Terrorism, 23 September 2014, UN Doc A/69/397, para 37; UN Doc A/HRC/27/37 (n 19) para 25; ECtHR, *Szabó and Vissy* v. *Hungary*, App No 37138/14, 12 January 2016.

[106] See also Human Rights Council, Summary of the Human Rights Council Panel Discussion on the Right to Privacy in the Digital Age, 19 December 2014, UN Doc A/HRC/28/39, paras 58–9.

recommendations that states parties should recognise and regulate domestically the challenges arising from modern forms of digital surveillance. Against this backdrop, it has identified insufficient and non-transparent regulation of surveillance activities and the lack of accountability of intelligence services as major obstacles to the effective protection of the right to privacy. Some states have relied on outdated laws that were designed to deal with more rudimentary forms of surveillance in order to justify bulk surveillance. But such laws are not adequate to deal with the deep intrusion into the private sphere that new technology makes possible.[107]

While some advances have recently been made on the national level regarding domestic surveillance, existing safeguards and available remedies remain insufficient and intelligence-sharing and cooperation continue to lack sufficient regulation. With respect to transnational surveillance there is a need for more concrete regulation for intelligence-sharing and cooperation. States parties are called upon to enact a statutory basis regulating the conditions for intelligence exchange, including due diligence standards,[108] that must be met for information to be shared. Furthermore, the authorisation and the necessary safeguards for all exchanges of intelligence need to be regulated domestically.[109]

Future pronouncements by the Human Rights Committee will need to deal in more detail with the distinction between targeted surveillance and general surveillance and the respective standards. Many states parties seem to depart from the assumption that targeted surveillance requires a higher standard of protection than general surveillance, which is purportedly less intrusive. Admittedly, the consequences of targeted surveillance for criminal prosecution are more far-reaching for suspects. On the other hand, existing safeguards provide that targeted surveillance requires a reasonable suspicion of illegal conduct and that such measures must be aimed at and tailored to collecting relevant evidence.[110]

[107] UN Doc A/69/397 (n 105) paras 37–8.

[108] For due diligence requirements see Anja Seibert-Fohr, 'From Complicity to Due Diligence: When Do States Incur Responsibility for Their Involvement in Serious International Wrongdoing?' in Kerstin von der Decken, Nele Matz-Lück and Andreas von Arnauld (eds.), *German Yearbook of International Law* (Duncker & Humblot 2018); Joana Kulesza, 'Protecting Human Rights Online – An Obligation of Due Diligence', Jean Monnet Working Paper No. 24/14, 2014.

[109] See UN Doc A/HRC/14/46 (n 3) paras 45–50.

[110] Anne Peters therefore considers mass surveillance 'far more troubling than targeted surveillance'; see Peters (n 18) 159.

With respect to general surveillance, domestic standards are usually less demanding. Nevertheless, for privacy concerns it usually does not make a big difference, practically speaking, whether a person is subject to targeted surveillance or whether communication is subject to general surveillance. The complete personal profile that can be put together from mass surveillance leads to a grave intrusion into the privacy of those affected. In addition, the chilling effect of general surveillance should not be underestimated. The constant apprehension of surveillance is likely to have a detrimental effect on the exercise of rights and liberties more generally. There are thus good reasons for the Committee to further specify the guarantees of Article 17 with respect to general surveillance in the future and to consider whether and under what circumstances it can be reconciled with the principle of proportionality.

While the Committee has emphasised procedural protection so far, it will need to deal in more detail with substantive issues in the future. This will require foremost a general consideration of the meaning of the protection of privacy in the digital age. By recognising that Article 17 of the Covenant applies also to information shared in public areas, it has already acknowledged that the protection of privacy is not limited to shielding intimacy but extends to all aspects of the individual's self-development and personality.[111] This personal development feeds on social interaction and the ability to communicate with others.[112] It is not limited to communication but also extends to other aspects of self-development, individual autonomy and personality. Therefore, non-discriminatory access to cyberspace, protection against undue interference and the right to exercise control over information and data pertaining to oneself, including the right to be forgotten, arguably are a necessary precondition for the free development of personality.

In the face of the ever growing challenges for the protection of privacy and correspondence in the digital age, the Committee's interpretation will also need to address further technological innovations, including new forms of surveillance such as IMSI-Catchers (used to intercept mobile phone traffic and to track location data of mobile phone users), mandatory secret backdoors for encryption technologies, data

[111] For the free development of personality, see *Case of Murillio et al.* v. *Costa Rica* (2012) Inter-Am Ct HR, Judgement of 28 November 2012, (Ser C) No 257, 143.

[112] Peters (n 18) 147.

mining, malware and data manipulation, stockpiling vulnerabilities, the use of biometric recognition technology for identification and monitoring of public places and the threats arising from new data. It will also need to deal with new modes of interference. Some states, in an effort to gain complete oversight over the vitreous human, have started to push for the surrender of comprehensive personal data from individuals in exchange for economic and other benefits, allowing them to construct complete personal profiles and exercise oversight on allegedly voluntary grounds. This practice requires a new reflection on the concept of interference with individual rights and the notion of voluntariness.

Furthermore, the Committee will need to give a closer look to the threats arising for privacy protection from non-state actors. Considering the rising risks caused by private companies, the Committee is called upon to consider in more depth the obligations by states parties to protect individuals against such threats.[113] A first step was taken when the Committee in its consideration of Italy's sixth report criticised that private companies in the state party sold surveillance equipment to governments with a record of serious human rights violation, and complained about the absence of any legal safeguards or oversight mechanisms regarding the export of surveillance equipment.[114] It called upon the state party to take measures to ensure that all corporations under its jurisdiction, such as technology corporations, respect human rights when engaging in operations abroad.[115] The concluding observation reminded the state party of its regulatory functions vis-à-vis private actors and affirmed the transnational application of the Covenant even in cases where companies act abroad. It thus clarified that states parties are called upon to take positive measures of protection against threats to privacy protection originating in their jurisdictions.

In conclusion, it is fair to say that, though the Committee has not been able to deal with all issues related to digital surveillance, the above survey demonstrates that its interpretation has significantly advanced in recent years in an effort to keep pace with new challenges for the right to privacy. The Committee has laid important groundwork in the context of the reporting procedure. It is in the Committee's prerogative to decide when it is time for an updated General Comment on Article 17 ICCPR.

[113] For the issue of private actors' accountability in cyberspace, see Laidlaw (n 4).
[114] UN Doc CCPR/C/ITA/CO/6 (n 41) para 36.
[115] ibid para 37.

In any case, by unpacking the right to privacy, it has already gone some way towards clarifying the exigencies under this provision. By specifying legal standards applicable to surveillance, meta data and foreign intelligence cooperation, the Committee has made and will continue to make a pertinent contribution to the international rule of law.

3

Some Reflections upon Access to Justice, in the Transnational Setting, as a 'Right to Law'

GIANLUIGI PALOMBELLA

The chapter presents access to justice, in the transnational setting, as a 'right to law'. By referring to several examples and decisions of higher courts, access to justice is seen, of course, as a right and as a basic premise to the realisation of human rights. What is its conceptual consistency? As I submit, access to justice is much more than a 'human right', in so far as it resembles the value of a 'right to have rights': it is a 'foundational right' insofar as it features as a kind of 'right to law'. At the same time it shows a dual nature: as a rule of law essential element or as an individual right; as a procedural or a substantive right; as a derivative or core right. Unsurprisingly, it is by upholding it in one of its different semblances that courts, legislatures, and scholars are able to enhance or downplay its potential. Finally, despite the fact that access to justice should be conceived of as a foundational right, that is, a premise to overcoming arbitrariness and lawlessness, it is often denied based on legal arguments, or in truth, prevented by observance of the rule of law: in the transnational setting, when countervailing norms endowed with alleged primacy are at stake.

access to justice, international courts, conceptions of access to justice, human rights

1 A 'Right to Have Rights'?

The fact that justice in the transnational sphere depends upon the realisation of human rights might appear both as a platitude and as the permanent challenge of our times. While the concepts of justice and human rights are moral constructions, whose political and philosophical nature are constantly under inquiry, their legal status has progressed through increased realisation. Disavowal of human rights seems legally unconceivable, according to the normative commitments which most or all states have undertaken at least since the Universal Declaration of Human Rights. Still, situations where human rights are devoid of effective protection remain plentiful.

The international or transnational sphere has become a leading example of a new stage where crowds of people lose effective protection and are left to experience unfairness, iniquity, injustice, as in the case of present migratory fluxes. In most cases, such fluxes are a consequence also of tragic impairment of human rights in the places of origin. This confirms that injustice is currently spreading within and outside the states.

At the forefront of the quest for the realisation of justice and human rights in the aftermath of World War II, Hannah Arendt defined citizenship as the 'right to have rights'[1], preeminent upon and a premise of any other right. Rather than a fundamental right, the legal belonging to a nation state was thought of, I believe, as a *foundational right*.

However, realities have ended up turning such an assumption into an ambiguity. As things stand, despite 'the momentous development of the international system for protection of human rights since World War II, the citizenship of a person determines how she is treated by this system; the rights people effectively have are still generally determined with a reference to the country they belong to'.[2] As Rhoda E. Howard-Hassmann and Margaret Walton-Roberts write, citizenship itself is a slippery right and a slippery concept, its import varying depending on the relevant states, whether wealthy or poor, democratic or undemocratic, so that it makes for 'lucky holders of hard citizenship rights' or, on the other extreme, stateless people enjoying 'neither de jure nor de facto citizenship anywhere'.[3] Although the status of stateless people[4] is obviously worthy of human rights protection, it is clear that the universalisation of human rights should better confront the need for overcoming limitations deriving from controversial fluctuations in the protection afforded by citizenship and their relationship to human rights.[5]

[1] Hannah Arendt, *The Origins of Totalitarianism* (Harcourt 1973) 296.

[2] Rainer Bauböck and Vesco Paskalev, 'Cutting Genuine Links: A Normative Analysis of Citizenship Deprivation' (2015) 30 Georgetown Immigration Law Journal 47, 49.

[3] Rhoda E. Howard-Hassmann and Margaret Walton-Roberts, 'Introduction: The Human Right to Citizenship', in Hassmann and Walton-Roberts (eds), *The Human Right to Citizenship: A Slippery Concept* (University of Pennsylvania Press 2015), 5.

[4] David Owen, 'On the Right to Have Nationality Rights: Statelessness, Citizenship and Human Rights' (2018) 65 Netherlands International Law Review 299.

[5] Howard-Hassmann and Walton-Roberts (n 3) 17, in their 'Introduction' to the volume, note that 'the increasing importance of human rights protections for everyone within a

The effort towards promoting human rights, including establishing their definition and advancing their entrenchment, made in the last seventy years presents to us a further candidate to play a role comparable to Arendt's notion of citizenship, as preeminent vis-à-vis liberty or justice, also being their fundamental premise. As I surmise below, the candidate for such a foundational place is the right of *access to justice*. It amounts, in depth, to a right to enjoy the protection of law itself: something that, in the present international positivisation of human rights, resembles to a large extent the significance of a *right to have rights*.

2 Justice through Law (Beyond Borders)

In principle, a first general question should be raised, one that concerns the conceivability of justice in a transnational or extra-state setting. At this level, the question of *accessing* justice depends, first and foremost, on the existence, availability and credibility of *justice* in a beyond-the-states environment.

In brief, one should acknowledge that, despite the fact that international relations among states and other non-state entities have been conceived of as involving questions of self-interest and power, legal international arrangements have gradually had an impact, and brought many actors and commentators to accept the idea that legal norms matter.[6] Nevertheless, as famously maintained by Thomas Nagel, an argument has been made that global justice would demand coercion by a world state. Since a global coercive power does not exist,[7] the promise of justice in the supra-state sphere is not completely tenable. Such a critique perhaps would not dismiss 'justice' served within the state, but it certainly undermines the very possibility that supranational rules can guide states' behaviour or, in general, ensure international protections of

state means that Arendt's dictum that only state citizenship can guarantee human rights is now obsolete. This may be the case for liberal democracies, but is not for many developing countries such as Myanmar, Bangladesh, India or many African countries, where legal citizenship is becoming more important and exclusivist as entitlements to social and economic rights are realizable.'

6 The literature is huge; see for example the chapter by Friedrich V. Kratochwil, 'How Do Norms Matter?' in Michael Byers (ed), *The Role of Law in International Politics: Essays in International Relations and International Law* (Oxford University Press 2001), or the book by Nicholas Greenwood Onuf, *World of Our Making: Rules and Rule in Social Theory and International Relations* (University of South Carolina Press, 1989).

7 Thomas Nagel, 'The Problem of Global Justice' (2005) 33 Philosophy & Global Affairs 113.

human rights. For sure, through those lenses, entire sets of fundamental international law, quasi-universal treaties concerning human rights, norms protecting global public goods or prescribing *erga omnes* obligations (binding even non-consenting states), would be pointless, and empty, should we insist that a global coercive power (now inexistent) would be necessary for them to create effective legal obligations.

As already mentioned, justice is strictly connected, by Nagel, to the monopoly of power: a monopoly that, in modern political thought, explains how a civil state has superseded a sheer 'state of nature'. However, in that very tradition of thought, the appearance of justice, more than depending on the rise of power, is made dependent on the rise of a civil power, that is, the rise of *law*. The creation of a coercive authority is relevant to the institution of law and legality, but would not of itself be a direct generator of justice, say, in a lawless state. Law makes for the birth of a public, collective sphere of 'justice', managing disagreements over collective issues, beyond isolated individuals ('monads'), according to Bentham.[8] For Kant, it is the generator of publicness, combining the creation of legal parameters with the pursuit of justice.[9] In Kant's reasoning, a legal society is a condition of conceivability for justice, and both law and justice are resorted to conceptually in order to avoid a lawless state and to leave a 'condition that is not rightful',[10] since the abuse of personal liberty and dependence upon external control are in such a state unobjectionable.[11] The institution of a civil society is connected to the condition of law, and as it seems, it provides for the very possibility of access to justice.

Much of the effort of bringing about a civil state is seen as affording the chance to access justice, for some justice to be delivered. Accordingly,

8 Jeremy Bentham, *Of Laws in General*, ed. HLA. Hart (Athlone Press 1970) 192. Gerald J. Postema, 'Bentham on the Public Character of Law' (1989) 1 Utilitas 41, addresses the problem of the public character of law in Bentham, as a coordinative service of law, but he stresses as well that: 'To focus only on the law's ability to put some questions beyond further debate obscures the role the law plays structuring the debate which continues. Legal arrangements, far from calming the political waters in the way Bentham's theory predicts, often attract and even invite disagreement and contention' (60).

9 In Kant's view, unless mankind 'wants to renounce any concepts of right, the first thing it has to resolve upon is the principle that it must leave the state of nature, in which each follows its own judgment, unite itself with all others (with which it cannot avoid interacting), subject itself to a public lawful external coercion, and so enter into a condition in which what is to be recognized as belonging to it is determined by law'; see Immanuel Kant, 'Metaphysical First Principles of the Doctrine of Right' in Mary Gregor (trans), *Kant: The Metaphysics of Morals* (Cambridge University Press 1996/2003) 33, §44, 90.

10 ibid. For that reason, man 'ought above all else to enter a civil condition', and accordingly 'each may impel the other by force to leave this state and enter into a rightful condition'.

11 ibid 42, 86.

more than being a fundamental right in any legal sense, like, for example, the Kantian natural right to liberty, access to justice is better meant as a different right. It is not just a fundamental but a *foundational* right, marking the birth of (positive) law as such: it separates violence from law, and in this sense it is a right to be ordered by law, abandoning a 'state of nature' that Kant defines as 'devoid of justice'.

Moreover, notwithstanding Nagel, as things stand as a sheer matter of fact, the international legal context survives the absence of a global power, and the normativity of extra-state and international law survives the absence of a global sovereign: demands of justice can be raised, although in a multilayered and admittedly plural or fragmented universe, accepting the principle of international legality, despite the lack of a world coercive power.

This said, however, it is consistent with such a claim to inquire upon the *state of the art*, at least in some areas of law. In what follows I will briefly look at some manifestations (admittedly among many) of access to justice.

3 The Dual Nature of Access to Justice

3.1

As is known, access to justice introduced in the Magna Carta Libertatum finds expression in instruments such as the Universal Declaration of Human Rights Articles 8 and 10, and a large number of subsequent international and regional norms, providing for fair trial, effective remedy, access to information and so forth.[12]

Evidently, access to justice speaks to the *conditions of legality* in its fundamental quality. Unsurprisingly, the foundational nature of access to justice also stems from a further account, that is, it being inherent in the ideal of the *rule of law*. It features among the general requirements that

[12] Among the major provisions: Articles 2(3) and 14 of the UN International Covenant on Civil and Political Rights (ICCPR), the 1998 Aarhus Convention on Access to Information, Public Participation in Decision-Making and Access to Justice in Environmental Matters, the 2006 Convention on the Rights of Persons with Disabilities. In European human rights law, Article 13 of the European Convention on Human Rights (ECHR) guarantees a right to an effective remedy, and Article 6 a right to a fair trial; in the section concerning Justice, the European Charter of Fundamental Rights (CFR) protects access to a fair trial and to an effective remedy at Article 47. Notably, according to Article 53, rights enshrined in the Charter are given the same meaning and scope as the corresponding ones laid down in the ECHR.

accounts of the rule of law, aptly defined as morphological or anatomical,[13] enumerate as essential to it. If one takes the virtue of the rule of law as defined by Joseph Raz, violations of human rights are considered largely compatible with the rule of law, since it cannot be equated to the 'rule of the good law'. However, 'the principles of natural justice' must be observed.[14] Among them one finds open and fair hearing, absence of bias and the like, which are themselves necessary in order to fulfil the primary raison d'être of law, that is, to guide behaviour. Therefore, guarantees of access to justice should be considered among those that are obviously essential to the correct application of the law and thus, through the very same considerations mentioned above, to its ability to guide action. The capacity of law to guide action is at the basis of the independence of the judiciary as well (in order 'to apply the law correctly').[15] Access to justice becomes a requirement at the service of law, structurally belonging to the rule of law. It survives the *contingent content* of law itself, including the current erosion of human rights or of democracy. Its foundational role stands, regardless of its current presentation as a fundamental right. Again, since any social system governed by law cannot do without it, access to justice proves to be at the cleavage between law and lawlessness.

Access to justice, however, is most often spelled as an individual *right*: this comes from a connected but separate route, i.e., as a consequence (for those who think) of justice as a necessary protection of personal dignity. In the well-known theory of Lon Fuller, requirements of legality basically work against arbitrary power and thereby prevent harm to the dignity of human beings as responsible agents.[16]

Accordingly, at issue is what I would call the *dual nature* of access to justice. That is due to multiple reasons. On the one hand, its foundational nature – as a structural requirement for law and the chance of justice – co-exists with its recognition as a fundamental right of individual persons. On the other hand, as we shall see in the following segment, a second reason for its dual character concerns its *essentialist* or *derivative*

[13] Martin Krygier, 'The Rule of Law: Legality, Teleology, Sociology' in Gianluigi Palombella and Neil Walker (eds), *Relocating the Rule of Law* (Hart 2009) 45.

[14] Joseph Raz, 'The Rule of Law and Its Virtue' in Joseph Raz (ed), *The Authority of Law: Essays of Law and Morality* (Clarendon Press 1979) 216–17. Raz lists (at 214–19) a number of requirements that all derive from the two principles according to which citizens must be guided by law, obey the law and it must be *possible* to obey the law.

[15] ibid 216–17.

[16] Lon L. Fuller, *The Morality of Law* (Yale University Press 1969).

nature, and a third pertains to the justification for the right itself, upon the *public or individual interest.*

In order to understand the first duality, between a *structural* requirement and an independent *right* of its own, one can resort, for example, to the reasoning of the Supreme Court of the United States in cases concerning Guantanamo detainees, striving to obtain *habeas corpus* rights. In *Rasul* v. *Bush* (2004)[17] the Court rejected the administration's position that the detainees had no access to federal courts, granted *habeas corpus* and resorted, in the end, to the principles regulating the aims and manner of exercise of public power. According to the Court, Congress provided district federal courts, within their respective jurisdictions, the power to hear applications for *habeas corpus* by any person who claims to be held in custody on an illegal basis. The historical reason and justification for this authority is found in the *limitation* of preponderant and therefore dangerous *powers of the executive.*

Since the principle justifying the authority of courts is said to be the limitation of the executive power, a limitation of the courts' jurisdictions in order to guarantee to the executive an area free of jurisdictional control should not be accepted. For this reason, *habeas corpus* should also be granted in a territory – Guantanamo Bay – over which the United States does not possess 'ultimate sovereignty' but exercises plenary and exclusive jurisdiction.[18] If the main thrust of the decision means that it is illegitimate to create a place where the executive power is released, as if by magic, from judicial control, such intrinsic unlawfulness is taken as the precondition allowing for the infringement of human rights. This *structural* justification largely prevails and precedes any conception of access to justice as a matter of fundamental rights.[19] It is worth

[17] *Rasul* v. *Bush*, 542 US 466 (2004).

[18] It is to be borne into account that the jurisdiction area refers to the place to which 'custodians' belong, not to the place where prisoners are held. In his dissenting opinion, Justice Scalia states the need to strictly observe the provision of law as to courts' jurisdiction, since as he writes, 'Normally, we consider the interests of those who have relied on our decisions. Today, the Court springs a trap on the Executive, subjecting Guantanamo Bay to the oversight of the federal courts ... the Court boldly extends the scope of the habeas statute to the four corners of the earth.' See ibid 497–8.

[19] The reading in terms of human rights is instead supported by Ronald Dworkin: according to Dworkin, the basic meaning of the Court's judgments is that 'the Constitution does not permit the government to hold suspected enemy combatants or terrorists indefinitely without charging and convicting them of crimes, according them all the traditional protections of our criminal law process, unless they are treated in effect as prisoners of war. They would then have the benefits and protections allowed by international law,

mentioning that the Military Commission Act of 17 October 2006 overruled the decision of the Supreme Court in the *Rasul* case, eliminating *habeas corpus* for aliens.[20] As a consequence, one can say that access to justice became, possibly, just a *right* of the individual *citizen*. Acting on this basis, the District of Columbia Court of Appeals maintained that *habeas corpus*, as a constitutional right, was to be denied to aliens. Interestingly, the dissenting opinion of the Court of Appeal's Judge Rogers resorted to *habeas corpus* as a structural feature of the legal system and opposed the argument that *habeas corpus* could be justified as a constitutional 'right': 'Far from conferring an individual right that might pertain only to persons substantially connected to the United States', the Suspension Clause (Article 9 US Const.: 'The privilege of the writ of habeas corpus shall not be suspended, unless when in cases of rebellion or invasion the public safety may require it') 'is a limitation on the powers of Congress'.[21]

Eventually, the Supreme Court in *Boumediene* v. *Bush*, published on 12 June 2008,[22] held that the MCA's withdrawal of jurisdiction violated the right to meaningful *habeas corpus* review by federal civilian judges. Still, by affirming that the Suspension Clause applies, the Court stressed that the framers of the Constitution were motivated by an 'inherent distrust of governmental power' and therefore wrote the Suspension Clause to protect the 'separation of powers' by 'ensur[ing] that, except during periods of formal suspension, the Judiciary will have a time-tested device, the writ, to maintain the delicate balance of governance that is itself the surest safeguard of liberty'.[23]

3.2

As mentioned above, a further reason for the dual nature of access to justice lies in the recurrent oscillation between essentialist or instrumental accounts of it as a right. As may often be the case for procedural rights, European Union case law alternates between instrumental arguments

including the Geneva Conventions.' See Ronald Dworkin, 'What the Court Really Said', *New York Review of Books*, 12 August 2004, 1.

20 As a consequence of the Military Commissions Act, judges in the US Court of Appeals dismissed the pending *habeas* petitions of tens of Guantanamo detainees.

21 *Boumediene* v. *Bush*, 476 F.3d 981, 994–5 (DC Cir. 2007). Of course, the idea of human rights is completely out of the discourse of the courts.

22 *Boumediene* v. *Bush*, 533 US 723 (2008).

23 ibid 15.

(valuing access to justice as a matter of community interest) to essentialist ones: in the latter case by stressing, for instance, that procedural participation should be granted even when in a specific context that would not be contributing at all to getting either further information or advancement towards truth and the public interest. On the other hand, in administrative procedures, access to a hearing or being informed about negative implicating evidence, is upheld as instrumental to the public interest, not just serving individual interest.[24]

A largely connected issue concerns the nature of the right itself, whether it is autonomous and self-standing or rather serving the *substantive right* which is the reason for which justice is sought (and therefore the reason of access). A derivative right would depend on the interest or value that another, substantive, not procedural, right protects. The derivative right would then be subordinate to the ultimate value, say, of (defending) the right to liberty, or property, or life, and so forth.[25] For example, 'the right of every person to be heard, before any individual measure which would affect him or her adversely is taken' is listed as a component of a preeminent *right to good administration* by Article 41 of the Charter of Fundamental Rights of the European Union (CFR).

For sure, the most typical relationship between procedural and substantive rights allow for a derivative construction of access to justice; in such a case, the substantive right is determinative for the issue at stake. For instance, the right to know essential information which facilitates viable access to justice, might be superseded in an easier way if it is intended to *serve* a substantive right (for example, to property) that is taken to be of a lower value than countervailing interests and rights (e.g. industrial secrets or environmental policies). Courts can describe a right as a core or derivative right, depending on the fundamental interests that are used to justify it and those that are going to be prioritised in given circumstances.[26]

As Francesco Francioni has pointed out, although worthy of legal protection, access to justice is construed in the main texts of human

[24] E. Barbier de la Serre, 'Procedural Justice in the European Community Case-Law Concerning the Rights of the Defence: Essentialist and Instrumentalist Trends' (2006) 12 European Public Law 225.

[25] On instrumental or ultimate value of a right, see, for example, Joseph Raz, *The Morality of Freedom* (Clarendon Press 1986) 192.

[26] As to the right to know, they accordingly can decide between closure and disclosure. Cf Shannon M. Roesler, 'The Nature of the Environmental Right to Know' (2012) 39 Ecology Law Quarterly 989.

rights treaties more as a procedural guarantee depending on other substantive rights or necessary for their implementation than as an independent human right, in a core and unrestricted sense of its generalised value: Article 47 of the CFR creates 'a right of access to justice only for the situations where the rights and freedoms guaranteed in the Charter have been violated by the European Union's institutions'.[27] In a similar vein, Article 13 of the European Convention on Human Rights (ECHR) (the right to an effective remedy) does not allow for judicial protection as such, but only with reference to the rights enshrined in the Convention, which does not include, for example, economic or social rights.[28] However, Francioni shows, thereafter, that, as a matter of judicial reasoning, courts tend to expand the right of access to justice and make less clear-cut the distinction between it as a core right or a derivative one.

All in all, in order to meaningfully safeguard the right to access to justice, its 'autonomy' should not be opposed. The dignitary or associative basis for such an autonomy has long been construed, for instance, in American constitutional law as well.[29] One can draw here an analogy to other human rights: to torture someone is wrong and illegal, even should it turn out useful in ascertaining the facts and the truth, and regardless of the unreliability of the information that could thereby be extracted. In the same way, having a right to defence protects individual autonomy and the individual interest not to be unjustly convicted, and it would maintain its value even if the substantive right at stake in the trial could not be saved.

The relevance of access to justice as a 'core' right can be inferred through judicial interpretation, when courts expand the right beyond its ordinary textual scope. Famously, in the *Golder* case, a detainee had been barred from consulting a lawyer to sue his accuser.[30] At the ECtHR the UK argued that Article 6 was not infringed, since it encompasses only

[27] Francesco Francioni, 'The Rights of Access to Justice under Customary International Law' in Francioni (ed), *Access to Justice as a Human Right* (Oxford University Press 2007) 32.

[28] There is better and 'broader' basis of access to justice in arts 8 and 25 of the American Convention on Human Rights, Pact of San Jose, Costa Rica (entered into force 18 July 1978) 1144 UNTS 123, including fundamental rights recognised by the state concerned; see Fancioni (n 27) 32.

[29] Frank I. Michelman, 'Formal and Associational Aims in Procedural Due Process' (1977) 18 Nomos 126; Robert Summers, 'Evaluating and Improving Legal Process – A Plea for Process Values' (1974) 60 Cornell Law Review 1.

[30] He found himself unable to sue a warden of his prison for defamation, for lack of authorisation to consult a lawyer, to be granted by the interior minister.

the right to a fair trial, that is, fairness and due process requirements, only when the proceeding has started: accordingly, not a right to start the proceeding itself. Going beyond the text, the Court referred to the rule of law and to European legal traditions to infer – from Article 6 – a wider and self-standing sense of access to justice, including to legal assistance.[31]

4 Faces of Access to Justice as 'Effective Remedy'

4.1

The very right to an *effective remedy* has been traditionally viewed as essential to and implied by the right of access to justice.

Access to justice, however, can face different forms of indirect denial (not formally foreclosing access), that is, being undermined through oblique routes. One category of relevant obstacles concerns the requirement of judicial independence. Belonging to the oft-mentioned natural justice requirements, judicial independence partakes in granting access to (sound) justice. It is a premise of Article 47 of the CFR providing for an effective remedy. An expedient strategy to drain and empty access to justice, by way of circumventing its core sense without denying formal access to a judge, seeks to undermine the functional substance of the justice system through submitting the judiciary or parts of it to political bias and whim. Imposing governmental directives on judicial assessments weakens the rule of law and inevitably deprives access to justice of its raison d'être. Recent examples, like Hungarian or Polish legislation[32] modifying age retirement of members of the judiciary, and subsequent acts aimed at reducing the freedom of judges to protect constitutional rights, are cases in point.

It is not rare that political power gets into a conflict with the judiciary. The general issue here, however, is that should the independence of the judiciary be in jeopardy, access to justice would be substantively in danger too. The famous court packing that President Roosevelt had in

[31] See ECtHR, *Golder* v. *UK*, App no 4451/70, 21 February 1975, 1.

[32] Gabor Halmai, 'The Early Retirement Age of the Hungarian Judges' in Fernanda Nicola and Bill Davies (eds), *Eu Law Stories* (Cambridge University Press 2017). On 24 June 2019, the CJEU decided that Poland had violated EU law by forcing judges into early retirement. However, Poland had already reinstated the judges after protests and international pressure; see 'European Commission Statement on the Judgment of the European Court of Justice on Poland's Supreme Court Law', European Comission: Press Release Database, 24 June 2019, http://europa.eu/rapid/press-release_STATEMENT-19-3376_en.htm.

mind in order to allow his 'new deal' legislation to pass constitutional review by the Supreme Court, reflects such a tension between the executive and the judiciary. Indeed, the point to be made is not about what positions courts could have had against Polish, Hungarian or American executives' desiderata, but how free and 'independent' from the executive power the delivering of justice remains (or is going to be). Access to justice, and judicial independence as part of it, are not so much a question of whether a court must be progressive in furthering substantive rights, but of which legal guarantees are in place for justice to be effectively claimed by and delivered to the citizens. In that sense, recent Polish or Hungarian heavy-handed undermining of judicial independence or the threatened but never realised Rooseveltian court packing, are all on the same level insofar as access to justice is concerned, although they certainly seek to advance opposite values from a substantive policy perspective, related to the liberal-democratic and social intent behind them.

As a rule of law issue, the more access to justice is safeguarded, through protecting the independence of the judiciary, the less it is subordinate to serving governmental policies, and to the contingent will to weaken or strengthen substantive rights. This means, in the end, that the autonomy of access to justice vis-à-vis substantive rights or public interest directives can often work in favour of the rule of law. It can do so by safeguarding what I call 'jurisdictio'-related guarantees vis-à-vis programmes decided by sovereign power affecting the public. All of them are essential to a sound and effective protection of liberty from the monopoly over interpretation and application of the law in the hands of the most powerful, which ideally is the ultimate objective of the rule of law.[33]

4.2

There are certainly many ways to weaken the effectivity of rights. We have learned for example that social and economic rights have an uncertain fate, and what makes them devoid of substance is often the lack of access to justice. For example, the European CFR goes significantly further than the ECHR, as it enshrines rights of social and economic relevance that are mainly included in its chapter under the label 'solidarity'. Nevertheless, much of the practical significance of that

[33] See Gianluigi Palombella, 'The Rule of Law at Home and Abroad' (2016) 8 Hague Journal on the Rule of Law 1.

chapter is controversial since international bodies as well as several domestic courts often doubt the justiciability of socioeconomic human rights. Here, access to justice as an effective remedy recedes due to stereotyped motivations, mainly revolving around the dubious assumption that courts should not intrude into the sphere of socioeconomic policies, whether for lack of democratic legitimacy vis-à-vis distributive issues or for lack of capacity or competence.[34] This is a recurrent question that courts have, however, successfully started to address, especially by providing definitions of some rights, like adequate housing, or a fair wage, and by approaching the issues through the canon of reasonableness. But the setting I wish to focus upon for its emerging significance in relation to the empowering potential of access to justice, relates to the justiciability of environmental rights and interests of the people. The impression here is that of some virtuous circle, along which achieving access to justice fosters understanding, clarification and possibly the recognition of rights previously felt much more as principles of good practice for governments, including legislators, than individual rights entailing the power to stand before a court.

The EU is committed to granting access to justice, even in matters such as the environment, having ratified the Aarhus Convention in 2005. But the pivotal question remains how to improve access by reducing the impediments for private entities to bring actions to courts: lack of standing, that is, the entitlement of NGOs or individuals to gain direct access to courts against EU acts (or national acts failing to comply with EU directives and regulations) impacting on the environment or public health. Neither the ECHR nor the EU provides a right to *actio popularis*, that is, a public interest litigation defending rights collectively enjoyed by the public. The Court of Justice of the European Union (CJEU) has been facing in this regard the interpretation of the standing requirements provided by Article 263(4) of the Treaty on the Functioning of the European Union (TFEU).[35] The general standing requirements were

[34] See the dedicated site 'Key Concepts on ESCRs – Can Economic, Social and Cultural Rights be Litigated at Courts?' United Nations Human Rights Office of the High Commissioner, www.ohchr.org/EN/Issues/ESCR/Pages/CanESCRbelitigatedatcourts.aspx, and the ESCR-net site providing a database of relevant cases worldwide, www.escr-net.org.

[35] Cf. Hendrik Schoukens, 'Access to Justice in Environmental Cases after the Rulings of the Court of Justice of 13 January 2015: Kafka Revisited?' (2015) 31 Utrecht Journal of International and European Law 46. See Consolidate versions of the Treaty on the Functioning of the European Union [2012] OJ C 326/47: art 263(4) of the Treaty reads as follows: 'Any natural or legal person may, under the conditions laid down in the first

often said to be still governed by the so-called Plaumann doctrine. In relation to environmental legal standing, the doctrine results in banning NGOs from courts, since they cannot be considered individually affected by environmental measures.[36] However, the European Court seems to apply such a limitation to itself, not at the level of its member states, or at least that would result after the *Protect* case (2017)[37] brought by the referring Austrian Court to the CJEU. In this case, the European Court ruled that environmental NGOs have access to justice in water law proceedings, and must be able to contest a permit for water uses that might infringe the obligation provided by the EU's Water Framework Directive to prevent the deterioration of water resources.[38] The Court established that all environmental law must be applied in conformity with the Aarhus Convention by national courts, so as to allow NGOs' participation. Another matter, however, is whether such a right of standing can extend to individuals, by virtue of Articles 9(3) and 2(5) of the Aarhus Convention. A preliminary reference (April 2018) from the German Federal Administrative Court has asked the CJEU about such a question.

As I wish to submit, the role played by access to justice in the evolution of environmental issues is a testament to a peculiar and insufficiently noticed function: especially after the Paris Agreement (2015), where states agreed to take climate action on the basis of equity and to keep global temperature increase below 1.5°C or maximum 2, access to justice is going to become a generator of further substantive protection of the environment. This means not just a method to make 'existing' substantive rights justiciable. The progress achieved through litigation is of particular value and impact in environmental legal settings. In diverse cases, claimants have asked courts to accept their right of standing, have

and second paragraphs, institute proceedings against an act addressed to that person or which is of direct and individual concern to them, and against a regulatory act which is of direct concern to them and does not entail implementing measures.'

36 See Ludwig Krämer, 'The EU Courts and Access to Environmental Justice' in Ben Boer (ed), *Environmental Law Dimensions of Human Rights* (Oxford University Press 2015).

37 Case C-664/15 *Protect Natur-, Arten- und Landschaftsschutz Umweltorganisation* v. *Bezirkshauptmannschaft Gmünd* (CJEU, 27 December 2017), http://curia.europa.eu/juris/document/document.jsf?text=&docid=195440&doclang=EN.

38 Notably, this holds outside Directive 2011/92/EU of 13 December 2011 on the assessment of the effects of certain public and private projects on the environment [2011] OJ L 26/1, known as the Environmental Impact Assessment directive (as itself amended by Directive 2014/52/EU of 15 May 2014 [2014] OJ L 124/1) which already granted access to NGOs.

challenged traditional interpretations of the law, and prompted courts to rethink the issue in the light of the many converging legal documents interweaving national and international norms, so to develop quite new scenarios. Access to justice becomes, through wider and deeper implementation of the Aarhus Convention, a powerful channel for policy-making, information and participation. In many cases, indeed, it not only allows for the vindication of existing substantive rights (at the ECtHR, for example, the right to life, to health, to property) to gain further purchase in environmental matters; it also promotes a new sensibility, which is slowly leading to the much awaited definition of a newly forged substantive *right to a healthy environment*. Professor Knox – an independent special rapporteur appointed by the Human Rights Council in 2012 – has written in his 2018 Report that international human rights bodies need to recognise in a coherent manner a right to a safe, clean, healthy and sustainable environment, something that some national and regional documents or courts have explicitly or implicitly recognised already.[39] That seems indispensable also because it helps to establish the causal link between GHG emissions and emitters and human rights breaches, while a weaker protection, for example by 'greening' other first or second generation human rights, is insufficient to shield fundamental rights from climate change. That has a further advantage in respect of accessing justice. As Alan Boyle writes, on one side, '[c]larifying the

[39] See John H. Knox, Report of the Special Rapporteur on the Issue of Human Rights Obligations Relating to the Enjoyment of a Safe, Clean, Healthy and Sustainable Environment, 19 July 2018, UN Doc A/73/188, para 37: 'The time has come for the United Nations to formally recognize the human right to a safe, clean, healthy and sustainable environment, or, more simply, the human right to a healthy environment. It is understandable that the central United Nations human rights instruments – the Universal Declaration of Human Rights, the International Covenant on Economic, Social and Cultural Rights and the International Covenant on Civil and Political Rights – do not include an explicit right to a healthy environment.' And for already given recognition in Europe, see para 35: 'Although the Convention for the Protection of Human Rights and Fundamental Freedoms does not include any explicit references to the environment, the jurisprudence of the European Court of Human Rights has repeatedly referred to the right to a healthy environment. For example, in a case involving the dangers of using sodium cyanide for gold mining in Romania, the European Court concluded that the State's failure to take positive steps to prevent an environmental disaster violated the rights to life, private and family life and, more generally, to the enjoyment of a healthy and protected environment. Similarly, the European Committee of Social Rights has interpreted the right to protection of health in article 11 of the European Social Charter to include an implicit right to a healthy environment.' Available at https://documents-dds-ny.un.org/doc/UNDOC/GEN/N18/231/04/PDF/N1823104.pdf?OpenElement.

existence of such a right would entail giving greater weight to the global public interest in protecting the environment and promoting sustainable development'; and on the other side, 'NGOs are already entitled to protect the human rights of victims of violations, and there is no need to extend their standing for that purpose. Extending their *standing in environmental matters makes sense only if the public interest in the environment itself is to be protected* – that is the point of Aarhus.'[40]

Eight hundred and eighty-six Dutch citizens represented by the Urgenda Foundation were able to access justice before The Hague District Court (2015)[41] and obtain a positive decision in respect of their claim requiring the Dutch government to adopt a number of measures to mitigate climate change. Pending in the United States is a challenging and controversial claim brought by twenty-one young people suing the federal government for allowing the exploitation of fossil fuels, damaging thereby the climate and violating their fundamental rights (*Juliana* v. *United States*, also known as the '*Kids' Climate* Case'). Rejecting the motion for dismissal from the federal government,[42] Judge Ann Aiken accepted the case in 2016, and in order to confirm the right to *access justice*, she remarked that plaintiffs have demonstrated sustained injuries, and then, acknowledging that damages are reaching an unsustainable catastrophic level, articulated a new right to a 'climate system capable of sustaining human life', stating that 'defendants' actions and inactions – whether or not they violate any specific statutory duty – have so profoundly damaged our home planet that they threaten plaintiffs' fundamental constitutional rights to life and liberty'.[43] Of the same significance, both for access to justice and for environmental law, is the so-called *People's Climate* Case,[44] which was accepted by the European General Court, and filed in May 2018 by ten families and the Sami Youth

[40] Alan Boyle, 'Human Rights and the Environment: Where Next?' (2012) 23 European Journal of International Law 613, 641, 626.

[41] See details at 'Climate Case Heard before Supreme Court on 24 May 2019', Urgenda, www.urgenda.nl/en/themas/climate-case.

[42] The bases for the dismissal are so resumed in the decision; see *Juliana* v. *United States*, 217 F. Supp. 3d 1224, 1235 (D. Or. 2916): 'They contend plaintiffs' claims must be dismissed for lack of jurisdiction because the case presents non-justiciable political questions, plaintiffs lack standing to sue, and federal public trust claims cannot be asserted against the federal government. They further argue plaintiffs have failed to state a claim on which relief can be granted.'

[43] ibid 1261ff.

[44] Case T-330/18, *Carvalho and Others* v. *Parliament and Council* [2018], https://eur-lex.europa.eu/legal-content/EN/TXT/PDF/?uri=OJ:C:2018:285:FULL&from=EN.

Association from Sweden, 'Sáminourra'. Here the plaintiffs claim that the EU's existing climate target to reduce domestic greenhouse gas emissions by at least 40 per cent by 2030 (as compared to 1990 levels) is inadequate with respect to the real need to prevent dangerous climate change and insufficient to protect their fundamental rights to life, health, occupation and property.[45]

5 The Law against Access to Justice?

Despite the fact that access to justice should be conceived of, as I have attempted to suggest, as a *foundational* right, that is, a premise to overcoming arbitrariness and lawlessness, it has often been rejected, based on *legal* arguments, or in truth, prevented by observance of the rule of law: namely, when relevant countervailing norms endowed with hierarchical primacy were at stake. I shall briefly consider the Kadi case before the ECJ and the *Germany* v. *Italy* case, concerning the victims of war crimes, before the ICJ and the Italian Constitutional Court. I shall read those cases – widely commented upon by scholarship in the light of their many facets of relevance to international, constitutional and European law – in the light of access to justice. The hypothesis that law might foreclose access to justice sounds like an oxymoron: where access to justice is denied, the law is deprived of its own raison d'être. But what makes the oxymoron even clearer, is the opposition that it exposes between two legalities, two different normative orders, like the international law order and the domestic system or European Union law.

The *Kadi* case can well be framed as concerning the denial of the right to a judge and to a defence (along with the right to property). The European Court of First Instance (CFI) held that the resolutions of the Security Council placing Mr Kadi on the blacklist of Al Qaeda affiliates and therefore obliging the EU to freeze his patrimonial assets without allowing him a right of defence and access to justice, fall 'outside the

[45] Of no less importance is the Torres Strait Islanders' claim filed at the UN Human Rights Committee in May 2019, and alleging that Australia's government violated their human rights both for contributing to and for not taking adequate measures against climate change: the latter is literally washing away their homes, their infrastructures and in one word their life. Standing at the UNHRC is a challenge of itself, because the claimants should be able to prove the preliminary exhaustion of domestic remedies. On the other hand, the latter appear to be lacking, since the available national administrative courts would not be able to accept claims that cannot be referred to the legality of single administrative provisions, but relate to the the whole of governmental policies.

ambit of the Court's judicial review and that the Court has no authority to call in question, even indirectly, their lawfulness in the light of Community law'.[46] Thus, it is the rule of international law, given its supremacy over any other states' obligations (pursuant to Article 103 of the UN Charter), that denies the expected protection of Kadi's rights. Later on, the European Court of Justice[47] found that Kadi's fundamental rights had been infringed by the EU regulation implementing the Security Council resolution against him. According to the ECJ, however, those rights are not simply part of a well-founded individual claim, they are pillars of European primary law. Rule of law in the European order requires that internal regulations are unlawful, regardless of a Security Council mandate, when they violate the fundamental norms of Community law. In a sense, it made an argument for European primary law – which protects access to justice – to prevail over the obligations stemming from international law (resulting in disregard of Article 103 of the UN Charter). Scholars either criticised the Court's failure to comply with international law or praised its defence of access to justice. In truth, the reasoning of the Court missed the opportunity to admit that instead of a question simply concerning an EU internal regulation, the matter before it exposed a failure of the international system, and particularly the Security Council system, to conform with the basic human rights recognised by international law itself, of which access to justice is of the highest prominence.

Another well-known case showing a 'legal' impediment to the recognition of access to justice was brought in 2012 before the ICJ[48] by Germany, claiming that Italy had failed to respect state immunity by allowing civil claims to compensation before Italian courts in respect of crimes committed by German military personnel during the Second World War. The ICJ declared that the violation of *jus cogens* norms by Germany does not displace its right to immunity, since the latter is endowed with logical priority, on a procedural plane, and prevents any further judgment on the merits by domestic courts. Moreover, the Court ascertained that a customary rule does exist granting state immunity for

[46] Case T-315/01, *Kadi* v. *Council of the European Union and Commission of the European Communities* [2005] ECR II-3649, [225].

[47] Joined Cases C-402/05 P and C-415/05 P, *Yassin Abdullah Kadi and Al Barakaat International Foundation* v. *Council of the European Union and Commission of the European Communities* [2008] ECR I-06351.

[48] *Jurisdictional Immunities of the State (Germany* v. *Italy: Greece Intervening)*, judgment [2012] ICJ Rep 99.

acta jure imperii, to which cases of grave war crimes do not provide an exception, and notwithstanding the absence of any other means of redress. When the question reached the Italian Constitutional Court[49] in 2014, the latter held that the customary international law rule of state immunity could not ever 'enter' the Italian legal order and could not prevail in the constitutional system. Despite the obligation under Article 94 of the UN Charter to comply with decisions of the ICJ, and Article 10 of the Italian Constitution notwithstanding ('the Italian legal system conforms to the generally recognized principles of international law'), supreme constitutional principles found in Articles 2 and 24 of the Constitution work as a *counter-limit* imposing the guarantee of human rights and access to justice. As a consequence, legislation implementing the ICJ decision in *Germany* v. *Italy* was declared unconstitutional.[50]

Access to justice was therefore a *casus belli* between two legal orders. However, as I have submitted elsewhere, unlike the ECJ in the *Kadi* case, the Court considered in depth the normative strength of the assessment by the ICJ of the primacy of states' immunity, and carefully reasoned on the linkage between the two legal orders, balancing between the principle of states' equality, immunity and the right of access to justice in the circumstances of the case.[51]

What we can learn from both cases concerns the autonomy of the right of access to justice as a core right. Beyond the relevance of the substantive claims to regain property rights in the *Kadi* case and to obtain civil compensation in the Italian proceeding, the reasonings used by the courts were centred upon the question of whether any higher international norm and public interest could be taken as displacing domestic norms enshrining access to justice.

The two values opposing access to justice have been, in one case, international peace and security (in the fight against terrorism) and, in

[49] Italian Constitutional Court, Judgment No. 238 of 22 October 2014, www.cortecostituzionale.it/documenti/download/doc/recent_judgments/S238_2013_en.pdf.

[50] I must refer, for a more complete account and comment on the case, to Gianluigi Palombella, 'German War Crimes and the Rule of International Law' (2016) 14 Journal of International Criminal Justice 607. For a wider theoretical frame, see Gianluigi Palombella, 'Theory, Realities and Promises of Inter-legality: A Manifesto' in Jan Klabbers and Gianluigi Palombella (eds), *The Challenge of Inter-legality* (Cambridge University Press 2019).

[51] Also part of the balancing are the principles underlying *jus cogens* norms, which are countervailing parameters that are found both as part of international law and as domestic 'constitutionalised' commitments. These *jus cogens* commitments work as a bridge between the two normative orders.

the other case, the customary law on states' immunity. When facing the problem of access to justice, the absence of any procedural guarantees for the defendants before the Sanctions Committee of the Security Council seemed to undermine its very authority, and make its action look lawless and arbitrary. The position taken by the Italian Constitutional Court that states' immunity would not be compatible with primary constitutional principles – if immunity covers crimes against humanity and the violation of *jus cogens* norms – has a twofold lesson to teach. According to the Italian Court, immunity cannot hold especially when no remedies and no other fora would be available to the victims. Accepting immunity in such cases of grave crimes would be equivalent to accepting the fading out of the international rule of law that the Italian constitution committed to, and to making the inter-state setting a lawless land. The protection of access to justice has, in fact, forced the European and the Italian courts to find their own way to circumvent the dogma of hierarchy, but has also paved the way to an implicit statement that legality devoid of access to justice ends up missing its basic reference to justice itself.

6 Concluding Remarks

As things stand, access to justice gains its value, through episodes mentioned above, because its 'autonomy' is defended also as a matter of more fundamental importance than other norms and principles protected by the primary law of the EU or the Italian Constitution. One could dare to say that the arguments from the ECJ were, as much as those of the Constitutional Court, not just to be perceived as gate-keeping, that is, defending idiosyncratic and supreme beliefs proper to the European or the Italian legal order; nor were they a mere reaffirmation of identity-based reasons against external and international law primacy. The further underlying sense of their reasoning can well be understood as hinting at the largely common conviction that both the Security Council and the ICJ were undermining the fundamental premises of legality to which they have all subscribed.

Despite the many setbacks, fortunes and misfortunes, the importance of access to justice, through its many semblances, is almost universally felt. The reason for that has been the question underlying the foregoing pages: depriving access to justice of its full-fledged effectivity, simply is tantamount to making the *law* fade away, not just to undermining an individual, albeit fundamental right. The distinction might be rather nuanced, but it suggests that while the disregard of some human right by a legal order might make its compliance record at odds with its international law obligations, or expose the authoritarian, conservative or discriminatory features of its legal culture, the denial of access to justice undermines the legal status of the normative structures that are in place, and the more extensive such a denial is, the deeper is the crisis of the legal order, as a whole. Access to justice, then, is not just a fundamental right, among others. Rather it is a foundational right, or *melius*, a right to law, in the absence of which the entire edifice of legal civilisation falls apart.

4

Human Rights Treaty Bodies as Standard-Setting Mechanisms

The Case of Family Law in CEDAW

RUTH HALPERIN-KADDARI*

This chapter introduces the evolution of a new field in family law – international human rights family law (IHRFL) – and traces the major role of one of the human rights treaty-monitoring bodies, the Committee on the Elimination of All Forms of Discrimination against Women (CEDAW Committee), in forming this field. In this new field, issues that have traditionally been thought of as solely part of the domestic legal order (i.e., under the jurisdiction and authority of each state) are now perceived to be part of international human rights law: protection from domestic violence; aspects of child custody; inheritance and property distribution upon dissolution of family relations. This means that family law should be understood as also governed by international human rights standards, whether they are hard law provisions in international treaties, or soft law jurisprudence of treaty bodies. States that have ratified the Convention on the Elimination of All Forms of Discrimination against Women (CEDAW) must scrutinise their family laws and bring them in line with the standards set by the CEDAW Committee in such matters as property relations, inheritance, protection from domestic violence and child custody. Through its standard setting function (i.e., the adoption of Concluding Observations, Views in Individual Communications, and General Recommendations), the CEDAW Committee is gradually and consistently contributing to the substantive development of IHRFL.

CEDAW, international human rights family law, treaty bodies, monitoring mechanisms, standard setting, international family law, gender and international law

* I would like to thank Marsha Freeman, Yaël Ronen and Yuval Shany for invaluable comments on previous drafts of this chapter, as well as Sagy Watemberg Izraeli and Sapir Izralevitch for excellent research assistance.

1 Introduction

The years that David Kretzmer served on the Human Rights Committee (HRC) were among the most significant in his professional career. He often refers to his experience there as substantially formative for his professional identity and worldview. During those eight years Kretzmer served in a number of roles, including two years as Vice-President of the Committee, and two years as Rapporteur for New Communications – the sphere which he found to be the most challenging and where he felt he had the most to contribute. Kretzmer wrote a number of separate Views (concurring or even dissenting) from those of the Committee, where he articulated his own independent understanding of the complex legal issues put to the Committee. Thus, for example, in the famous Holocaust denial *Faurisson* case, where the Committee held that France had not violated the freedom of expression of the complainant by convicting him of Holocaust denial under a controversial French law, it is the concurring View of Kretzmer and his fellow Committee member at the time, Elizabeth Evatt, which offers much richer analysis and nuanced reasoning than the Committee's majority's View.[1] In a later scholarly reflection upon the Committee's communications work under the Optional Protocol, Kretzmer explained the dynamic for this discrepancy:

> There are, of course, institutional reasons why the Committee does not generally provide well-reasoned Views. It is a collegial body of 18 independent experts and finding consensus on lengthy reasoning is bound to raise difficulties. It is much easier to agree on the basics, and to provide minimal legal reasoning. At times this has spurred individual members to attach concurring opinions to the View of the Committee. Not subject to the constraints of finding consensus many of these opinions provide well-reasoned arguments for the legal positions taken.[2]

Indeed, more than any other treaty-monitoring body, the HRC is characterised by the presence of many jurists among its members: judges, academics, or legal civil servants. It is to be expected, then, that there will be significant differences in their approach to the role of law and particularly of international human rights law, and in their perception of treaty-monitoring bodies' mandate as actors within the field of

[1] HRC, *Faurisson* v. *France*, Communication No. 550/1993, views of 8 November 1996, UN Doc CCPR/C/58/D/550/1993.

[2] David Kretzmer on Communications, unpublished manuscript, p 40 (a copy with the author).

international human rights law. This, as we have just seen, is demonstrated in the Committee's activities on communications, which unlike the practice in the Committee's other activities, specifically allow for separate opinions.[3]

For Kretzmer, this course of writing separate concurring or even dissenting opinions offered a venue for expressing his overall take on the Committee's role within the field of international human rights. While his uncompromising commitment to demanding full compliance with the Covenant's provisions was indisputable, when it came to issues of interpretation, Kretzmer took a more conservative approach, reflected in a number of powerful and much quoted dissenting opinions. Thus, for example, in *Hopu* v. *France*, Kretzmer refused to expand the definition of 'family' to include 'all members of one's ethnic or cultural group', or to conceptualise connection to one's ancestors and visits to their burial grounds as part of one's right to privacy.[4] Another example is *Kennedy* v. *Trinidad and Tobago*, where Kretzmer objected to the Committee's novel interpretation of international law, and concluded that a reservation to the Optional Protocol that precluded the Committee from considering communications from persons sentenced to death was permissible, and that when it was clear that the state party had conditioned its accession to the Optional Protocol on a reservation, holding the reservation incompatible with the object and purpose of the treaty meant that the state party was not a party to the OP.[5] These two cases, as well as a couple of others,[6] demonstrate Kretzmer's careful attempt to accurately define

[3] HRC, Rules of Procedure of the Human Rights Committee, 9 January 2019, UN Doc CCPR/C/3/Rev.11. In its first session, the Committee decided to add the following footnote to Rule 52 to its Rules of Procedure, which originally provides for decisions to be taken by a majoritarian method: 'The members of the Committee generally expressed the view that its method of work should normally allow for attempts to reach decisions by consensus before voting.' On the other hand, Rule 103 which addresses Communications, specifically states that 'Any member of the Committee who has participated in a decision may write a separate opinion that should be appended to the Committee's Views or decision.'

[4] HRC, *Hopu* v. *France*, Communication No. 549/1993, views of 30 October 1995, UN Doc CCPR/C/51/D/549/1993.

[5] HRC, *Kennedy* v. *Trinidad and Tobago*, Communication No. 845/1999, views of 2 November 1999, UN Doc CCPR/C/67/D/845/1999. Individual opinion (dissenting) of Committee members Nisuke Ando, Prafullachandra N. Bhagwati, Eckart Klein and David Kretzmer.

[6] HRC, *Hendrick Winata and So Lan Li* v. *Australia*, Communication No. 30/2000, views of 16 August 2001, UN Doc CCPR/C/72/D/930/2000; HRC, *Thompson* v. *Saint Vincent & Grenadines*, Communication No. 806/1998, views of 18 October 2000, UN Doc CCPR/C/70/D/806/1998.

the Committee's competence vis-à-vis other actors in the field, and to determine the limits of its inherent interpretive power. Upon reflection, this seems to represent his basic approach towards human rights treaty-monitoring bodies as standard-setting entities.

2 Standard-Setting by Treaty Bodies

One of the major responsibilities of the treaty bodies is standard-setting. This function is not explicitly named in the various treaties, but, as Kretzmer and Eckart Klein have noted in their comprehensive account of the Human Rights Committee's work, 'setting standards became an inherent part of [the Committee's] function'.[7] To fully appreciate this function, we need to reflect upon the manner in which international law is formed. International law develops differently from domestic law. It is a much more complex and diverse exercise than domestic law. Whereas in domestic law the norm-setting function is separate from the implementing organ and the judicial branch under the basic separation of powers principle, in international law the lines between the three branches are not so clear. International law is inherently dispersed and is characterised by the lack of central legislative, implementing and judicial authorities. This results in proliferation of processes emanating from various directions. In their book *The Making of International Law*, Alan Boyle and Christine Chinkin explain that 'Every society perceives the need to differentiate between its legal norms and other norms of social, economic and political behavior. But unlike domestic legal systems where this distinction is typically determined by constitutional provisions, the decentralized nature of the international legal system makes this a complex and contested issue'.[8]

Within this arena, treaty-monitoring bodies have a special position. They are constituted in accordance with the respective human rights treaties to promote and evaluate states' implementation of international human rights as stated in the treaties. Accordingly, the human rights treaty-monitoring bodies are required to engage in interpretation of the

[7] David Kretzmer and Eckart Klein, 'The Human Rights Committee: Monitoring States Parties Reports' (2015) 45 Israel Yearbook on Human Rights 133, 159.

[8] Alan Boyle and Christine Chinkin, *The Making of International Law* (Oxford University Press 2007) vii.

underlying human rights norms to meet new conditions and challenges. As Kretzmer and Klein explain:

> in a significant number of cases questions arise that require the Committee to take a position on the interpretation of provisions in the Covenant. In doing so, the Committee is involved in standard setting, or creating what has generally become known as 'soft law'. This has become quite an important part of the Committee's work as international and domestic courts begin relying on the Concluding Observations [issued by] the treaty bodies.[9]

And as noted elsewhere by Klein, 'treaty bodies contribute most to the interpretation, clarification and concretization of legal norms which is, at least partly a norm creating function'.[10]

And yet, a certain scepticism co-exists with recognition of the Committee's standard-setting competence, in the form of concerns as to the Committee's capacity to properly fulfil this task. In their reflection upon the Committee's work, Kretzmer and Eckart also raise doubts as to 'whether the process itself is conducive to the setting of standards that are well thought out and are suitable for general application'.[11] In an unpublished manuscript on the Committee's work on Communications, after explaining why standard-setting cannot be regarded as the primary purpose of this function, Kretzmer suggests that 'Justifying the communications procedure as one for laying down human rights standards would require far more persuasive reasoning in its Views and concentration on cases in which some new point of law arises.'[12]

Another reason for the cautious approach is noted in Kretzmer's discussion of the Committee's Views in the *Joslin* case, which held that New Zealand did not violate a lesbian couple's right to equality when its legislation, at the time, did not provide a way for them to marry.[13] In comparing the Human Rights Committee's approach to the question of same-sex marriage with that of the European Court of Human Rights, he concludes that the need for diverse international treaty bodies such as the

[9] See Kretzmer and Klein (n 7) 159.

[10] Eckart Klein, 'Impact of Treaty Bodies on the International Legal Order' in Rudiger Wolfrum and Volker Roeben (eds), *Developments of International Law in Treaty Making* (Springer 2005) 571, 575.

[11] Kretzmer and Klein (n 7) 159.

[12] See Kretzmer (n 2) 43.

[13] HRC, *Joslin* v. *New Zealand*, Communication No. 902/1999, views of 30 July 2002, UN Doc CCPR/C/75/D/902/1999.

Human Rights Committee to preserve legitimacy in the eyes of all the states parties results in slower progress in this area than that of regional mechanisms.[14]

While these observations were made within the context of individual communications, a preference for self-restraint seems to run through Kretzmer's approach towards all the venues in which the Committee engages in standard-setting, be it the issuing of Concluding Observations, the adoption of communications views, or the passage of general comments. As Kretzmer and Eckart note in another paper, discussing the practice of issuing general comments:

> Protection of human rights requires courage and commitment to universal values. However, at the same time it demands patience and an element of modesty. Generally, human rights will be better protected by a step by step approach. The Committee should beware of an all-or-nothing maxim in its protective endeavors.[15]

While treaty bodies' standard-setting now seems to be ubiquitous, this phenomenon has not generated much scholarly examination. In this contribution I wish to elaborate on this very function of the treaty bodies. In particular, and based on my personal experience, I shall highlight the standard-setting exercised in the area of family law by the sister Committee to the HRC, the CEDAW Committee, which monitors the implementation of the Convention on the Elimination of All Forms of Discrimination against Women (CEDAW),[16] to introduce a new field in family law: International Human Rights Family Law (IHRFL).[17]

During the years that I served on the CEDAW Committee, I had the privilege of enjoying countless discussions with Kretzmer, benefiting

[14] David Kretzmer and Yaniv Lushinsky, 'The Rights of LGBT in International Law' in Einav H. Morgenstern, Yaniv Lushinsky and Alon Harel (eds), *LGBTQ Rights in Israel: Gender Identity, Sexual Orientation and the Law* (Hebrew University Press 2016) 1072.

[15] David Kretzmer and Eckart Klein, 'The UN Human Rights Committee: General Comments – The Evolution of an Autonomous Monitoring Instrument' (2015) 58 German Yearbook of International Law 189, 219.

[16] Convention on the Elimination of All Forms of Discrimination against Women 'Adopted and opened for signature, ratification and accession by General Assembly resolution 34/180 of 18 December 1979' (entered into force 3 September 1981), in accordance with Article 27(1) (UNGA). I should add that this project also bears a personal account, as my own twelve years on the CEDAW Committee have largely contributed to the process that I trace and describe here.

[17] I develop this thesis more broadly in a larger theoretical essay: see Ruth Halperin-Kaddari, 'Parenting Apart in International Human Rights Family Law: A View from CEDAW' (2020) 22 Jerusalem Review of Legal Studies 130.

from his wise advice, and learning immensely from his experience. His writing and thinking have shaped my understanding of the intricacies and the politics of international human rights, and taught me the importance of caution, precision and other critical aspects of the human rights enterprise. His work has contributed to my own work in the international arena – even if I sometimes think that had we served together on the same Committee, our approaches would not have always aligned.

3 The Evolution of International Human Rights Family Law

The concept of international human rights norms relating to the family has originally only addressed a general right to marry and to form a family, as stated in Article 16 of the Universal Declaration of Human Rights and in Article 23(2) of the International Covenant on Civil and Political Rights;[18] or has been limited to the prohibition of polygamy and of child marriage, and noting the states' obligation to ensure registration of marriages. These minimal obligations are reflected in the first treaty dedicated to marriage, the Convention on Consent to Marriage, Minimum Age for Marriage and Registration of Marriages (1962).[19]

I argue that international human rights law has substantially evolved since those formative years, and has generated a growing body of family law that addresses issues that have traditionally been thought of as solely part of the domestic legal order (i.e., under the jurisdiction and authority of each state), but are now also perceived to be part of international human rights law: domestic violence; aspects of child custody; inheritance and property distribution upon dissolution of family relations. Another way to look at it is as tracing the process of turning family law from an issue in the sole domain of domestic private law (possibly with some influence of constitutional law) into a sphere that is highly influenced by international human rights norms. This is not just a question of terminology or labelling. It means that family law should be understood as governed by international human rights standards, whether they are

[18] Universal Declaration of Human Rights, UNGA Res 217A(III), 10 December 1948, UN Doc A/810 (1948) Article 16; International Covenant on Civil and Political Rights (entered into force 23 March 1976) 999 UNTS 171 (ICCPR), art 23(2).

[19] Convention on Consent to Marriage, Minimum Age for Marriage and Registration of Marriages (entered into force 9 December 1964) 521 UNTS 231 (UNGA); Convention on the Nationality of Married Women (entered into force 11 August 1958) 309 UNTS 65.

hard law provisions in international treaties, or soft law jurisprudence of treaty bodies. It means that states that have ratified CEDAW, for instance, must scrutinise their family laws and bring them in line with the standards set by the CEDAW Committee in such matters as property relations, inheritance, domestic violence and child custody. This must not be taken lightly. Legislators and policy-makers should be aware that existing laws must be reviewed, and any new measure should be evaluated to ensure that the whole legislative framework complies with these international standards. Similarly, judges must adjudicate in light of these standards, and employ interpretive and other tools to reach greatest conformity. While all this may be obvious to an international human rights lawyer and scholar, it seems this is not the case for those in the area of substantive family law.

In family law scholarship, one usually distinguishes between domestic, comparative and international family law,[20] and the latter is usually perceived to be relevant only to 'international families', or as Gillian Douglas recently explained, to cases where families are formed 'living and changing across state borders'.[21] I argue that another field within family law has evolved, which I suggest naming 'international human rights family law' (IHRFL). It is 'international' not in the sense of addressing cross-border situations. On the contrary, it applies to all familial situations, regardless of their geographic circumstances. It is international simply because it derives its normative basis from international human rights law. My aim is to uncover this new body of law, follow its formation and analyse its substantive content, while recognising that its applicability varies according to the international law regime in each country. I recognise of course that issues relating to family law have been part of the international human rights regime since its inception, as reflected in the Marriage Convention above. I term these the first generation of IHRFL.

A number of observations may be made with respect to the differences between the first generation of IHRFL and the more recent developments that I am tracing. First, the scope of the norms of that first generation was rather narrow, while those that came later adopted a much broader and detailed reach, as demonstrated, for instance, in the language of

[20] Barbara Stark, *International Family Law: An Introduction* (Ashgate 2005) 1–3. See also Katharina Boele-Woelki, 'What Comparative Family Law Should Entail' (2008) 4(2) Utrecht Law Review 1, 4: 'Frequently, family law courses, for instance, which look beyond national boundaries, combine both comparative family law and international family law.'

[21] Gillian Douglas, *Obligations and Commitment in Family Law* (Hart 2019) viii.

CEDAW's Article 16 on Equality in Family Relations.[22] Second, the first generation's norms targeted practices that were and still are more prevalent in the Global South (i.e. child marriages, lack of registration of marriages), while the more recent developments address issues that are of universal concern (such as gender-based violence against women, as addressed by CEDAW's General Recommendation 35 on gender-based violence against women, updating General Recommendation 19, 2017), or even of more relevance to the Global North (such as the economic consequences of marriage, as addressed by CEDAW's General Recommendation 29 on economic consequences of marriage, family relations and their dissolution, 2013), as will be discussed below. I develop these themes elsewhere.[23] In this contribution I focus on another difference, which has to do with the manner in which the norms have been generated. The first two generations of IHRFL were a product of traditional law-making through international treaties between states. The new body of IHRFL builds upon those first generations, and develops and expands it to the extent of creating something new. This process takes place on both the regional and the international levels, not between states, but by different entities entrusted with monitoring and interpreting the treaties. On the regional level, this is carried out not only by various treaty-monitoring mechanisms, such as the Inter-American Commission which oversees the Belém do Pará Convention or the GREVIO that oversees the Istanbul Convention,[24] but also by international courts, such as the European Court of Human Rights or the Inter-American Court of Human Rights, whose contributions to this development will be examined at a later stage of my project. On the international level, where my current work centres, it is mostly the product of standard-setting by treaty bodies' monitoring mechanisms, composed of independent experts. As monitoring mechanisms, their work entails continuous interpretation and development of the

22 For the purpose of the current analysis, I place CEDAW as a category in itself, forming the second generation of IHRFL, as on the one hand, it too is an inter-state treaty, yet on the other hand it contains many of the elements which differentiate the more recent developments from the first generation.

23 See Halperin-Kaddari (n 17); Ruth Halperin-Kaddari, 'The Emergence of International Human Rights Family Law', work in progress.

24 Organization of American States Inter-American Convention on the Prevention, Punishment and Eradication of Violence against Women, 'Convention of Belém do Pará' (entered into force 5 March 1995); Council of Europe, The Council of Europe Convention on Preventing and Combating Violence against Women and Domestic Violence, November 2014.

treaties. My argument is that the process described here, based on the experience of the CEDAW Committee, demonstrates that in practice, in some cases their implementation-monitoring and interpretive tasks have led to new norm-generating and standard-setting, which some might even see as exceeding their original mandate.

The first two generations of IHRFL reflect the traditional consensus-seeking treaty-generating formation of international law, through negotiations between governments to reach understandings over which agreement may be formulated. The new body of IHRFL is the product of standard-setting by interpretation from the body which is entrusted with the implementation of one of those major agreements, namely CEDAW. The difference here is not just in form, but also in substance. As a treaty body, CEDAW is composed of experts, who act in their independent professional capacity. The standard-setting function here is not a result of state parties' agreements, but of an interpretive exercise by a group of individuals, nominated by their respective states but acting as impartial experts. This description may also fit the operation of international judicial tribunals. One difference stands out, however, namely the professional identity of their members. While members of international tribunals must always be jurists, perhaps even professional judges, that it not the case with members of treaty bodies.

This should not, however, lead one to conclude that this particular method of standard-setting lacks the inter-state agreement component. First of all, it is the states parties which drew up the treaties, designated the treaty bodies and entrusted them with the task of overseeing the implementation of the international agreements, entailing the task of interpretation leading to the development of norms set in those agreements. As explained by Bertrand Ramcharan:

> The adhering or ratifying governments have thus freely accepted human rights treaties. They are therefore the most solid consensual bases on which to build national, regional, and international human rights work in the twenty-first century ... it bears repeating that the human rights treaties and the body of jurisprudence arising from their treaty bodies represent the broadest consensual ground on which to build future human rights work.[25]

[25] Bertrand Ramcharan, 'The Law- Making Process: From Declaration to Treaty to Custom to Prevention' in Dinah Shelton (ed), *The Oxford Handbook of International Human Rights Law* (Oxford University Press 2013) 518.

Second, and more important, while there is ongoing debate as to the normative weight attributed to the different outputs of the treaty bodies in general and to the Concluding Observations in particular, the idea of states' acceptance through acquiescence plays an important role in the literature.[26] Since my interest here is not so much with the question of the precise normative weight, but rather with identifying the element of state parties' consent in the ongoing treaty bodies' standard-setting exercise, I suggest that the component of the inter-state agreement may be there, if – once the treaty body comes up with a progressive interpretation that can be viewed as a new norm – the states parties do not express objection, and in time even relate to it in a manner that reflects acceptance. This may be taken as an implied, ex-post facto endorsement. In other words, the manner in which these norms are established inherently involves this implied retroactive agreement by the states parties. It is evidenced by the approach they take towards the norms. Experience shows that in most cases not only do states parties not reject the Committee's interpretations as formulated in its Concluding Observations, but they in fact attempt to prove their compliance with it, as seen in the periodic reports. It is therefore inaccurate to assume that state acceptance is necessarily lacking.

3.1 Gender-based Violence against Women

Gender-based violence against women (VAW) is a good case study demonstrating the method of standard-setting and its evolutionary binding character. When CEDAW was drafted in the 1970s, the time was not yet ripe for openly addressing violence against women. Thus, there is no specific provision on the issue in the Convention. Building on provisions of CEDAW on state obligation and equal protection within the family, and anchoring their arguments on the lived experiences of women, feminists argued for the need to address the issue of violence within the umbrella of CEDAW. This led in 1992 to the CEDAW Committee's adoption of General Recommendation 19 (GR 19) on violence against women which considers gender-based violence as a form of discrimination 'that seriously

[26] ibid; Steven Wheatley, 'Introduction to Human Rights Institutions: Legitimacy and Authority' in Gerd Oberleitner (ed), *International Human Rights Institutions, Tribunals, and Courts* (Springer 2018) (offering a comprehensive analysis of treaty bodies' ways of achieving legitimacy through states' responses to their pronouncements, including by remaining silent when a response might have been expected).

inhibits women's ability to enjoy rights and freedoms on a basis of equality with men'.[27] In showing how specific articles of CEDAW are violated by VAW, the General Recommendation makes clear that it is firmly based on the Convention itself.[28] This is the channel through which states' primary and original obligation is maintained. By citing specific provisions, the committee clarifies that at issue is not a new obligation but merely interpretation of one that is already binding upon states parties. As put by Boyle and Chinkin, 'it is now clear that violence against women may violate human rights treaty obligations'.[29]

The adoption of GR 19 meant that states parties were expected to report on their efforts geared towards addressing VAW. Concluding Observations from the Committee demanded VAW data, called out VAW and other harmful practices, and reiterated the state's obligation as set out in GR 19. States parties started to routinely devote large parts of their periodic reports to describe the efforts taken for complying with this newly formed norm, thus expressing their acceptance of the General Recommendation as part and parcel of their obligations under the Convention. The Optional Protocol process also enriched the view on VAW. Views adopted by the Committee made clear the scope of states' obligations to respect and fulfill women's human rights, including their protection from violence. It developed further the concept of 'due diligence', namely the state's responsibility to take measures against such violations by non-state actors within what is considered to be the private sphere. Throughout the years, the CEDAW Committee further enriched and made visible different forms of gender-based violence against women and expanded its guidance to states through its General Recommendations including a focus on state obligation (General Recommendation 28), gender-based violence against women in the context of armed conflict (General Recommendation 30), as well as access to justice (General Recommendation 33).[30] Then, upon the twenty-fifth

[27] Committee on the Elimination of Discrimination against Women, 'General Recommendation 19: Violence against Women', Eleventh Session, 1992.

[28] See Boyle and Chinkin (n 8) 155; Krissi Shaffina Twyla Rubin, 'Realizing CEDAW's Transformative Power: The Role of CEDAW Jurisprudence in Addressing Violence against Women', LLM Thesis, SOAS University of London, 2018.

[29] See Boyle and Chinkin (n 8) 155.

[30] Committee on the Elimination of Discrimination against Women, 'General Recommendation 28 on the Core Obligations of States Parties under Article 2 of the Convention on the Elimination of All Forms of Discrimination against Women', CEDAW/C/GC/28, 16 December 2010; Committee on the Elimination of Discrimination

anniversary of the adoption of GR 19, the Committee adopted General Recommendation 35 on gender-based violence against women, updating General Recommendation 19 (GR 35). GR 35 states the following:

> For over 25 years, the practice of States parties has endorsed the Committee's interpretation. The *opinio juris* and State practice suggest that the prohibition of gender-based violence against women has evolved into a principle of customary international law. General Recommendation 19 has been a key catalyst for this process.[31]

By this, the Committee left no doubt that its jurisprudence has evolved into binding law, beyond the original purview of the Convention.

3.2 Economic Consequences of Family Relations and Their Dissolution

The evolution of the prohibition of gender-based violence against women into an international human rights norm has been noted by numerous international law and feminist scholars.[32] While this may be the best-known case, I argue that it is not an isolated one. To better understand the significance of norm creation through interpretation which CEDAW has engaged in within this area of family law, I suggest examining the topic of economic aspects of marriage and its dissolution as a less-known case study. First-generation IHRFL did not include gender equality within family relations as a strong tenet of international human rights

against Women, 'General Recommendation 30 on Women in Conflict Prevention, Conflict and Post-Conflict Situations', CEDAW/C/GC/30, 18 October 2013; Committee on the Elimination of Discrimination against Women, 'General Recommendation 33 on Women's Access to Justice', CEDAW/C/GC/33, 3 August 2015.

[31] Committee on the Elimination of Discrimination against Women, 'General Recommendation 35 on Gender-based Violence against Women, updating General Recommendation 19,' CEDAW/C/GC/35, 14 July 2017, para 2. In a lengthy footnote the Committee compiles a long list of international documents (including reports by special rapporteurs, acceptance of recommendations of the UPR, regional instruments and more) as well as domestic laws and policies (including of those states who are not parties to the CEDAW Convention), all demonstrating this statement.

[32] To name only a few: Sally Engle Merry, 'Constructing a Global Law-Violence against Women and the Human Rights System' (2003) 28(4) Law & Social Inquiry 941; Christine Chinkin, 'Violence against Women: The International Legal Response' (1995) 3(2) Gender and Development 23; Marsha A. Freeman, Christine Chinkin and Beate Rudolf (eds), *The UN Convention on the Elimination of All Forms of Discrimination against Women: A Commentary* (Oxford University Press 2012); Yakın Ertürk, 'Feminist Advocacy for Family Law Reform: Cross-Country Overview' in Mahnaz Akhami, Yakın Ertürk and Ann Elizabeth Mayer (eds), *Feminist Advocacy, Family Law and Violence against Women* (Routledge 2018) 11.

governing the family. It goes without saying that none of those first-generation early instruments included any reference to women's property rights within marriage, or to the issue of distribution of marital property upon dissolution of marriage through death or divorce. The first time that these matters appear on the international human rights scene is in CEDAW's Article 16, which establishes a comprehensive and unequivocal standard of equality between women and men in and throughout all family relationships. States parties are now obligated to eliminate discrimination against women at all stages of the marriage or partnership, from betrothal through dissolution by separation, divorce or death. Article 16 is remarkable in its reach, extending beyond marriage to 'family relations'. Most relevant for present purposes is its radical reach in extending principles of equality to issues that had historically been left to management behind the closed doors of the household, beyond the reach of state intervention. Likewise, it extends the reach of international human rights law to issues that had traditionally been left to the domestic regulation of each state, without intervention by international law.[33]

Among these new issues, Article 16(h) provides for gender equality 'in respect of the ownership, acquisition, management, administration, enjoyment and disposition of property, whether free of charge or for a valuable consideration'.[34] Notably, even this bold provision on family property rights did not expressly include equal inheritance rights, due to strong objections raised by Islamic states.[35] As for the delineation of all other aspects of property rights, as novel as it is, it can hardly be viewed as setting a clear standard of gender equality in the area of marital property, whether during the marriage or upon its dissolution by death or divorce. Hence, even though women's economic capacity is clearly a critical factor in their decision to enter or leave marriage, the

[33] As noted above, the issues of child marriage and consent to marriage were subject to international prohibition and regulation at an earlier period, but they were exceptions to the general reluctance to address these issues.

[34] The Convention on the Elimination of all Forms of Discrimination Against Women (entered into force 3 September 1981) 1249 UNTS 13 (CEDAW), art 16(1)(h): '1. States Parties shall take all appropriate measures to eliminate discrimination against women in all matters relating to marriage and family relations and in particular shall ensure, on a basis of equality of men and women: ... (h) The same rights for both spouses in respect of the ownership, acquisition, management, administration, enjoyment and disposition of property, whether free of charge or for a valuable consideration.'

[35] Ruth Halperin-Kaddari and Marsha A. Freeman, 'Economic Consequences of Marriage and Its Dissolution: Applying a Universal Equality Norm in a Fragmented Universe' (2012) 13(1) Theoretical Inquiries in Law 323, 329.

Committee's record on dealing with economic aspects of family relations (or with issues pertaining to family law at large, for that matter) during its first two and a half decades, was rather weak. Thus, for example, in its twenty-third session (June 2000), in which seven states parties reported, only two of the Concluding Observations (Cuba and Romania) mentioned issues pertaining to the economic aspects of marriage and its dissolution, and even that was in a rather dismissive fashion.[36] This was not unusual. In fact, a preliminary study of the Committee's Concluding Observations on these issues, randomly examining one session each year between 2000 and 2006, shows an almost complete absence of reference to the economic aspects of marriage and its dissolution.[37] Marsha Freeman and I have previously suggested that lack of deep family law expertise among Committee members was one of the reasons for this absence, as well as lack of detail in the state party reporting.[38] For anyone familiar with preparing states' reports to treaty bodies, it is obvious that this last point is related to the lack of a clear normative framework to guide the states parties in this area.

All this probably explains why the Committee remained relatively silent on these issues well into the first decade of the twenty-first century, despite the important step forward that the Committee took in 1994 when it adopted General Recommendation 21, which elaborated upon many aspects of Article 16 as well as its relationship to Articles 9 (nationality) and 15 (equality before the law, legal capacity and choice of domicile).[39] The General Recommendation touched upon property issues, clearly stating that existing discriminatory norms and practices must be eradicated,[40] but it did not suggest a framework for new provisions. This was the background against which I concluded that an elaborate normative

36 See CO Cuba A/55/38 (SUPP) (2000) para 268: 'The Committee encourages the Government to monitor carefully the implementation of divorce by consent, and in particular any negative impact this option might have for women with regard to issues such as alimony payments, custody and maintenance of children and distribution of property'; CO Romania A/55/38(SUPP) (2000) para 319: 'The Committee invites the Government to consider how women's rights, including with regard to alimony and child custody, can be protected following dissolution of domestic partnerships.'

37 With one exception, that of the Philippines in the thirty-sixth session (July 2006). Art 16 and family relations broadly speaking were addressed in many of the Concluding Observations, but none of them related to the economic aspects.

38 Halperin-Kaddari and Freeman (n 35) 327.

39 Committee on the Elimination of Discrimination against Women, 'General Recommendation 21: Equality in Marriage and Family Relations', 1994, para 1.

40 ibid paras 38–41.

framework on the economic aspects of family relations is urgently needed, and the way to do it was through a new General Recommendation. Together with Prof. Marsha Freeman, who volunteered her consultancy work, we embarked on a five-year strenuous exercise to carefully formulate principles that could accommodate all states parties, in the Global North and Global South alike, and would still contain accurate substantive provisions to guide the states parties in this sensitive family law area; and after all that – to have the CEDAW Committee adopt the resulting text. In 2013, in its fifty-fourth session, the Committee adopted General Recommendation 29, on Economic Consequences of Marriage and Family Relations (GR 29). In its fifty-five paragraphs, the General Recommendation acknowledges the various forms of contemporary family relationships that give rise to property rights, including registered partnerships, same-sex relationships and de facto unions. It notes the many forms of property that should be subject to distribution or inheritance, from pensions and social security benefits through 'human capital' to use rights in communally held land, indicating that women's equal rights to property must be globally recognised regardless of its form, and in all world regions and legal systems. It also addresses the discriminatory nature of multiple family legal systems within a state, concluding that all family laws, regardless of their origin, must adhere to the equality norms of the Convention.[41]

CEDAW's GR 29 is an apt demonstration of standard-setting through interpretation. All its provisions are rooted in the Convention's obligations to ensure 'the same rights and responsibilities during marriage and at its dissolution', including with respect to 'ownership, acquisition, management, administration, enjoyments and disposition of property'.[42] It runs chronologically from the formation of marriage, through ongoing family relations, to their end by divorce, separation or death. At each of these junctions, it specifies what is required by the principle of equality. Prior to navigating through the different stages of family relations, it addresses two themes that the Committee identified as overarching and present in many of the dialogues with the states parties on the

[41] Committee on the Elimination of Discrimination against Women, 'General Recommendation 29 on art 16 of the Convention on the Elimination of All Forms of Discrimination against Women: Economic Consequences of Marriage, Family Relations and Their Dissolution,' CEDAW/C/GC/29, 30 October 2013.

[42] CEDAW (n 16) art 16(1)(c).

implementation of Article 16: plural legal systems (namely the existence of a plurality of legal systems within the state), and various forms of family relations. Here, too, the General Recommendation builds upon preceding Concluding Observations pertaining to states' reports, developing them into coherent instructions to the states. On plural legal systems, it requires states parties to 'adopt written family codes or personal status laws that provide for equality between spouses or partners', or 'provide for individual choice as to the application of religious law, ethnic custom or civil law at any stage of the relationship' and ensure that personal laws 'embody the fundamental principle of equality between women and men' and are 'fully harmonized with the provisions of the Convention so as to eliminate all discrimination against women in all matters relating to marriage and family relations'.[43] On various forms of family, the General Recommendation starts by outlining them, giving precise description and definition for each type of relationship, itself an unusual but a much needed endeavour.[44] Having encountered so many different kinds of families, with so little consistency in states' treatment of them, the Committee saw the urgent need to clarify what legal framework states are required to adopt in order to abide by Article 16.[45] Thereafter, guided by the principle of gender equality, the General Recommendation proceeds to specify how each family form should be treated, and what protection must be accorded to women in each of them.[46]

The main part of GR 29, and its paramount novelty, is the guidance it provides to the states parties with respect to all economic, property and financial aspects of spousal relations and their dissolution. Economic issues embody the most concrete expression of inequality in the family and of the power relationships between family members across generations as well as between spouses or de facto partners. The economic issues appear at every stage of family formation, from the inception of relationships to dissolution through divorce or death. In a previous paper Freeman and I analysed the structure of the General Recommendation and explained how each of its provisions is set to facilitate the

[43] GR 29 (n 41) para 15.
[44] ibid paras 16–24.
[45] For a broader discussion of the different family formations that had to be accounted for, and the manner in which these considerations impacted the General Recommendation, see Halperin-Kaddari and Freeman (n 35).
[46] GR 29 (n 41) paras 25–31.

implementation of Article 16 and to realise gender equality in spousal property relations.[47] We discussed the way such practices as betrothal payment, polygamy and husband's authority contravene the Convention in general and Article 16 in particular, and the manner in which they are addressed in the General Recommendation. As much as these were already tackled in GR 21, they were now handled with stronger, clearer terms, preceded by richer reasoning.

Undoubtedly, the paragraphs addressing women's economic equality upon divorce or separation or in case of death are the most elaborate and innovative. That's where the Committee stated that 'The guiding principle should be that the economic advantages and disadvantages related to the relationship and its dissolution should be borne equally by both parties',[48] and introduced such concepts as 'lost economic opportunity' on the one hand and 'development of human capital' on the other, as well as the tool of 'post-dissolution spousal payments as a method of providing for equality of financial outcome'.[49] Setting globally applicable guiding principles for the legal regulation of the economic consequences of dissolution of family relations is an enormous and formidable task. The resulting text deals directly with all the core issues in this area, and sets clear provisions, including the following: women should have legal capacity to own and manage property, including land; women should share equally in property accumulated during the relations; women should have the right to inherit, equal to that of a surviving husband or male partner; the default property regime offered by the state should be one that treats men and women equally; the definition of marital property available for division between the spouses should include employment-related benefits, and should recognise nonfinancial contribution, including loss of economic opportunity and financial or nonfinancial investment in development of a spouse's economic activity. The CEDAW Committee did not shy away from any of these issues, and produced a far-reaching scheme to guide all states parties' normative frameworks on the economic consequences of dissolution of family relations.

General Recommendations – while an important part of a treaty body's standard-setting operation – should not be viewed in isolation. No less important is the way a General Recommendation is integrated

[47] Halperin-Kaddari and Freeman (n 35).
[48] GR 29 (n 41) para 45.
[49] ibid para 47.

into the treaty body's ongoing work, as the case of GR 19 on violence against women has shown. A preliminary empirical study of CEDAW's Concluding Observations (COs) starting five years before it was adopted in early 2013 reveals the strong impact that the draft GR 29 has had on the Committee's performance, even prior to its adoption, as can be seen in the following table:[50]

Year	# of countries' reports	COs addressing marital property	Per cent
2007	39	8	21
2008	28	10	36
2009	18	4	22
2010	21	11	52
2011	23	12	52
2012	21	11	52
2013	22	8	36
2014	25	10	40
2015	27	15	56
2016	27	12	44
2017	28	9	32

The table clearly shows that the scant attention to the economic aspects of family relations and their dissolution continued throughout the first decade of the twenty-first century, with only an eighth (in 2005), a fifth (in 2007 and 2009) or a third (in 2008) of the COs addressing these issues. Then, in 2010, things changed: for three years in a row, more than half of the COs addressed them. What happened in between was the intensive discussion within the Committee on these issues, as part of the process of drafting the General Recommendation. At the forty-third session, in July 2009. The Committee was presented with a Concept Note, which was then posted on the Internet, inviting input from all

[50] The table depicts the results of a search conducted in the Human Rights Index, which included data up to the end of 2017. We searched for twenty-two search terms throughout the text of all Concluding Observations between 2007 and 2017. The search included such terms as 'property regimes', 'marital property', 'economic consequences', 'administration of property', 'distribution of property', 'inheritance', 'non-monetary contribution' and more.

stakeholders.[51] A Working Group on the General Recommendation was established in the following session, and various drafts were discussed throughout the subsequent sessions,[52] until the final adoption in February 2013. It is clear, then, that this process raised the Committee's awareness of the subject-matter, and generated substantive discussion with the reporting states parties, which resulted in its inclusion in about half of the Concluding Observations in the years preceding the adoption of the General Recommendation. In terms of the contents of those Concluding Observations, a more thorough analysis is still being carried out. However, a telling finding is the following: out of 127 sets of Concluding Observations adopted from 2013 to 2017, over half (70) make specific reference to GR 29.[53]

In addition to the larger number of Concluding Observations addressing the matter of distribution of marital property in particular, as shown in the table above, the contextual characteristic of the Concluding Observations on these issues has also evolved. The focus has shifted from addressing what I termed 'first generation IHRFL', mostly relating to child and forced marriages, husband's authority over wife, and transmission of nationality, which are more Global South issues, to the economic consequences of divorce, and more recently to specific aspects of issues related to parents and children, which (perhaps somewhat superficially) are more Global North issues. Their structural style has also changed, from abstract and open-ended language to specific and detailed targeting of the issues. Once again, all these observations will be tested in light of the more thorough content analysis which is still being carried out.

4 Conclusion

The jurisprudence of the Committee on the economic consequences of dissolution of family relations, including the final adoption of GR 29 and the transformed Concluding Observations following its adoption, are only part of the process of standard-setting, and of the creation of IHRFL. A significant factor is the question how this General Recommendation was treated by the relevant stakeholders, and how it

[51] Ruth Halperin-Kaddari, 'General Recommendation on Economic Consequences of Marriage and Its Dissolution: Concept Note', CEDAW/C/2009/II/WP.2/R, 2009.

[52] These included an informal session held in Istanbul in November 2012, during a Committee's retreat hosted by the Turkish government.

[53] Computerised and manual search conducted through the Universal Human Rights Index.

was greeted by its addressees, namely the states parties. These also form part of the larger study, and go beyond the scope of this chapter. My aim here was more modest: to draw attention to the role of the treaty-monitoring bodies, composed of individual experts, in setting standards in international human rights law, as demonstrated by the particular development of international human rights family law by the CEDAW Committee.

5

The Applicability of the Law of Occupation to UN Administration of Foreign Territory

EYAL BENVENISTI

In this chapter I examine the UN position with respect to the legal status of the administration of territory by UN-authorised actors. The essay first explores whether the law of occupation applies to direct administration of foreign territory by the UN or its authorised organs. It then examines as a case study the practice of the UN administration of Kosovo. The essay argues that unfettered discretion for civil servants, even international civil servants, undermines the functionality of any administration. Embracing the discipline of accountability embedded in the law of occupation for UN-led administration of territories is therefore required. This discussion provides the grounding for the argument that as a matter of both *lex lata* and *lex ferenda* any administration of territories without a valid sovereign consent, even when exercised by the UN, qualifies as an occupation, and is hence subject to the requirements of the law of occupation.

international organisations, law of occupation, international human rights, United Nations, UMNIK, UN administration of Kosovo

I dedicate this essay to my teacher David Kretzmer as a tribute to his determined and rigorous efforts to explore the discrepancies between the requirements of the law of occupation and their implementation in practice. In his writings[1] and by his involvement in public affairs,[2] Dave has inspired me and many of my colleagues. Taking the

[1] His books, - David Kretzmer, *The Occupation of Justice: The Supreme Court and the Occupied Territories* (State University of New York Press 2002) and *The Legal Status of the Arabs In Israel* (Westview Press 1990) - are only part of a long list of publications, in Hebrew and English, that carefully and critically assessed the jurisprudence of the Israeli Supreme Court with respect to infringements of human rights under domestic and international law.

[2] Kretzmer was among the founders of the Association for Civil Rights in Israel and of B'Tselem - The Israeli Information Center for Human Rights in the Occupied Territories.

Israeli Supreme Court to task for its treatment of the law of occupation was at that time a rare act of selfless courage among Israeli legal academics. His was a model of an involved scholar who unwaveringly maintains personal integrity, not afraid to speak truth to power, including to the judicial power. In hindsight, Kretzmer's oeuvre signifies a shift in Israeli public law scholarship on matters subject to international attention towards critical engagement that is driven by deep commitment to human values and to democracy in Israel.

1 Introduction

Beginning with the intervention in Somalia in December 1992, the UN Security Council acted under Chapter VII to authorise the non-consensual administration of territories of member states in internal or international post-conflict situations.[3] The preferred policy was to rely formally on domestic institutions, as was the case in Cambodia (1991),[4]

As an advocate he led several petitions to the Supreme Court on matters related to the administration of the Occupied Territories. In one of the key petitions he brought, Kretzmer petitioned that the President of the Court, Judge Meir Shamgar, recuse himself due to his personal involvement in setting the very regime that the petition sought to challenge (HCJ 785/87 *Al-Afou* v. *IDF Commander in the West Bank* 1988 PD 42 (2) 1).

3 For reviews of these interventions, see Eric De Brabandere, *Post-Conflict Administrations in International Law: International Territorial Administration, Transitional Authority and Foreign Occupation in Theory and Practice* (Martinus Nijhoff 2009); Gregory H. Fox, *Humanitarian Occupation* (Cambridge University Press 2008); Carsten Stahn, *The Law and Practice of International Territorial Administration: Versailles to Iraq and Beyond* (Cambridge University Press 2008); Ralph Wilde, *International Territorial Administration: How Trusteeship and the Civilizing Mission Never Went Away* (Oxford University Press 2008); Bernhard Knoll, *The Legal Status of Territories Subject to Administration by International Organisations* (Cambridge University Press 2008); Jane Stromseth, David Wippman and Rosa Brooks, *Can Might Make Rights? Building the Rule of Law after Military Interventions* (Cambridge University Press 2006); Simon Chesterman, *You, The People: The United Nations, Transitional Administration, and State-Building* (Oxford University Press 2005); Richard Caplan, *International Governance of War-Torn Territories: Rules and Reconstruction* (Oxford University Press 2006); Ioannis Prezas, *L'administration de collectivités territoriales par les Nations Unies: Étude de la substitution de l'organisation internationale à l'État dans l'exercice des pouvoirs de gouvernement* (Anthemis 2012).

4 See Michael W. Doyle, *UN Peacekeeping in Cambodia: UNTAC's Civil Mandate* (Lynne Rienner 1995); Steven R. Ratner, 'The Cambodia Settlement Agreements' (1993) 87 American Journal of International Law 1.

Haiti (1994)[5] and Bosnia (1995).[6] But when reliance on the consent of the local population and on domestic bodies was not available, the Security Council either assigned responsibility to the forces which were in control of the foreign area, as in the case of Somalia (1992), or, as in the cases of Kosovo (1999) and East Timor (1999), it assumed direct control over the territory. The administration of Kosovo (by UNMIK) and East Timor (by UNTAET) was based on Chapter VII of the UN Charter. In all these cases the Security Council never made reference to the law of occupation, and implicitly rejected the proposition that the law of occupation applied to these exercises of authority over the indigenous populations.[7]

This contribution seeks to critically examine the UN position by questioning its grounding and demonstrating its normative weaknesses and its harmful consequences. The essay first explores whether the law of occupation applies to direct administration of foreign territory by the UN or its authorised organs. It then examines as a case study the practice of the UN administration of Kosovo. This discussion provides the grounding for the argument that as a matter of both *lex lata* and *lex ferenda* any administration of territories without a valid sovereign consent, even when exercised by the UN, qualifies as an occupation, and is hence subject to the law of occupation.

2 The Law Applicable to UN Administration of Territories

Which law applies to a UN-led administration of territories? The UN never articulated its view on this matter.[8] Nor did it commit itself, or the

[5] UNSC Res 940 (1994), 31 July 1994, UN Doc No. S/RES/940 (1994), para 4 (calling, inter alia, for 'the prompt return of the legitimately elected President and the restoration of the legitimate authorities of the Government of Haiti').

[6] UNSC Res 1031 (1995), 15 December 1995, UN Doc No. S/RES/1031 (1995), para 1 (referring to the peace agreement that delineated the allocation of authorities between the parties to the internal dispute and 'call[ing]s upon the parties to fulfil in good faith the commitments entered into in that Agreement').

[7] On the applicability of the law of occupation to the non-consensual administration of territories by international organisations, see Eyal Benvenisti, *The Law of Occupation* (2nd edn, Oxford University Press 2012), Chapter 10.

[8] For the view of one of its legal advisers, see Daphna Shraga, 'Military Occupation and UN Transitional Administrations – the Analogy and Its Limitations' in Marcelo G. Kohen (ed), *Promoting Justice, Human Rights and Conflict Resolution through International Law / La promotion de la justice, des droits de l'homme et du règlement des conflits par le droit international* (Martinus Nijhoff 2007). On the need for international organisations to state clearly their international legal obligations, see Kristina Daugirdas and Sachi Schuricht,

specific territorial administrations which it set up, to any legal discipline or judicial scrutiny. In the case of Somalia, the first post-Cold War UN-authorised intervention without the consent of the sovereign, the Security Council addressed only the functional aspect when it authorised the Secretary-General and 'Member States cooperating' to 'use all necessary means to establish as soon as possible a secure environment for humanitarian relief operations in Somalia'.[9] Neither did the administrating units acknowledge any legal constraints. Only the Australian contingency responsible for some parts of Somalia chose to apply the law of occupation to the areas under its authority.[10]

The same silence as to the applicable legal framework reflects the treatment in 1999 of the administration of both Kosovo and East Timor. With respect to Kosovo, Chapter VII-based Security Council Resolution 1244 of 19 June 19 1999 established 'international civil and security presences' (Article 5), and granted the UN Interim Administration Mission in Kosovo (UNMIK) wide-ranging powers, including to 'protect[] and promot[e] human rights' (Article 11(j)), without any restriction. Upon gaining office, the Special Representative of the Secretary-General (SRSG), in charge of directing UNMIK, issued a regulation declaring that 'All legislative and executive authority with respect to Kosovo, including the administration of the judiciary, is vested in UNMIK and is exercised by the Special Representative.'[11] This assertion of unbridled authority was subject to unspecified 'internationally recognized human rights standards' and 'the mandate given to UNMIK under United Nations Security Council Resolution 1244'.[12]

'Breaking the Silence: Why International Organizations Should Acknowledge Customary International Law Obligations to Provide Effective Remedies' (forthcoming) AIIB Yearbook of International Law; University of Michigan Public Law Research Paper No. 659; University of Michigan Law & Econ Research Paper No. 20-018. Available at SSRN: https://ssrn.com/abstract=3539178.

9 UNSC Res 794 (1992), 3 December 1992, UN Doc No. S/RES/794 (1992), para 10.

10 For an in-depth analysis of the applicability of the law of occupation to UN-supported peace-enforcement operations in general and the operation in Somalia in particular, see Michael J. Kelly, *Peace Operations: Tackling the Military, Legal and Policy Challenges* (Australian Government Public Service 1997).

11 UNMIK, Regulation No. 1991/1 on the Authority of the Interim Administration in Kosovo, 25 July 1999, UN Doc UNMIK/REG/1999/1, art 1(1), www.legislationline.org/documents/id/3936.

12 ibid arts 2–3. See also European Commission for Democracy through Law (Venice Commission), 'Opinion on Human Rights in Kosovo: Possible Establishment of Review Mechanisms', Opinion No. 280/2004, CDL- AD (2004) 033, 8–9 October 2004.

With respect to East Timor, Chapter VII-based Security Council Resolution 1272 established the United Nations Transitional Administration in East Timor (UNTAET) and endowed it with 'overall responsibility for the administration of East Timor ... empowered to exercise all legislative and executive authority, including the administration of justice' (Article 1). As opposed to UNMIK, the Resolution concerning UNTAET did express commitment to 'consult and cooperate closely with the East Timorese people ... with a view to the development of local democratic institutions, including an independent East Timorese human rights institution' (Article 8). In its foundational Regulation, the UNTAET's Special Representative of the UN Secretary-General imposed the duty of 'all persons undertaking public duties or holding public office in East Timor' to abide by the entire set of international human rights conventions as well as by relevant Security Council resolutions,[13] but without committing itself to the same legal restraints, nor providing for processes for monitoring compliance.[14]

The silence of the UN Security Council with respect to the legal framework constraining the exercise of authority stems from a long-held self-perception of being an inherently impartial and infallible body,[15] a conviction that has been endorsed by the International Court of Justice since 1945. In a series of Advisory Opinions given during this formative period, the Court extolled the virtues of the UN and of international organisations in general as, in the words of Jan Klabbers, 'the harbingers of international happiness'.[16] This unqualified trust in the UN and in other international organisations led the Court to assert, quite enigmatically and even tautologically, that as independent legal personalities, international organisations are subject to 'any obligations *incumbent upon them* under general rules of international law, under their constitutions or under international agreements to which they are

[13] UNTAET, Regulation No. 1999/1 on the Authority of the Transitional Administration in East Timor, 27 November 1999, UN Doc UNTAET/REG/1991/1, art 2, https://peacekeeping.un.org/en/mission/past/etimor/untaetR/etreg1.htm.

[14] ibid. The list included also the Universal Declaration on Human Rights.

[15] Dag Hammarskjöld, 'The International Civil Servant in Law and in Fact (Lecture delivered to Congregation at Oxford University, 30 May 1961)' reprinted in *Servant of Peace: A Selection of the Speeches and Statements of Dag Hammarskjöld, Secretary-General of the United Nations, 1953–1961* (Harper & Row 1962) 329.

[16] Jan Klabbers, 'The Life and Times of the Law of International Organizations' (2001) 70 Nordic Journal of International Law 287, 288; see also Eyal Benvenisti, 'Upholding Democracy amid the Challenges of New Technology: What Role for the Law of Global Governance?' (2018) 29 European Journal of International Law 9, 11.

parties' (my emphasis).[17] More specifically, the same deferential attitude was reflected by the Secretary-General of the UN's 'somewhat circular'[18] formulation of the applicability of the laws of armed conflict to UN operations, issued in 1999 after several years of engagements in peacekeeping operations.[19] The Secretary-General's Bulletin recognises that a limited and simplified set of 'fundamental principles and rules of international humanitarian law set out in the present bulletin are applicable to United Nations forces when in situations of armed conflict they are actively engaged therein as combatants, to the extent and for the duration of their engagement'.[20] Hence these principles do not apply to the crucial post-hostilities stage including during occupation.

In fact, several arguments have been raised to absolve UN-led occupations from obedience to this law. The UN, some say, is not subject to the laws of war in general, and to the law of occupation in particular.[21] More specifically, it was claimed that the law of occupation is inapplicable because the ousted sovereign should be regarded as having consented to the unfettered exercise of authority of the Security Council in the sovereign's territory when becoming a party to the UN Charter; that the law of occupation applies to the UN, but only when it is directly involved

[17] *Interpretation of the Agreement of 25 March 1951 between the WHO and Egypt*, Advisory Opinion [1980] ICJ Rep 73 [37]. On this see Benvenisti (n 16) 22–3.

[18] Terry D. Gill et al. (eds), *Leuven Manual on the International Law Applicable to Peace Operations* (Cambridge University Press 2017) 96.

[19] Observance by United Nations Forces of International Humanitarian Law, 6 August 1999, UN Doc ST/SGB/1999/13. For background on the Bulletin and its contents, see Daphna Shraga, 'UN Peacekeeping Operations: Applicability of International Humanitarian Law and Responsibility for Operations-Related Damage' (2000) 94 American Journal of International Law 406.

[20] Compare the much more straightforward and comprehensive Institut de Droit International, 'Conditions of Application of Humanitarian Rules of Armed Conflict to Hostilities in which United Nations Forces May be Engaged' 1971 Zagreb Resolution, 2 September 1971, art 2, www.idi-iil.org/app/uploads/2017/06/1971_zag_03_en.pdf; see also (n 29).

[21] For a view supporting the inapplicability of the law (but noting that the law can inspire the administration), see Shraga (n 8); Erika de Wet, 'The Direct Administration of Territories by the United Nations and Its Member States in the Post Cold War Era: Legal Bases and Implications for National Law' (2004) 8 Max Planck Yearbook of United Nations Law 291, 323–6; Moritz P. Moelle, *The International Responsibility of International Organisations: Cooperation in Peacekeeping Operations* (Cambridge University Press 2017) 308; Caplan (n 3) 3–4; Robert Kolb, Gabriele Poretto and Sylvain Vité, *L'application du droit international humanitaire et des droits de l'homme aux organisations internationales : Forces de paix et administrations civiles transitoires* (2005) 216–32 (calling for de facto respect for the principles of the law of occupation).

in an international armed conflict; that the telos of the law of occupation is to constrain a potentially biased and unreliable foreign power, whereas the UN-led administration will by definition be fair and balanced, or be subjected to its own accountability mechanisms that ensure impartiality toward the inhabitants, thereby rendering the law of occupation superfluous; that the restrictive demands of the law of occupation would undermine efforts to make the necessary changes in the law of the foreign country in the quest for restoring and maintaining global peace and security of which the Security Council is the guardian; finally, that acting under Chapter VII frees the Security Council from the constraints of otherwise applicable law, and so even if all the arguments *supra* were wrong, and the law of occupation did apply to the UN, this law would be most likely superseded by the specific Security Council Chapter VII-based resolutions. To sum up: a trusted institution such as the Security Council-authorised territorial administration will only be burdened by the law of occupation. Applying the law of occupation would needlessly impede the international organisation and excessively limit its mandate to ensure good governance and protect human rights in the foreign territory.[22]

Unfortunately, experience gained with international organisations in general and with the UN in particular, has belied the mythical belief in the sanctity of these organisations.[23] Much of the evidence for the simple truth that there is nothing inherently trustworthy in international organisations, that they are as fallible as any human endeavour, is laid bare in the practice of UN-led administration of territories. As the following section will demonstrate, potential conflicts of interest between occupiers and occupied that inhere in almost any occupation[24] exist also in UN-led occupations. The triangular conflict of interests that characterises foreign occupations – between the occupier, the occupied population and the

[22] *See* Charles H. B. Garraway, 'Applicability and Application of International Humanitarian Law to Enforcement and Peace Enforcement Operations' in Terry D. Gill and Dieter Fleck (eds), *The Handbook of the International Law of Military Operations* (Oxford University Press 2010) 129, 130–1; Christopher Greenwood, 'International Humanitarian Law and United Nations Military Operations' (1998) 1 Yearbook of International Humanitarian Law 3, 28–30, 33–34; Adam Roberts, 'What Is Military Occupation' (1985) 55 British Yearbook of International Law 249, 256, 290. Michael Matheson, 'United Nations Governance of Postconflict Societies' (2001) 95 American Journal of International Law 76, 83–5; David J. Scheffer, 'Beyond Occupation Law' (2003) 97 American Journal of International Law 842, 851.

[23] See Benvenisti (n 16); Klabbers (n 16).

[24] On these conflicts see Benvenisti (n 7) Chapter 1.

ousted government – exists also in UN-led administration of territories. Although the local population may be less wary about an international organisation than about a foreign state, conflicts of interest and conflicting visions about the future of the territory could arise, and do arise as we shall see in Section 3. As a consequence, none of the teleological arguments against the applicability of the law of occupation is fully convincing.[25] Such arguments will certainly not convince an occupied population weary of external intervention in their domestic affairs.[26]

As a matter of *lex ferenda*, it is also unclear why the law should allow the UN to ignore the accumulated experience with occupations when dealing with the trilateral conflicts of interest between occupier, occupied and ousted government, and allow a foreign actor to relieve itself of the discipline that the law of occupation imposes on governing others.[27] The law of occupation provides basic guidelines on the exercise of wide-ranging governmental powers by occupiers, including in so-called transformative occupations.[28] Recourse to the framework of the law of occupation would enable both the government and the governed to draw upon the rich experience that has accumulated over the years with respect to foreign administration of territories and to inform their policies and expectations accordingly.

The applicability of the law of occupation is not only a matter of *lex ferenda*. It is also a matter of *lex lata*, despite the above arguments. There is little doubt that UN-led operations are subject to the full panoply of the laws of war concerning the conduct of hostilities during international and non-international armed conflicts. As the law of occupation is part and parcel of these bodies of law, and enjoys the same status as customary law, it is part of the law applicable to the UN and other international organisations. As stated by the Institut de Droit International in 1971,

[25] Steven R. Ratner, 'Foreign Occupation and International Territorial Administration: The Challenges of Convergence' (2005) 16 European Journal of International Law 695, 702 ('the legal frameworks governing these two types of operations have witnessed significant convergence. As a result, it becomes more difficult to see them as governed by separate sets of norms').

[26] W. Michael Reisman, 'Why Regime Change Is (Almost Always) a Bad Idea' (2004) 98 American Journal of International Law 516, 522 (noting the potential indigenous opposition also to a UN-led occupation).

[27] Siobhan Wills, *Protecting Civilians: The Obligations of Peacekeepers* (Oxford University Press 2009) 241–4.

[28] Adam Roberts, 'Transformative Military Occupation: Applying the Law of War and Human Rights' (2006) 100 American Journal of International Law 580; Roberts (n 22) 290.

> The humanitarian rules of the law of armed conflict apply to the United Nations as of right, and they must be complied with in all circumstances by United Nations Forces which are engaged in hostilities . . . includ[ing] in particular: b) the rules contained in the Geneva Conventions of 12 August 1949; [and] c) the rules which aim at protecting civilian persons and property.[29]

Obviously, the inclusion of all the Geneva Conventions, including the Fourth Convention that covers relations with 'protected persons' outside the zone of combat, implies applicability in occupied territories. Any sophisticated interpretation of the Fourth Geneva Convention must bear in mind the fact that there are human beings at the end of the interpretative exercise whose rights are not necessarily protected by benevolent UN administrators.

The applicability of the law of occupation is derived also from first principles of sovereignty and non-intervention. The law of occupation is not only about regulating armed conflicts. It is also, if not primarily, about sovereignty and the protection of sovereign rights. The nineteenth-century notion of occupation as a temporary regime that does not confer sovereign authority can be understood as the culmination of a long process in which the concept of sovereignty was refined. Indeed, the evolution of the concept of occupation can be seen as the mirror-image of the development of the concept of sovereignty. The inclusion of the regime of occupation in the codification of the laws of war was a consequence of the fact that hitherto, conquest through war would extinguish sovereign title. The obligation to respect the sovereign rights of the ousted government reflects the final stages of the crystallisation of the concept of sovereignty as a nation's claim for exclusive and permanent control over its territory and nationals.[30] During the twentieth century, emerging principles of self-determination, democracy and

[29] Zagreb Resolution (n 20) art 2. See also Institut de Droit International, 'The Application of International Humanitarian Law and Fundamental Human Rights, in Armed Conflicts in which Non-State Entities are Parties', 1999 Berlin Resolution, 25 August 1999, art 1(2), www.idi-iil.org/app/uploads/2017/06/1999_ber_03_en.pdf ('All parties to armed conflicts in which non-State entities are parties, irrespective of their legal status, as well as the United Nations, and competent regional and other international organizations have the obligation to respect international humanitarian law as well as fundamental human rights').

[30] Edward James Kolla, *Sovereignty, International Law, and the French Revolution* (Cambridge University Press 2017) (outlining the impact of the French call for national self-determination on the evolution of international law and the reconceptualisation of sovereign title).

human rights that pierced the veil of national sovereignty and limited it affected also the law of occupation. By the end of the twentieth century, the occupier would, for example, be required to respect the human rights of indigenous populations, who, in turn, would be entitled to promote their collective interests against the oppressive sovereign. Indeed, the law of occupation can be seen as indirectly defining the concept of sovereignty just as tort law defined the common law private right to property by providing causes of action for its violation.[31]

If we take account of the fact that the law of occupation is designed not only to protect the rights of occupied inhabitants, but also to respect state sovereignty and self-determination – a *jus cogens* norm[32] – it becomes clear that there are, as a matter of *lex lata*, legal limits to UN-led administrations.[33] The law of occupation internalises a delicate balance between conflicting interests of occupier and occupied, and reflects the obligation to respect the indigenous people's right to continue exercising

[31] Eyal Benvenisti, 'The Origins of the Concept of Belligerent Occupation' (2008) 26 Law and History Review 621; Benvenisti (n 7) Chapter 1, fn 3 and accompanying text.

[32] For a discussion of derogation from *jus cogens* rights by the Council, see Case T-315/01 *Kadi* v. *Council* [2005] ECR II–3649, [230]; Erika de Wet, 'The Role of Human Rights in Limiting the Enforcement Power of the Security Council: A Principled View' in Erika de Wet et al. (eds), *Review of the Security Council by Member States* (Intersentia 2003) 22; Dapo Akande, 'The International Court of Justice and the Security Council: Is There Room for Judicial Control of Decisions of the Political Organs of the United Nations?' (1997) 46 International & Comparative Law Quarterly 309, 322. See also Katharina Parameswaran, *Besatzungsrecht im Wandel* (Nomos 2008) 196–201; Marten Zwanenburg, 'Existentialism in Iraq: Security Council Resolution 1483 and the Law of Occupation' (2004) 86 International Review of the Red Cross 745, 760–6. But see FOX (n 3) 211–13. For the principle of self-determination as an *erga omnes* obligation, see *East Timor (Portugal* v. *Australia)*, Judgment [1995] ICJ Rep 90, 102. For the principle as also a *jus cogens* right, see International Law Commission, Draft Articles on Responsibility of States for Internationally Wrongful Acts, with Commentaries (2001) UN Doc A/56/10 (2001) 113 *et seq* (in the context of Article 41); Antonio Cassese, *Self-Determination of Peoples: A Legal Reappraisal* (Cambridge University Press 1995) 320.

[33] For the view that the UN is or should be subject to the laws of armed conflict and the law of occupation, see Michael Bothe and Thilo Marauhn, 'UN Administration of Kosovo and East Timor: Concept, Legality and Limitations of Security Council Mandated Trusteeship Administration' in Christian Tomuschat (ed), *Kosovo and the International Community: A Legal Assessment* (Kluwer International 2002) 237; Tobias H. Irmscher, 'The Legal Framework for the Activities of the United Nations Interim Administration Mission in Kosovo: The Charter, Human Rights, and the Law of Occupation' (2001) 44 German Yearbook of International Law 353, 383–7; Hansjoerg Strohmeyer, 'Collapse and Reconstruction of a Judicial System: The United Nations Mission in Kosovo and East Timor' (2001) 95 American Journal of International Law 46, 58–9; Umesh Palwankar, 'Applicability of International Humanitarian Law to UN Peacekeeping Forces' (1993) 33 International Review of the Red Cross 227.

self-determination.[34] Therefore, authorising an occupier to derogate from its responsibilities under the law of occupation and thereby intervene in the indigenous exercise of self-government carries the danger of infringing the *jus cogens* right to sovereignty and self-determination.[35]

The final source of *lex lata* limitation on the Security Council's authority is derived from the structure of the UN. In no way may the UN purport to extinguish the right to sovereignty of a member state, which the regime of occupation seeks to protect. As Oscar Schachter emphasised, when discussing UN Security Council Resolution 1483 concerning Iraq,

> the principles of the Charter require respect for 'sovereign equality' and the right of states to political independence and territorial integrity. These principles and the related Charter purposes may be considered to limit the authority of the Council to impose a regime on the defeated aggressor . . . The people of the country would still be entitled to self-government and basic political rights.

Similarly, the Security Council is obligated to protect the rights, including the human rights, of the protected persons in a territory it controls directly or through sub-organs.[36] If, according to the General Comment of the Human Rights Committee, 'the rights guaranteed under the Covenant belong to the people living in the territory of a State party, and . . . once the people are accorded the protection of the rights under the Covenant, such protection devolves with territory and continues to belong to them, notwithstanding changes in the administration of that territory',[37] then it is

[34] Benvenisti (n 7) Chapter 1, fn 91 and accompanying text, Chapter 4, fn 113 and accompanying text.

[35] Robert Kolb and Sylvain Vité, *Le droit de l'occupation militaire: Perspectives historiques et enjeux juridiques actuels* (Bruylant 2009) 213–14, 250–60.

[36] Alexandre Faite, 'Applicability of the Law of Occupation to United Nations-Mandated Forces' in Alexandre Faite & Jérémie Grenier (eds), *Report of Expert Meeting on Multinational Operations: Applicability of International Humanitarian Law and International Human Rights Law to UN Mandated Forces, Geneva, December 11–12, 2003* (ICRC 2004) 71, 76 ('one may wonder if the Security Council could institute a regime that falls short of the protection provided for protected persons by the Fourth Geneva Convention and adopt lower standards of protection. This would appear contradictory to the underlying rationale of international humanitarian law, as reflected in Articles 7, 8 and 47 of the Fourth Geneva Convention'). See also Venice Commission (n 12).

[37] HRC, General Comment No. 26 (1997). On this comment and its applicability to UNMIK in Kosovo, see Benvenisti (n 7) Chapter 10, fn 73.

not clear to what extent the Security Council can, even acting under Chapter VII, instruct the administering regime to ignore those protections.

Therefore, there can be no legally valid UN-based regime 'beyond occupation law';[38] as it strives to protect individual and collective rights, the law of occupation also applies to UN-led missions.[39] The application of this law could allow for a wider interpretation of the scope of the occupier's authority, to the extent that as a UN-led body, the administration promises to be impartial and unbiased.[40] While it is safe to assume that the Security Council or its sub-organs would be more trustworthy administrators than any national army,[41] and therefore could maybe benefit from more leeway in implementing the law, the lack of any discipline could lead to concerns about corruption that any exercise of unbridled power raises.

Finally, it should be recalled that the law of occupation, as well as human rights law, would certainly apply to states whose forces take part in implementing the UN-led mission. To the extent that the operation is attributed to the member states (rather than to the UN), they would be expected, when complying with the UN mandate, to observe, as much as the text allows them, their general obligations under international law, including human rights law.[42] This principle has received in recent years sound support from national[43] and international[44] courts.

38 Cf. Scheffer (n 22).

39 See also ICTY, *Prosecutor* v. *Tadić*, Decision on the Defense Motion for Interlocutory Appeal on Jurisdiction, IT-94-1-A, Appeals Chamber, 2 October 1995, [93] (noting that Article 1 of the four Geneva Conventions 'lays down an obligation that is incumbent, not only on states, but also on other international entities including the UN').

40 Sylvain Vité, 'L'applicabilité du droit international de l'occupation militaire aux activités des organisations internationales' (2004) 86 International Review of the Red Cross 9, 25–6 (the law of occupation should apply at the start of UN-led occupations, but then could then be progressively adjusted to meet the specific needs of populations under international administration).

41 On these see Wilde (n 3); Stahn (n 3). During the occupation of Iraq by the United States and the United Kingdom, it is safe to assume that their interests were somewhat checked by the involvement of other permanent members, most notably China and Russia.

42 Jann K. Kleffner, 'Human Rights and International Humanitarian Law: General Issues' in Gill and Fleck (n 22) 76 ('Article 103 does not free States from their international obligations under applicable international law, if action authorized by Chapter VII can be taken in a manner that conforms to those obligations').

43 *R (on the application of Al-Jedda) (FC)* v. *Secretary of State for Defence* [2007] UKHL 58.

44 ECtHR, *Al Jedda* v. *United Kingdom*, App No. 27021/08, 7 July 2011. See also the judgment of the European Court of Justice in Case T-315/01 *Kadi* v. *Council* [2005] ECR II-3649, [230].

3 Case Study: UNMIK in Kosovo

To demonstrate the embeddedness of the trilateral conflict of interests – between the foreign administration, the local population and the ousted government – also in a UN-led administration, as well as to show the consequences of the dismissive attitude towards the need for legal constraints on UN-led administration, this section will assess the experience of the UN administration of Kosovo. This was the first attempt by the UN to exercise direct plenary administrative powers in a territory of a member state, after control over Kosovo had been wrestled from the Serbian government by NATO forces.[45] This brief description of the regime in Kosovo underscores the impact of a regime that is intent on having no checks or balances. It highlights the need to impose legal discipline of the sort provided by the law of occupation.

3.1 *The Legal Framework*

UNMIK administrated a territory subject to Serbian sovereignty, following a NATO campaign that sought to end the repression of the Kosovars and force the Rambouillet draft agreement on Serbia.[46] The Serbian government capitulated, and withdrew its forces from Kosovo, while

> Underst[anding] and agree[ing] that [the NATO-led force, KFOR] will deploy following the adoption of the Security Council resolution . . . and operate without hindrance within Kosovo and with the authority to take all necessary action to establish and maintain a secure environment for all citizens of Kosovo and otherwise carry out its mission.[47]

This agreement is clearly one-sided, as one would expect from an agreement obtained after seventy-eight days of relentlessly punishing NATO air strikes that could easily qualify as coercion. The Serbian government does not insist on any guarantees to the Serbian population remaining in

[45] The Secretary-General, Report of the Secretary-General pursuant to Paragraph 10 of Security Council Resolution 1244 (1999), 12 June 1999, UN Doc S/1999/672. On this administration see also Guglielmo Verdirame, *The UN and Human Rights: Who Guards the Guardians?* (Cambridge University Press 2011) 244–69; Chesterman (n 3).

[46] 'Press Statement by Dr. Javier Solana, Secretary General of NATO', NATO Press Release, Press No. 040, 23 March 1999.

[47] Military-Technical Agreement between the International Security Force (KFOR) and the Governments of the Federal Republic of Yugoslavia and the Republic of Serbia from 9 June 1999, 15 June 1999, UN Doc S/1999/682, art 1, https://undocs.org/S/1999/682.

Kosovo (except for entreating for KFOR's goodwill). The agreement details Serbia's obligations to cease and refrain from hostilities and withdraw its forces from Kosovo. The KFOR commander is, according to Article 5, 'the final authority regarding interpretation of [the] agreement and the security aspects of the peace settlement it supports. Its determinations are binding on all Parties and persons.'

The following day, on 10 June 1999, the Security Council passed Resolution 1244. This Chapter VII-based Resolution clearly indicates that it is imposed on Serbia. While KFOR effectively controls Kosovo, the actual administration of public order and civil life is assigned by Resolution 1244 to an international civil presence in Kosovo. Pursuant to paragraph 10, the Secretary-General established UNMIK as the international civil presence, headed by the SRSG.[48] The SRSG would have overall authority to manage the mission and to coordinate the activities of the various participating international organisations.[49]

The huge task of reconstructing Kosovo and leading it to a 'substantial autonomy' formally within Serbia was too much for the UN body which lacked the expertise and the capacity to perform these functions. Indeed, it is not clear whether the authors of this complex legal structure were anticipating that the UNMIK authorities would be able actually to shape, coordinate and implement the policies of UNMIK and how much would be decided by the European states and the European Union on which UNMIK was relying.[50] Although they were called 'Special Representatives of the Secretary-General' it is not clear how much power the Secretary-General had over its representatives. The first SRSG appointed for this task was Bernard Kouchner, a prominent French politician who had never served in a UN position. The succeeding SRSGs, all from Europe, were either top politicians or high-level civil servants in their countries, except one who had been working at the UNHCR.[51] As a matter of fact, it is not very clear how much clout the

[48] Report of the Secretary-General (n 45).

[49] ibid para 3.

[50] Matthias Ruffert, 'The Administration of Kosovo and East-Timor by the International Community' (2001) 50 International & Comparative Law Quarterly 613, 619.

[51] See UNMIK's website: http://www.unmikonline.org/Pages/SRSGs.aspx; Ruffert (n 50) even doubted the legal authority the Security Council had over the SRSG(!), mentioning that 'Conflicts of competence that might arise between the organizations must be solved on a more or less consensual basis. It would not be convenient for the UN to make use of Chapter VII in this respect, leaving aside that Security Council action is only binding upon UN members, i.e. States.'

SRSGs enjoyed while in office. Seven people served as SRSG in the first ten years of UNMIK, none holding office for more than two years, and none having the opportunity or the personal incentive to study the problems facing its administration and to make long-term plans for implementation.

3.2 The Structure of Governance

The SRSG held effectively all three branches of government, due to its vast legislative and executive powers,[52] as well as its significant authority in the context of the administration of justice, including the authority to appoint or remove judges from office.[53] Armed with an extensive mandate from the Security Council, and constrained normatively by the obligation to protect and promote human rights, the SRSG issued its first order on 25 July 1999 (with retroactive effect).[54] Regulation No. 1999/1 on the Authority of the Interim Administration in Kosovo asserted that all three branches of government – the legislative, executive and judiciary – were vested in the SRSG. It stipulated that the administration of Kosovo will be based on respect for 'internationally recognized human rights standards and shall not discriminate against any person'.[55]

UNMIK embarked on rewriting the existing criminal and criminal procedure codes, to render them compatible with international human rights standards.[56] UNMIK conducted reviews of all legislation related to the creation of an independent judiciary, and amended and superseded inconsistent laws by subsequent UNMIK Regulations.[57] Furthermore, UNMIK introduced extensive modifications of the local civil laws. A major intervention in the domestic law, one that significantly altered

52 Regulation No. 1999/1 (n 11) art 1(1).

53 UNMIK, Regulation No. 2001/2 Amending UNMIK Regulation No. 2000/6, as Amended, on the Appointment and Removal from Office of International Judges and International Prosecutors, 12 January 2001, UN Doc UNMIK/REG/2001/2.

54 Regulation No. 1999/1 (n 11). The retroactive effect is provided by section 6.

55 The Secretary-General, Report of the Secretary-General on the United Nations Interim Administration Mission in Kosovo, delivered to the Security Council, 12 July 1999, UN Doc S/1999/779. The report mentions that the SRSG 'may change, repeal or suspend existing laws to the extent necessary for the carrying out of his functions, or where existing laws are incompatible with the mandate, aims and purposes of [UNMIK]' (para 39).

56 Strohmeyer (n 33).

57 Fredrick Lorenz, 'The Rule of Law in Kosovo: Problems and Prospects' (2000) 11 Criminal Law Forum 127, 139.

the regime imposed by the Serbian sovereign, was effected when the Albanian Kosovars pressed to regain their rights under the autonomous regime they had enjoyed prior to the Serb annulment of that regime in 1989.[58] Caving in to their pressure, the SRSG corrected that foundational Regulation by setting the date of the applicable local law back to 22 March 1989, that is, just before Kosovo's autonomy status had been revoked by the Serbian government.[59]

As head of UNMIK, the SRSG was the 'highest international civilian official' in Kosovo, thereby enjoying 'maximum civilian executive powers' and the 'final authority on their interpretation'.[60] It also had the authority to appoint and remove persons in administrative functions in accordance with the existing laws and UNMIK Regulations.[61] Because the SRSG is both the supreme legislator and head of the executive branch, it would assign to itself, in Regulations, the authority to issue administrative acts called 'Administrative Directions' to implement the Regulations. But the hierarchy between the two types of orders was more practical than legal. The SRSG regarded both as having the same legal status, and thus Directions could amend Regulations even retroactively. In one instance, concerning the Human Rights Advisory Panel, a Direction that 'implemented' a Regulation actually altered it significantly.[62] As administrator, UNMIK intervened in and regulated all areas of commercial life as any other government, including regulation of the banks, the media and public services. One of the tasks that UNMIK faced was management of the tense relations between the Albanian majority and the Serb minority and the protection of Serb, Roma and other minorities from acts of discrimination, violence and what was called 'reverse ethnic cleansing'.

Aside from its legislative and executive powers, the SRSG also had authority regarding the administration of justice. The task proved to be

[58] Ibid 128–9.

[59] UNMIK, Regulation No. 1999/24, as amended by Regulation No. 1999/59 Amending UNMIK Regulation No. 1999/24 on the Law Applicable in Kosovo, 27 October 2000, UN Doc UNMIK/REG/2000/59, at section 1. Regulation No. 1999/1 was thereafter repealed by UNMIK, Regulation No. 1999/25 Amending UNMIK Regulation No. 1999/1 on the Authority of the Interim Administration in Kosovo, 12 December 1999, UN Doc UNMIK/REG/1999/25.

[60] The Secretary-General Report of 12 July 1999 (n 55) para 44.

[61] ibid para 40.

[62] For a significant example, see the modification of the Regulation establishing the Human Rights Advisory Panel, Benvenisti (n 7) Chapter 10, text accompanying fnn 78–80.

particularly problematic. The dissolution of Kosovo's autonomy within Serbia in 1989 was reflected not only in the elimination of Kosovo's legislature and government, but also the dissolution of its autonomous judicial system and the removal or resignation of most Albanian Kosovars from the Bench. In 1999, those who remained judges were deemed collaborators by the Albanian majority, and judges belonging to the Serb minority resigned due to intimidation or refusal to collaborate with UNMIK. The judiciary had to be reconstituted in a very short space of time. But then a new problem emerged: the newly appointed judges, Kosovar Albanians, tended to discriminate against the Serb and other minorities.[63]

UNMIK reacted immediately by establishing an emergency judicial system.[64] On 28 June 1999, the SRSG issued an emergency degree creating the Joint Advisory Council on Provisional Judicial Appointment[65] that provided recommendations for three-month, renewable appointments of judges and prosecutors and was engaged in setting up the Judicial System Mobile Units, a mobile court travelling around the area to adjudicate the most pressing cases. Thereafter, UNMIK focused on the establishment of a permanent judiciary. To facilitate this process, the SRSG issued two Regulations, each creating a specific body. UNMIK Regulation 1999/6 established the Technical Advisory Commission on Judiciary and Prosecution Service that was mandated to evaluate the requirements for the judiciary in the long term.[66] UNMIK Regulation 1999/7 created the Advisory Judicial Commission on Appointment of Judges and Prosecutors that replaced the Joint Advisory Council.[67] This Regulation, asserting 'the purpose of establishing an independent and multi-ethnic judiciary in

[63] On the judicial crisis and the responses thereto, see Michael E. Hartmann, 'International Judges and Prosecutors in Kosovo: A New Model for Post-Conflict Peacekeeping' USIP Special Report, 13 October 2003, www.usip.org/publications/international-judges-and-prosecutors-kosovo-new-model-post-conflict-peacekeeping; Strohmeyer (n 33).

[64] Wendy S. Betts, Scott N. Carlson and Gregory Gisvold, 'The Post-Conflict Transitional Administration of Kosovo and the Lessons-Learned in Efforts to Establish a Judiciary and Rule of Law'(2001) 22 Michigan Journal of International Law 371, 377–9.

[65] ibid referring to Organization for Security and Cooperation in Europe, Legal Systems Monitoring Section, Kosovo: Review of the Criminal Justice System, February–July 2000 (2000).

[66] UNMIK, Regulation No. 1999/6 on the Recommendations for the Structure and Administration of the Judiciary and Prosecution Service, 7 September 1999, UN Doc UNMIK/REG/1999/6.

[67] UNMIK, Regulation No. 1999/7 on the Appointment and Removal from Office of Judges and Prosecutors, 7 September 1999, UN Doc UNMIK/REG/1999/7.

Kosovo', authorised the SRSG to appoint and remove from office judges and prosecutors on the basis of the recommendation of an 'independent' commission of local and foreign legal experts who would be selected, appointed (for one-year renewable terms) and remunerated by the SRSG.[68] A similar procedure provided for the appointment, removal and remuneration of 'lay-judges'.[69]

But this was not deemed sufficient to ensure the impartiality of judges and prosecutors. Therefore a novel solution was found by the inclusion of 'international judges'.[70] But similar to the way local judges were appointed or dismissed, the Regulation concerning international judges allowed the SRSG wide discretion concerning their appointment, renewal of term and removal from office: a judge's 'failure in the due execution of office' was one of the grounds authorising the SRSG to terminate a judge's term.[71]

3.3 Accountability (or Lack Thereof)

Despite the concentration of authority in a single position, the SRSG has not offered any effective mechanism for administrative review of its policies or of their implementation. Review mechanisms have been established only in a few technical matters related to the implementation of UNMIK policies, such as tax matters, but even so appeals would be before courts appointed by the SRSG.[72] In addition, UNMIK Regulation 2000/47 granted a general immunity from legal process to KFOR and

[68] ibid ('For the purpose of establishing an independent and multi-ethnic judiciary in Kosovo'). For a critique, see Carsten Stahn, 'Justice under Transitional Administration: Contours and Critique of a Paradigm' (2005) 27 Houston Journal of International Law 311, 331–2.

[69] Regulation No. 1999/18 on the Appointment and Removal from Office of Lay Judges, 10 November 1999, UN Doc UNMIK/REG/1999/18.

[70] UNMIK, Regulation No. 2000/64 on Assignment of International Judges/Prosecutors and/or Change of Venue, 15 December 2000, UN Doc UNMIK/REG/2000/64.

[71] Regulation No. 2001/2 (n 53).

[72] Andreas Zimmermann and Carsten Stahn, 'Yugoslav Territory, United Nations Trusteeship or Sovereign State? Reflections on the Current and Future Legal Status of Kosovo' (2001) 70 Nordic Journal of International Law 423, 448, referring in note 124 to UNMIK, Regulation No. 2000/20 on Tax Administration and Procedures, 12 April 2000, UN Doc UNMIK/REG/2000/20, creating an Independent Review Board in the area of Tax Administration, or UNMIK, Regulation No. 2000/36 on the Licensing and Regulation of the Broadcast Media in Kosovo, 17 June 2000, UN Doc UNMIK/REG/2000/36, establishing the Media Appeals Board. On the substandard accountability mechanisms provided for by UNMIK, see also Caplan (n 3) 199–211.

UNMIK and effectively placed both beyond the reach of the local courts.[73] The same Regulation provided that

> Third party claims for property loss or damage and for personal injury, illness or death arising from or directly attributed to KFOR, UNMIK or their respective personnel and which do not arise from 'operational necessity' of either international presence, shall be settled by Claims Commissions established by KFOR and UNMIK, in the manner to be provided for.[74]

But UNMIK did not establish any commission to settle 'third party claims'. Instead, it relied on a rather opaque procedure which exists in the UN concerning such claims,[75] based on a broad UN General Assembly Resolution from 1998.[76] In some cases, individuals who presented legal claims were offered compensation.[77] The SRSG reacted angrily to a handful of domestic court decisions that refused to enforce executive orders or regulations, and in one case refused to follow a contrary decision by a local court because it was, in his view, 'without legal basis' and 'unenforceable'.[78]

[73] UNMIK, Regulation No. 2000/47 on the Status, Privileges and Immunities of KFOR and UNMIK and Their Personnel in Kosovo, 18 August 2000, UN Doc UNMIK/REG/2000/47. See generally, Margaret Cordial, 'Outline of Presentation of the Situation in Kosovo' in Faite and Grenier (n 36) 52–5; Sylvain Vité, 'Case Study: The Applicability of International Human Rights Law in Kosovo' in Faite and Grenier (n 36) 87, 92.

[74] Regulation No. 2000/47 (n 73) at section 7.

[75] This process is referred to in the Human Rights Advisory Panel, 'Decision in Case No. 26/08 N.M. and Others against UNMIK', 31 March 2010, paras 5–7, www.worldcourts.com/unmik_hrap/eng/decisions/2010.03.31_NM_v_UNMIK.pdf, concerning a Roma camp located near a lead smelter. In that case the process was not finalised until more than four years after submission of the claim.

[76] UNGA Res 52/247(1998), 17 July 1998, UN Doc A/RES/52/247 (1998) on 'Third-Party Liability: Temporal and Financial Limitations' refers to 'Third Party Claims' as 'claims against the [UN] resulting from peacekeeping operations'. The Resolution defines the temporal and financial limitations for damage 'resulting from or attributable to the activities of members of peacekeeping operations arising from "operational necessity"'.

[77] E.g., Human Rights Advisory Panel , 'Decision in Case No. 04/07 Kadri Balaj et al. against UNMIK', 31 March 2010, www.worldcourts.com/unmik_hrap/eng/decisions/2010.03.31_Balaj_v_UNMIK.pdf. KFOR established, in 2003, a commission regarding claims only with respect to activities in its main headquarters. It delegated the responsibility to process other claims to the 'Troop Contributing Nations' regarding 'claims that arise from their own activities, in accordance with their own claims rules, regulations and procedures'. See Standard Operating Procedure 3023 for Claims in Kosovo (SOP) on 22 March 2003, reproduced in Didier Pacquée and Steven Dewulf, 'International Territorial Administrations and the Rule of Law: The Case of Kosovo' (2007) 4 Essex Human Rights Review 1, 8–9.

[78] Rebecca Everly, 'Reviewing Governmental Acts of the United Nations in Kosovo' (2007) 8 German Law Journal 21, 28.

The Ombudsperson Institution set up by the SRSG provided it with 'jurisdiction to receive and investigate complaints from any person or entity in Kosovo concerning human rights violations and actions constituting an abuse of authority by the interim civil administration', namely, the UN-led part of UNMIK; not the other parts of UMNIK, or KFOR.[79] The SRSG was to appoint the Ombudsperson for a term of two years, renewable for further terms of two years, and the SRSG was also authorised to remove the Ombudsperson from office, inter alia, for 'failure in the execution of his or her functions'.[80] The Ombudsperson has issued several reports criticising the immunities of the SRSG and UNMIK from judicial oversight and criticising several of their policies; however, the SRSG either disagreed with most of these reports or simply disregarded them.[81] For example, the Ombudsperson's Special Report No. 1 addressed Regulation 2000/47 on the Status, Privileges and Immunities of KFOR and UNMIK,[82] criticising it in the most unequivocal terms as infringing basic principles of human rights law, and lamenting that '[s]uch blanket lack of accountability paves the way for the impunity of the state.'[83] The report was simply ignored.

Ultimately the SRSG succumbed to mounting international pressure and formally exposed its policies to international scrutiny. Both the Human Rights Committee (HRC) and the Committee on Economic, Social and Cultural Rights (CESCR) extended in 2004 and 2005 (respectively) requests to UNMIK to submit reports, based on the theory expressed in the HRC's General Comment No. 26 (1977) on continuity of obligations towards the people concerned.[84] UNMIK complied and

[79] UNMIK, Regulation No. 2000/38 on the Establishment of the Ombudsperson Institution in Kosovo, 30 June 2000, UN Doc UNMIK/REG/2000/38.

[80] Carsten Stahn, 'Governance Beyond the State: Issues of Legitimacy in International Territorial Administration' (2005) 2 International Organisations Law Review 9, 36; Zimmermann and Stahn (n 72) 445.

[81] Everly (n 78) 32.

[82] Ombudsperson Institution in Kosovo, 'Special Report No. 1. On the compatibility with recognised international standards of UNMIK Regulation No. 2000/47 on the Status, Privileges and Immunities of KFOR and UNMIK and Their Personnel in Kosovo (August 18, 2000) and on the Implementation of the above Regulation', para 23. This document is available (in a draft version) at https://fer.org.rs/wp-content/uploads/2018/02/Final-special-report-1-Regulation-47.pdf.

[83] ibid para 23.

[84] '[T]hat the rights guaranteed under the Covenant belong to the people living in the territory of a State party, and that once the people are accorded the protection of the rights under the Covenant, such protection devolves with territory and continues to belong to them, notwithstanding changes in the administration of that territory'. HRC,

submitted reports to both bodies (in 2006 and 2008, respectively), and received highly critical reviews.[85] Among its critical observations, the HRC noted 'the legal uncertainty resulting from the failure to specify which provisions of the formerly applicable law are being replaced by those UNMIK Regulations and Kosovo Assembly laws' and 'the absence of adequate guarantees for the independence of international judges and prosecutors ... the low remuneration of local judges and prosecutors, the low representation of ethnic minorities in the judiciary'.[86] The CESCR expressed its concerns inter alia about the inadequate protection of minority rights against discrimination by the Albanian majority.[87]

UNMIK's insistence on immunity from public accountability was not only harmful to the Kosovar population, but it also nurtured an internal culture of corruption. In 2013, the UN Secretary-General filed an appeal against a judgment of the UN Dispute Tribunal (UNDT) in a case concerning a whistleblower who had reported the complicity of senior UNMIK officials in a kickback scheme related to a controversial proposed power plant in Kosovo. In retaliation, the informer was detained, his home and person were searched, his post was abolished and he was subjected to criminal and administrative investigations. The UNDT criticised the 'wholly unacceptable treatment in breach of his right to due process'.[88] It awarded the informer compensation, on the basis that 'the [UN's] conduct of the proceedings in deliberately and persistently refusing, without good cause, to abide by the orders of the Tribunal and not granting access to the ... investigation report constituted a manifest abuse of proceedings'.[89] Instead of endorsing the decision, the Secretary-General appealed against it, arguing that the UNDT lacked jurisdiction over the matter. In a two-to-one judgment, the UN Appeals Tribunal accepted the Secretary-General's appeal and, thereby, not only left the whistleblower without remedy but also weakened the internal system of

Concluding Observations of the Human Rights Committee Kosovo (Serbia), 14 August 2006, UN Doc CCPR/C/UNK/CO/1, para 4, https://undocs.org/en/CCPR/C/UNK/CO/1.

85 For the HRC observations see ibid; CESCR, Concluding Observations on the Document Submitted by the United Nations interim Administration Mission in Kosovo (UNMIK), 1 December 2008, UN Doc E/C.12/UNK/CO/1, https://tbinternet.ohchr.org/_layouts/15/treatybodyexternal/Download.aspx?symbolno=E%2fC.12%2fUNK%2fCO%2f1&Lang=en.

86 HRC, Concluding Observations (n 84), paras 8, 20.

87 CESCR, Concluding Observations (n 85) paras 12–13, 15, 18, 32.

88 UN Dispute Tribunal, *Wasserstrom* v. *Secretary-General of the United Nations*: Judgment, 21 June 2012, Case No. UNDT/NY/2009/044/JAB/2008/087, para 46.

89 ibid para. 43.

review.[90] This experience belies the belief that UN administrators would be impartial and effective and that subjecting them to legal discipline would therefore be unnecessary and even over-burdensome. The instances of UN-led territorial administration highlight a simple truth with respect to the relationship between functionality and accountability: these are not necessarily opposing goals that need to be pitched against one another but, actually, complementary elements in the organisation's quest for success. Accountability is necessary for ensuring functionality because unfettered discretion for civil servants, even international civil servants, is prone to abuse by those who exploit their privileged position in the pursuit of goals that are incompatible with the organisation's mandate.

3.4 Assessment

The observations of the Ombudsperson, the HRC and the CESCR were shared by many commentators who lamented the culture of unaccountability of the UNMIK regime and in particular the absence of a clear commitment to universal standards of human rights, the lack of reliable checks and balances, and of effective means of review of UNMIK policies and practices.[91] 'With regard to KFOR, the question of whether it is bound even by the applicable law has never been clearly answered and has led to KFOR's possessing seemingly unchallengeable authority.'[92]

Those observations also indicate shortcomings in the maintenance of public order and civil life by UNMIK. No doubt, a significant factor that contributed to these shortcomings was the tense inter-ethnic relations. Despite the autocratic nature of his position – or perhaps because of it – the SRSG has found it difficult to resist the intense pressures from the Kosovar Albanians. These pressures were present from the start, as the population simply refused to regard the law that existed prior to UNMIK's rule as legally valid. They insisted on the eradication of what was for them a symbol of the denial of their autonomy, and their demand

[90] UN Appeals Tribunal, *Wasserstrom* v. *Secretary-General of the United Nations*: Judgment, 27 June 2014, Case No. 2014-UNAT-457.

[91] The list is long and includes David Marshall and Shelley Inglis, 'The Disempowerment of Human Rights–Based Justice in the United Nations Mission' (2003) *Kosovo* 16 Harvard Human Rights Journal 95, 105; Stahn (n 68) and Stahn (n 80); Everly (n 78); Wilde (n 3); Pacquée and Dewulf (n 77).

[92] Marshall and Inglis (n 91) 103.

was met by the SRSG's retroactive resuscitation of the 1989 law.[93] These pressures were also reflected in legislation, such as a regulation which imposed unnecessary evidentiary demands on minority employees seeking to prove discrimination on ethnic grounds.[94] KFOR's capabilities for containing ethnic violence and fighting crime were also found wanting.[95]

The story told thus far raises a simple question: 'If organisations such as UNMIK and KFOR start acting like a state, should they not obey the same principles and rules that apply to states and limit their action? As they are essentially given "state-like" powers, should they not bear the same responsibilities?'[96] I would accentuate this question by asking: if states are subject to strict legal and institutional constraints on their treatment of their own citizens, on what grounds should a body that exercises state-like functions be exempted from the same constraints in treating *foreign nationals*? And finally, what difference would the application of the law of occupation make?

In retrospect, observers of UNMIK have suggested that it was the 'weak policy adopted in the early stages of deployment' in Kosovo and the 'kid gloves approach' that contributed to the breakdown of law and order and the failure to create a secure environment for vulnerable minorities; a tough stance based on martial law should have been preferred.[97] The fact that there is a preordained set of norms, especially legal norms that constitute part of the laws of war, provides a basis for the new administrator to restrain inhabitants who scramble to fill the political vacuum created by ousting the previous local regime, and to reject domestic pressures to ignore the law in force in the country. The lack of clarity regarding the applicable law which resulted from local pressure to revive 1989 law persisted for several years and was criticised by the HRC as late as 2006. The law of occupation provides an explanation for domestic stakeholders who query why the occupiers act like autocrats.

93 See Strohmeyer (n 33) 58–9; Irmscher (n 33) 392.

94 The *Termosistem Case*: see Eyal Benvenisti and Michal Saliternik, 'The Treatment of Occupation Legislation by Courts in Liberated Territories' in Edda Kristjansdottir, Andre Nollkaemper and Cedric Ryngaert (eds), *International Law in Domestic Courts: Rule of Law Reform in Post-Conflict States* (Intersentia 2012).

95 Cornelius Friesendorf, *The Military and Law Enforcement in Peace Operations: Lessons from Bosnia-Herzegovina and Kosovo* (Lit 2009) 125–8.

96 Pacquée and Dewulf (n 77) 14.

97 Ray Murphy, *UN Peacekeeping in Lebanon, Somalia and Kosovo: Operational and Legal Issues* (Cambridge University Press 2007) 153.

More generally, if it is not likely that a UN-led administration would have god-like traits such as omnipotence, omniscience, and impartiality, it is imprudent to allow it to rule without any normative constraints and institutional checks. The administration of Kosovo by UNMIK and KFOR suggests that UN-led administration is not inherently omnipotent, but suffers from limited personnel and budget, and is heavily dependent on the cooperation of domestic forces to avoid destabilising its mission; it is not omniscient, as it lacks experience and knowledge of local conditions; and it is not impartial, as it seeks the success of its self-defined 'civilizing mission' at minimal human and material costs, and this might lead it to pursue skewed policies and practices that unduly prefer some domestic interests over others.[98]

Reflecting on the administration of Kosovo by UNMIK and KFOR, Siobhán Wills observed,[99]

> it is oversimplification to suggest that the UN administration will always have no interest of its own. The Security Council . . . acts in the interests of maintaining international peace and security, as those interests are perceived by its Member States, particularly the Permanent Five. The inhabitants . . . may have a different perspective . . . to the UN . . . and may not always regard the UN as an impartial representative of their interests.

The experience in Kosovo provides sufficient reasons to expect UN-led administration missions to comply with international law 'like states' that occupy foreign territories, namely in line with the law of occupation. Compliance with the law of occupation is particularly useful for the success of a UN mission, even beyond the application of international human rights law, because the law of occupation is inherently geared towards the same triangular conflicts of interest that arise when a foreign actor rules a foreign community, especially during the aftermath of military crisis that destabilises the institutional framework of governance. This law offers established mechanisms to respond to immediate challenges upon assuming control and restoring public order. The strict demands of the law, to restore public order and civil life, by imposing martial law if necessary, while protecting individual rights, supply the necessary ingredients that can promote stability in a period of chaos and confusion. This law 'provides practical solutions to problems that armed

[98] Wilde (n 3).
[99] Wills (n 27) 227–8.

forces will necessarily have to face in the field'.[100] As opposed to human rights law that confers an aura of regularity and social legitimacy, the law of occupation preserves the exceptional status of the foreign regime and continues to question and limit the authority of the administration and its exercise of discretion.[101]

It is understandable that governing bodies seek to distinguish themselves from the notion of an 'occupier', which carries a negative connotation. But a population at odds with such a regime would sooner rather than later question its legitimacy regardless of any euphemistic title it adopted. And by recognising the applicability of occupation law the administrative organ would send an important signal of an accountable government that recognises strict limits to its authority. A government subjected to the law of occupation is by definition operating in the zone of the exception; its authority to form and implement policies is inherently suspicious and constantly questioned. This administration must offer reasons for its modifications of the status quo. Perhaps counter-intuitively, it is the undertaking of the administration to comply with the law of occupation which will generate trust and confidence among the inhabitants and outside observers, at the initial moments when the 'battle for hearts and minds' is most crucial, and also later on, during a potential transformative phase, which the law of occupation also provides for.[102]

The application of the law of occupation to UN administrations might be opposed with the concern that the precedents set by those regimes might be emulated by subsequent occupiers who would seek to follow the UN organ's exercising of greater leeway, in particular in cases of transformative occupation.[103] While this is a valid concern, the distinction between the UN and states as occupiers could be carefully monitored and distinguished to the extent that the UN-authorised government is impartial vis-à-vis the occupied territory. Moreover, to the extent that UN-led occupations act effectively and impartially, they could set a healthy precedent for what occupiers

[100] Marco Sassòli, 'Outline of De Jure and De Facto Applicability of the Law of Occupation to United Nations-Mandated Forces' in Faite and Grenier (n 36) 33.

[101] On the problematic recourse by foreign occupation regimes to the language of human rights that 'is based on the assumption that its preferences and moral sensibilities are broadly reflective of the preferences and sensibilities of the community in which it exercises its jurisdiction', see Martti Koskenniemi, 'Occupied Zone – "A Zone of Reasonableness"?' (2008) 41 Israel Law Review 13. On the need to keep referring to an occupation regime as exceptional, see also Benvenisti (n 7) 103–4.

[102] Roberts (n 28).

[103] I thank Jasmin Wennersbusch for this point.

should do, for example, as they involve the local population in governance, as UNTAET in East Timor has sought to do.[104]

4 Concluding Observations

The experience gained with the UNMIK-led administration of Kosovo belies the belief that UN administrators would be impartial and effective and that regulating them would therefore be unnecessary and even taxing. It demonstrates the fact that the typical triangular conflicts of interest that characterise foreign occupations – between the occupier, the occupied population and the ousted government – exist also in UN-led administration of territories, and implicates *jus cogens* issues of sovereignty and self-determination that test the limits on UN action under the UN Charter. The law of occupation offers norms and institutions designed to address these concerns.

The law of occupation is also useful when calling the administrator to take account of and give account to the foreign people subject to its authority, to the legitimate sovereign authority and to the international community. The experience in Kosovo expose the weaknesses of the assumptions that UN-led administrations of territories is inherently trustworthy, or that accountability is sufficiently secured through internal mechanisms. The experience in Kosovo is far from exceptional. As mentioned in the introduction, there have been several instances of territorial administration by UN-led forces. And there are other, more recent, examples of UN-authorised bodies that directly engage with individuals and communities and adversely affect their lives without proper accountability mechanisms. The more recent situation in Haiti is a glaring example of incompetence and lack of accountability of a UN peacekeeping force,[105] and similar observations are offered by Emma Dunlop with respect to the exercise of authority by the United Nations High Commissioner for Refugees (UNHCR) over individuals subject to its direct administration.[106] UN-led instances of territorial administration highlight a simple truth more generally with respect to the law that

[104] See (n 7). On the need to ensure public participation in the governance of occupied territories, see Benvenisti (n 7) 80.

[105] Devika Hovell, 'Due Process in the United Nations' (2016) 110 American Journal of International Law 9; José Alvarez, 'The United Nations in the Time of Cholera' (2014) 108 American Journal of International Law Unbound 22.

[106] Emma Dunlop, 'A Globalized Administrative Procedure: UNHCR's Determination of Refugee Status and Its Procedural Standards' in Sabino Cassese et al. (eds), *Global Administrative Law: The Casebook* (3rd edn IRPA IILJ 2012).

applies to international organisations and that treats them with kids gloves, fearing for their loss of 'functionality': accountability is not a burden on functionality. Rather, accountability enhances functionality, and in fact, it is necessary for ensuring functionality. Unfettered discretion for civil servants, even international civil servants, undermines the functionality of any administration. Embracing the discipline of accountability embedded in the law of occupation for UN-led administration of territories is therefore required both as *lex lata* and as *lex ferenda*.

6

The Responsibility of Businesses Operating in the Settlements in Occupied Territory

YAËL RONEN

This chapter examines standards of conduct applicable to businesses operating in civilian settlements in occupied territory, focusing on the Israeli settlements in the West Bank as a case study. It reviews the legal bodies which govern settlement projects and their applicability to businesses. Noting that businesses are not bound by international law directly, the chapter proceeds to examine the responsibility of businesses involved in settlements under the emerging soft law standards on businesses and human rights, namely the UN's 'Protect, Respect and Remedy' Framework. Some businesses directly contribute to violations of human rights on which the settlement project is inextricably dependent. Businesses operating on a regular basis in settlements benefit from such violations and contribute to their perpetuation. The chapter examines the practical implications of these forms of responsibility in light of the UN Framework and of domestic law.

businesses and human rights, Ruggie Principles, occupation, civilian settlements, Israel, UN Guiding Principles on Business and Human Rights, West Bank

1 Introduction

This chapter explores the applicability and implications of international law with regard to businesses operating in civilian settlements established in occupied territories. It was stimulated by various measures that have been taken over the last two decades in the international community with regard to businesses involved in the Israeli settlements in the West Bank.[1]

[1] This chapter proceeds on the understanding that the law of occupation, including GC IV, applies to Israel's presence in the West Bank. Israel applies the occupying power in the West Bank, but its position on the matter is ambiguous. Aeyal Gross, *The Writing on the*

There are hundreds such businesses, catering to all aspects of life of the communities and of individuals within them.[2] Businesses are involved in construction and real estate management, and in provision of finances, goods, utilities and services. Industrial and agricultural businesses maintain offices, facilities and plants in the settlements.[3] Other businesses, in Israel and around the world, are linked to such activities through supply chains, including producers, suppliers, exporters, intermediary agents and customers.

The BDS campaign, informally launched in 2001, calls upon 'people of conscience to play an effective role in the Palestinian struggle for justice' until Israel 'complies with international law' by ending the occupation and recognising Palestinians' rights. The campaign pertains to a host of Israeli policies that are allegedly unlawful, the settlement project being only one of them.[4] The BDS movement calls on individuals and legal entities to boycott Israeli products on the grounds that Israel profits from the violation of the individual and collective rights of Palestinians. It calls on financial institutions to divest from businesses complicit in the violation of Palestinian rights, and it encourages states to adopt economic sanctions against Israel.

Another development is the adoption by businesses around the world of policies grounded in principles of corporate social responsibility, namely adherence to a set of ethical standards that derive from the 'do no harm' principle. As its name suggests, corporate social responsibility

Wall: Rethinking the International Law of Occupation (Cambridge University Press 2017) Chapters 2, 3. The analysis is equally applicable to East Jerusalem and the Golan Heights, where Israeli domestic law is applied.

2 Databases relating to settlements in the West Bank include WhoProfits, www.whoprofits.org/involvement/settlement-industry, and the UN Database, discussed below. Databases on business activity in occupied territory (not only settlement-related) include the Eiris Foundation, www.businessinoccupiedlands.org, for the West Bank and Crimea, and Western Sahara Resource Watch, www.wsrw.org/a106x4348, for Western Sahara. See also Kohelet Policy Forum (n 11) for Nagorno-Karabakh and Northern Cyprus.

3 The Civil Administration (the civilian arm of the military government in the West Bank) reported over 370 businesses registered in the West Bank, of which about 140 are registered in Israeli settlements. Civil Administration Letter re Freedom of Information Request – List of Companies registered in the Area – Response of Civil Administration Judea and Samaria (24 April 2018), http://peacenow.org.il/wp-content/uploads/2018/05/Companies_List_Feb2018.pdf. WhoProfits lists over 420 businesses linked to the settlement project, https://whoprofits.org/?csearch=1&s=&companys=&involvement=283&industry=0&location=0&revenue=0&region=0&settlements=0.

4 What is BDS, www.bdsmovement.net/bdsintro. The broad scope of the campaign has led to criticism, including accusation that it is grounded in antisemitism.

is addressed to businesses rather than to states or to individuals. Its principal purpose is to protect the ethical integrity of the businesses themselves. While it relies on certain legal criteria to determine ethical standards, it is not limited to legal norms. Various businesses have instated policies of avoiding commercial interaction with partners based in the settlements or in Israeli projects in the West Bank more generally. Some financial and commercial institutions have distanced themselves from the settlements further, by divestment from businesses involved in the settlement project.[5]

Some states have enacted a labelling requirement to distinguish products originating in the Israeli settlements from products originating in Israel. This measure has been justified by domestic consumer protection law obligations that enable consumers to make informed shopping choices.[6]

EU trade and financial support regimes distinguish Israeli businesses and other entities based or operating in the settlements, from those that are based and operate within Israel.[7] These regimes deny settlement-based entities financial support and privileges from which Israel-based entities may benefit. The EU's measures are addressed to member states and are perceived by it as legally required 'to ensure the respect of EU positions and commitments in conformity with international law on the non-recognition by the EU of Israel's sovereignty over the territories occupied by Israel since June 1967'.[8] The EU policy is also based on a political view that the settlements 'constitute an obstacle to peace

[5] For a list of businesses that have adopted such policies, see Yonatan Levi, 'Molad Analysis – Updated Analysis: Economic Boycotts Against Israel' (21 January 2014) www.molad.org/en/articles/Boycotts-Against-Israel.

[6] E.g., Sasha Ingber, 'Canadian Court Rules West Bank Wines Are Not a "Product of Israel"', *NPR.org* (30 July 2019) https://www.npr.org/2019/07/30/746507056/canadian-court-rules-west-bank-wines-are-not-a-product-of-israel; CJEU, *Organisation Juive Européenne and Vignoble Psagot Ltd* v. *Ministre de l'Économie et des Finances*, Request for a Preliminary Ruling from the Conseil d'État, Judgment of the Court (Grand Chamber) ECLI:EU:C:2019:954 (12 November 2019) http://curia.europa.eu/juris/liste.jsf?num=C-363/l; Raphael Ahren, 'Israel Rejects Pretoria Compromise on Labeling Settlement Goods' (14 April 2013) www.timesofisrael.com/israels-rejects-pretoria-compromise-on-labeling-settlement-goods.

[7] Notice to importers – Imports from Israel into the EU, 2012 OJ (C 232) 5; Guidelines on the Eligibility of Israeli Entities and Their Activities in the Territories Occupied by Israel since June 1967 for Grants, Prizes and Financial Instruments funded by the EU from 2014 Onwards, 2013 OJ (C 205) 9.

[8] EU Guidelines, ibid art 1.

and threaten to make a two-state solution to the Israeli-Palestinian conflict impossible'.[9]

In March 2016, the UN Human Rights Council established a database of business projects that involved a ten-item list of settlement-related activities that raise particular human rights violations concerns.[10] The purpose of this database is to enable member states 'to take appropriate measures to ensure that business projects domiciled in their territory and/or under their jurisdiction ... that conduct activities in or related to the settlements respect human rights throughout their operations'.[11] In February 2020 the Office of the UN High Commissioner for Human Rights (OHCHR) issued a list of 112 businesses qualifying for inclusion under the mandate.[12] Even earlier, some states cautioned business activity in the settlements may entail legal and economic risks stemming from the settlements' illegality.[13] In December 2016, the UN Security Council adopted a resolution reaffirming that the establishment by Israel of settlements in the Occupied Territories has no legal validity and constitutes a flagrant violation under international law, and a major obstacle to the achievement of the two state solution and a just, lasting and

[9] Zoya Sheftalovich, 'EU Holds Firm on West Bank Settlements as US Eases Stance', *Politico* (19 November 2019) www.politico.eu/article/eu-holds-firm-on-west-bank-settlements-as-us-eases-stance.

[10] Human Rights Council, Resolution 31/36, 'Israeli Settlements in the Occupied Palestinian Territory, Including East Jerusalem, and in the Occupied Syrian Golan, UN Doc A/HRC/RES/31/36 (24 March 2016) para 17.

[11] Human Rights Council, Report of the Independent International Factfinding Mission to Investigate the Implications of the Israeli Settlements on the Civil, Political, Economic, Social and Cultural Rights of the Palestinian People throughout the Occupied Palestinian Territory, Including East Jerusalem, UN Doc A/HRC/22/63, para 117. For a critique of the Council for singling out Israel, see Kohelet Policy Forum, 'Who Else Profits' (November 2018) https://euiha41fnsb2lyeld3vkc37i-wpengine.netdna-ssl.com/wp-content/uploads/2018/11/WhoElseProfits-e-version.pdf.

[12] UN High Commissioner for Human Rights, 'Database of All Business Enterprises Involved in the Activities Detailed in Paragraph 96 of the Report of the Independent International Fact-Finding Mission to Investigate the Implications of the Israeli Settlements on the Civil, Political, Economic, Social and Cultural Rights of the Palestinian People throughout the Occupied Palestinian Territory, Including East Jerusalem: Report of the United Nations High Commissioner for Human Rights, UN Doc A/HRC/43/71 (12 February 2020) ('UN Database').

[13] Working Group on the Issue of Human Rights and Transnational Corporations and Other Business Enterprises; and UNHCHR, 'Statement on the Implications of the Guiding Principles on Business and Human Rights in the Context of Israeli Settlements in the Occupied Palestinian Territory' 7 https://www.ohchr.org/Documents/Issues/Business/OPTStatement6June2014.pdf.

comprehensive peace. Inter alia, the resolution demanded that Israel cease all settlement activities.[14]

The measures described above are grounded in both politics and law and reflect various conceptions of the role of businesses: as the soft underbelly of a state, as a pressure group, as socially and morally accountable actors, or as blameworthy accomplices in the commission or beneficiaries of violations of international law.

The Israeli settlement project is exceptional in terms of the international attention that it attracts. The analysis is nonetheless applicable, *mutatis mutandis*, to other settlement projects, such as in Western Sahara, Northern Cyprus, Crimea and elsewhere. In regions where the very presence of the occupying power in the territory is regarded as unlawful, concern over business activity is often related to the occupation more broadly.[15]

While occupation is not unlawful in itself, state-organised civilian settlement in occupied territory is.[16] This chapter therefore focuses on business activity related to settlements, and specifically on businesses operating in settlements rather than on their partners around the world. Since it is not obvious that businesses of the former type bear legal responsibility, businesses of the latter type, that are more remote from the settlement project, are even less likely to be implicated.[17]

Section 2 reviews the various bodies of international law which govern settlement projects and their relevance to businesses. Section 3 focuses on the emerging standards of international human rights law that apply directly to businesses and their relevance to businesses operating in the Israeli settlements. Section 4 examines what businesses operating in

[14] E.g., UN SC Res 2334, UN Doc S/RES/2334(2016) (23 December 2016) preambular para 4, operative paras 1, 5.

[15] This is reflected in the grounds cited for the few actions that have been taken with respect to these regions, e.g. Norges Bank's Decision to Exclude Kosmos Energy Ltd and Cairn Energy Plc (June 2016), www.nbim.no/en/the-fund/news-list/2016/decision-on-exclusion-of-companies-from-the-government-pension-fund-global. Also see Petroleum Fund's Council on Ethics: Recommendation on Exclusion from the Government Petroleum Fund's Investment Universe of the Company Kerr-McGee Corporation, Government of Norway (12 April 2005) http://www.regjeringen.no/nb/dep/fin/tema/statens_pensjonsfond/ansvarlige-investeringer/tilradninger-og-brev-fra-etikkradet/Recommendation-on-Exclusion-from-the-Government-Petroleum-Funds-Investment-Universe-of-the-Company-Kerr-McGee-Corporation.html?id=419582.

[16] GC IV Article 49(6); David Kretzmer and Yaël Ronen, *The Occupation of Justice* (2nd edn, Oxford University Press 2021) 186–89 .

[17] *Richardson* v. *Director of Public Prosecutions* [2014] UKSC 8, para 17.

settlements must do to discharge their responsibility, and some challenges that arise in that context. Section 5 briefly considers the implications of these challenges.

2 International Law, Settlement Projects and Businesses

International law applies ipso facto only to states.[18] For it to be applicable to businesses it must be extended to them under conventional or customary law. Judicial practice on the matter is not uniform. While the US Supreme Court majority expressed strong (but not unequivocal) reservations about the liability of businesses under international law, the Canadian Supreme Court in a narrow majority held that customary international law may allow businesses to be held directly liable for violations of 'obligatory, definable, and universal norms of international law'. It suggested that this would include peremptory norms, referring specifically to international crimes.[19] This innovative statement does not dispose of the need to examine the potential obligations of businesses under specific bodies of law.[20] The following sections review the main bodies of law which business activity in settlements is likely to involve.

2.1 Settlements, Businesses and the Law of Occupation

Under the law of occupation, the norm most prominently and directly implicated in the settlement project is Article 49(6) of the Fourth Geneva Convention (GC IV) that prohibits the transfer of the occupying power's own civilian population to the occupied territory.[21] The establishment

[18] James Crawford, *Brownlie's Principles of International Law* 3–19 (8th edn, Oxford University Press 2012).

[19] *Jesner* v. *Arab Bank, PLC*, 138 S Ct 1386 (24 April 2018) 17–18; *Nevsun Resources Ltd.* v. *Araya*, 2020 SCC 5, paras 113, 114.

[20] E.g. STL, *Al Jadeed SAL & Ms Khayat* (STL-14-05), Decision on Interlocutory Appeal Concerning Personal Jurisdiction in Contempt Proceedings' (2 October 2014) paras 45–60, where the Special Tribunal for Lebanon's Appeals Panel interpreted Rule 60bis of its Rules of Procedure and Evidence on contempt of court as encompassing the criminal liability of legal persons. The Tribunal relied on the UN Guiding Principles on Business and Human Rights, discussed below, and on the domestic law of various states, seemingly deducing the existence of a general principle of international law regarding legal responsibility of businesses.

[21] For the applicability of Article 49(6) to the Israeli settlement project, see Kretzmer and Ronen (n 16); Theodor Meron, 'The West Bank and International Humanitarian Law on the Eve of the Fiftieth Anniversary of the Six-Day War' (2017) 111 American Journal of International Law 1. This view has been confirmed in *Legal Consequences of the*

and the maintenance of the settlements may involve the violation of additional norms of the law of occupation. One is the prohibition on the use of public land other than by usufruct.[22] Another is the prohibition on the requisition of private property other than for the needs of the army.[23]

In addition to specific prohibitions, the establishment and maintenance of civilian settlements in occupied territories is contrary to the constitutional norm of the law of occupation, articulated in the 1907 Hague Regulations, Article 43. This provision protects the population and resources of occupied territory by requiring the occupying power to restore and ensure, as far as possible, public order and civil life; respecting, unless absolutely prevented, the laws in force in the territory. According to the prevailing interpretation of Article 43, changes to the law and administration in the occupied territory are permissible if they are necessary for military purposes or beneficial to the local population.[24] The settlement project is neither.[25] Changes to local law and

Construction of the Wall in the Occupied Palestinian Territory, Advisory Opinion, [2004] ICJ Rep 136, [120] (9 July 2004) ('*Wall Advisory Opinion*'). It is rejected by Israel, 'Israeli Settlements and International Law', Israel Ministry of Foreign Affairs (30 November 2015), www.mfa.gov.il/mfa/foreignpolicy/peace/guide/pages/israeli%20settlements%20and%20international%20law.aspx.

[22] Hague Regulations Annexed to Hague Convention (IV) respecting the Laws and Customs of War on Land, and its Annex: Regulations concerning the Laws and Customs of War on Land (entered into force 26 January 1910) *Martens Nouveau Recueil* (ser 3) 461 art 55 ('Hague Regulations'); James Crawford, 'Third Party Obligations with Respect to Israeli Settlements in the Occupied Palestinian Territories' (24 January 2012) paras 57, 63, 90, www.tuc.org.uk/sites/default/files/tucfiles/LegalOpinionIsraeliSettlements.pdf.

[23] Hague Regulations (n 22) arts 46, 52. HCJ 390/79 *Dweikat* v. *Government of Israel* (22 October 1979). In February 2017, the Israeli Parliament adopted the Regularisation of Settlement in Judea and Samaria Law, that purports to authorise and compel the military commander to expropriate private land on which private individuals have established settlements with governmental knowledge, setting aside any semblance of adherence to the international legal prohibition on the taking of private property for non-military purposes. For a critique, see Yaël Ronen and Yuval Shany, 'Israel's Settlement Regulation Bill Violates International Law' (20 December 2016) Just Security www.justsecurity.org/35743/israels-settlement-regulation-bill-violates-international-law.

[24] HCJ 393/82 *Jam'iyat Iskan* v. *Commander of IDF Forces in Judea and Samaria* (28 March 1983).

[25] The Israeli Supreme court has been willing to regard the *Israeli* settlers as part of the local population to whom the military authorities owe obligations: HCJ 256/72 *Jerusalem District Electric Company* v. *Minister of Defence* 1972 PD 27(1) 124; and HCJ 794/17 *Ziada* v. *Commander of IDF Forces in the West Bank* (31 October 2017) para 26. This view runs counter to the rationale of the law of occupation (Kretzmer and Ronen (n 16) ch 11) and is internationally rejected.

administration aimed at establishing and maintaining the settlements, such as restrictions on movement, diversion of natural resources for use in the settlements, and military legislation relating only to the settlements, are breaches of Article 43.[26]

The law of occupation is part of the law of international armed conflict, which applies to states. Businesses may be involved in an armed conflict,[27] but they are rarely direct parties to it. Even when they are, it is not in their corporate capacity but as armed groups. Moreover, a conflict in which a business is involved is by definition non-international, in which case the law of occupation is not applicable.

Businesses may nonetheless be involved in activities of the occupying power. Commercial activity of an occupying power and other states with regard to the occupied territory may be lawful if such activity ensures public life in the territory, including its economic well-being.[28] However, business activity specifically related to settlements does not promote the economic well-being of the territory, and may involve violation of specific prohibitions as noted above.[29] Against this background, measures taken by EU states, for example, can be regarded as grounded not only in political interests, but also in their legal obligation to ensure respect for the provisions of the law of occupation.[30]

International criminal law pertaining to violations of the law of occupation (or to any other international crime) does not apply to businesses as such, although corporate officers may be vulnerable to criminal charges for acts performed in an institutional capacity. None of the international tribunals' statutes extend to businesses, and proposals to include corporate entities in the International Criminal Court's personal

[26] Eyal Benvenisti, *The International Law of Occupation* (Oxford University Press 2012) 241.

[27] E.g., *The Presbyterian Church of Sudan* v. *Talisman Energy, Inc.*, No. 07-0016-cv (2d Cir, 2 October 2009).

[28] Eugene Kontorovich, 'Economic Dealings with Occupied Territories' (2014) 53 Columbia Journal of Transnational Law 584, 588, 634.

[29] In HCJ 2164/09 *Yesh Din* v. *IDF Commander in the West Bank* (26 December 2011) the Israeli Supreme Court suggested that employment in businesses in the West Bank was beneficial to the local Palestinian population because it provided employment and contributed to the economic development and modernisation of the area. For a critique see Kretzmer and Ronen (n 16) ch 8. The Court stopped short of holding that measures exclusively benefiting the settlers are lawful *Ziada* (n 25) para 26.

[30] GC IV art 1; Robin Geiß, 'The Obligation to Respect and to Ensure Respect for the Conventions' in Andrew Clapham et al., *The 1949 Geneva Conventions: A Commentary* (Oxford University Press 2015) 111,118 mn 11.

jurisdiction have been deliberately rejected. Even in Nuremberg corporate activity was put on trial only figuratively. It was not the businesses themselves that were indicted but their officers.[31]

2.2 *Settlements, Businesses and the Right to Self-Determination*

The transfer of civilian population to occupied territory may determine the future of that territory by changing its demographic foundations. It is thus an impediment to the realisation of right to self-determination.[32] Since the late 1970s, the Israeli settlement project has openly been pursued with the objective of minimising the possibility for the development of a Palestinian state.[33] While not every impediment to the right necessarily amounts to a violation,[34] the illegality of the project under the law of occupation and its declared purpose of undermining the realisation of the right to self-determination preclude it from being regarded as legitimately grounded. It is thus a violation of the right to self-determination.

The obligation to respect the right to self-determination, including sovereignty over natural resources, and the prohibition on deprivation of the local population of its wealth, lies with states.[35] Exploitation of natural resources may be compatible with the principle of sovereignty over natural resources if it is conducted for the benefit of the people in the territory recognised as a self-determination unit, on their behalf or in

[31] But see STL (n 20), and STL STL-14-06 *Akhbar Beirut SAL and Ibrahim Mohamed Ali Al Amin*, 'Decision on Interlocutory Appeal Concerning Personal Jurisdiction in Contempt Proceedings' (23 January 2015) paras 72–3 .

[32] Christian Tomuschat, 'Prohibition on Settlements' in Clapham et al. (n 30), 1551, 1559 mn 21, 1567–8 mns 48–9; Human Rights Council, Resolution 34/29 'Right of the Palestinian People to Self-Determination' UN Doc A/HRC/RES/34/29, preambular para 11, operative para 3. The Canadian Supreme Court's dictum (n 19) on the potential liability of businesses for violation of peremptory norms is difficult to apply to the right to self-determination, given the requirement that the norms be 'definable'.

[33] For official statements, see Kretzmer and Ronen (n 16) 180.

[34] *ICJ Advisory Opinion* (n 21), separate opinion of Judge Kooijmans, para 32.

[35] E.g., C-104/16 *P Council* v. *Front Polisario* ECLI:EU:C:2016:973 (21 December 2016) para 92; C-266/16 *Western Sahara Campaign* UK ECLI:EU:C:2018:118 (27 February 2018) paras 62–3. Exceptionally see UN Council for Namibia, Decree No 1 for the Protection of the Natural Resources of Namibia, UN Doc A/AC.131/33. The status of the Decree as a matter of international law has never been decided. 'Implementation of Decree No 1 for the Protection of the Natural Resources of Namibia: Study on the Possibility of Instituting Legal Proceedings in the Domestic Courts of States: Report of the United Nations Commission for Namibia' (1986) 80 American Journal of International Law 442.

consultation with their representatives.[36] Businesses involved in exploitation activities may be affected by states' obligations.[37] This aspect of the right to self-determination has been prominent in legal action concerning businesses operating in Western Sahara, but is not directly related to settlement projects.

2.3 *Settlements and International Human Rights Law*

In theory, not every settlement project necessarily involves limitations to the human rights of individual members of the local population.[38] In practice, the establishment and maintenance of the Israeli settlements in the West Bank involves limitations on the rights to private property, freedom of movement and access to water. These limitations in turn affect numerous other rights, among them the rights to equality, employment, education, health, social services and an adequate standard of living.[39] In many areas of law, the law applicable to Israelis resident in the settlements differs from that applicable to Palestinians, in breach of the prohibition on discrimination.[40] After half a century of practices that benefit the settlements' existence and development by depriving the Palestinian population of land and resources, and almost two decades characterised by the imposition of harsh restrictions on property and movement within the West Bank by the separation barrier, it is difficult to conceive of the settlement project as one which does not encroach on these rights.[41]

[36] UN Under-Secretary-General for Legal Affairs, the Legal Counsel, Letter dated 29 January 2002 addressed to the President of the Security Council, UN Doc S/2002/161 (12 Feb 2002) para 24.

[37] Eastern Cape High Court, Port Elizabeth, South Africa, *Saharawi Arab Democratic Republic and Another* v. *Owner and Charterers of the MV 'NM Cherry Blossom' and Others* [2017] ZAECPEHC 31 (15 June 2017) paras 47, 51.

[38] The present analysis assumes that IHRL applies in occupied territory. For the government of Israel's contrary position, see, e.g., Committee on Economic, Social and Cultural Rights, Replies of Israel to the List of Issues (27 August 2019) UN Doc E/C.12/ISR/Q/4/Add.1, para 9.

[39] B'Tselem, 'By Hook and By Crook: Israeli Settlement Policy in the West Bank' (July 2010) www.btselem.org/download/201007_by_hook_and_by_crook_eng.pdf.

[40] For a comprehensive review not limited to the settlement context, see Association for Civil Rights in Israel (ACRI), 'One Rule, Two Legal Systems: Israel's Regime of Laws in the West Bank' (24 November 2014) https://law.acri.org.il/en/2014/11/24/twosysreport.

[41] In Northern Cyprus the main violation is of the right to property, resulting from the allocation to Turkish settlers of private properties of Greek Cypriots who fled during the 1974 war or left earlier. In Western Sahara the allocation of jobs to settlers is a

Rights may be subject to limitations and derogations. However, the illegality of the settlement project under the law of occupation precludes the limitations it entails from being regarded as required to achieve a legitimate aim.

International human rights treaty law is formulated in terms of states' obligations.[42] Yet its applicability to businesses has been generating international legal interest since the 1970s. This interest originated in concern over the impact of multinational corporations based in Europe and North America and operating in developing countries. The inability to rein in such businesses, because the of limited jurisdiction of home states and the political weakness of host states, prompted an attempt to impose international human rights obligations directly on them. This attempt, the 2003 Draft Norms on the Responsibilities of Transnational Corporations and Other Business Projects with Regard to Human Rights,[43] failed to gain formal binding status due to a deeply divisive debate between the business community and human rights advocacy groups, which elicited little support from governments. In 2005 the UN Secretary-General initiated another project to identify and clarify non-binding standards for businesses. This led to the adoption in 2011 by the Human Rights Council of the 'Protect, Respect and Remedy' (PRR) Framework, and its operationalisation through the UN Guiding Principles on Business and Human Rights (UNGP).[44]

The PRR Framework rests on three pillars. The first is the state's duty to protect individuals against human rights abuses committed by third parties, including businesses. Under the second pillar businesses have a non-legally binding responsibility to respect human rights, which means

discriminatory practice with regard to the right to employment. Robert F. Kennedy Human Rights and others, 'Report on the Kingdom of Morocco's Violations of the International Covenant on Economic Social and Cultural Rights in the Western Sahara' (August 2015) https://tbinternet.ohchr.org/Treaties/CESCR/Shared%20Documents/MAR/INT_CESCR_CSS_MAR_21582_E.pdf.

[42] Yaël Ronen, 'Human Rights Obligations of Territorial Non-State Actors' (2013) 46 Cornell International Law Journal 21.

[43] Commission on Human Rights, 'Economic, Social and Cultural Rights: Draft Norms on the Responsibilities of Transnational Corporations and Other Business Enterprises with Regard to Human Rights', UN Doc E/CN.4/Sub.2/2003/12 (26 Aug 2003).

[44] UN Human Rights Council, 'Report of the Special Representative of the Secretary-General on the Issue of Human Rights and Transnational Corporations and Other Business Enterprises, John Ruggie: Guiding Principles on Business and Human Rights: Implementing the United Nations "Protect, Respect and Remedy" Framework', paras 2–5, UN Doc. A/HRC/17/31 (21 March 2011) ('UNGP').

to act with due diligence to avoid infringing on the rights of others and to address adverse impacts that do occur. This responsibility applies across the business's activities and through its relationships with third parties connected with those activities. The third pillar is the provision by both states and businesses of greater access for victims of human rights abuses to effective remedy. The UNGP apply to businesses of all commercial sectors and geographic regions.[45]

Human rights are understood, under the UNGP, at a minimum 'as those expressed in the International Bill of Human Rights [the Universal Declaration of Human Rights, the International Covenant on Civil and Political Rights (ICCPR) and International Covenant on Economic, Social and Cultural Rights (ICESCR)] and the principles concerning fundamental rights set out in the International Labor Organization's Declaration on Fundamental Principles and Rights at Work'.[46] These include the rights affected by the settlement project, including the right to property, freedom of movement, economic and social rights and more.

The right to self-determination, so central to the critique of the settlements, is entrenched in the ICCPR and ICESCR. Nevertheless, it stands out among the rights enumerated in these instruments. While 'ordinary' human rights concern the exercise of power, the right to self-determination concerns the political choice in allocation of power itself.[47] Furthermore, it is a collective right rather than an individual one. Its exceptional character is evident in the evolution of the PRR Framework. The 2003 Draft Norms covered a wide range of economic, social and cultural rights as well as civil and political rights, and even a controversial mention of the right to development, but they did not mention self-determination. There is nonetheless no reason why businesses could not be required to respect the right to self-determination.[48]

The Commentary accompanying the UNGP indicates that in situations of armed conflict businesses should also respect the standards of

45 ibid Guiding Principle)GP(14.

46 ibid GP 12.

47 Henry J. Steiner and Philip Alston, *International Human Rights in Context: Law, Politics, Morals* (2nd edn, Clarendon Press 2000) 1249.

48 The Petroleum Fund's Council on Ethics (n 15) classified economic activities off the Western Sahara shore on behalf of Morocco as contribution to 'a possible strengthening of Morocco's sovereignty claims regarding the territory', falling under 'particularly serious violations of fundamental ethical norms' *other* than violations of human rights, on the grounds that the violation is not of individual rights.

international humanitarian law.[49] While this includes restrictions under the law of occupation on taking of property, it is not clear whether the UNGP cover GC IV Article 49(6). The prohibition on transfer of civilian population to occupied territory is not considered a human rights norm. However, if the right to self-determination is regarded as falling within the scope of the UNGP, it stands to reason also to include the absolute prohibition that aims to protect that right.

The PRR Framework does not set for itself as a goal to become a binding international obligation.[50] Nevertheless the UNGP have been adopted as an authoritative standard for evaluating business conduct by governments,[51] international organisations,[52] civil society and workers' organisations, national human rights institutions, investors, and the business sector itself.[53] They are becoming a statement not merely of what is desirable that businesses do, but of what is increasingly required of them.[54]

[49] UNGP (n 44) Commentary to GP 12.

[50] Penelope Simons, 'International Law's Invisible Hand and the Future of Corporate Accountability for Violations of Human Rights' (2012) 3 Journal of Human Rights and the Environment 5, 9–10.

[51] For a repository of national action plans incorporating the UNGP, see www.ohchr.org/EN/Issues/Business/Pages/NationalActionPlans.aspx.

[52] Human Rights Council, 'Report of the Independent International Factfinding Mission to Investigate the Implications of the Israeli Settlements on the Civil, Political, Economic, Social and Cultural Rights of the Palestinian People throughout the Occupied Palestinian Territory, Including East Jerusalem', UN Doc A/HRC/22/63 (7 February 2013) para 117; OECD, Guidelines for Multinational Enterprises (2011 edn) www.oecd.org/daf/inv/mne/48004323.pdf; additional examples in ILA Study Group on Business and Human Rights, 'Final Report in the International Law Association, Report of the Seventy-Eighth Conference held in Sydney 19–24 August 2018' (16 November 2018) 1098, 1105, 1101–2.

[53] UN Global Compact, www.unglobalcompact.org/HowToParticipate/Business_Participation/index.html; International Organization for Standardization, 'ISO 26000: Guidance on Social Responsibility' (2010) www.iso.org/obp/ui/#iso:std:iso:26000:ed-1:v1:en; Voluntary Principles on Security and Human Rights www.voluntaryprinciples.org; International Finance Corporation, 'Sustainability Framework: Policy and Performance Standards on Environmental and Social Sustainability' (1 January 2012) www.ifc.org/wps/wcm/connect/topics_ext_content/ifc_external_corporate_site/sustainability-at-ifc/publications/publications_handbook_pps.

[54] E.g., Office of the UN High Commissioner for Human Rights, 'The Business and Human Rights Dimension of Sustainable Development: Embedding "Protect, Respect and Remedy" in SDGs implementation', Information Note, Geneva, 30 June 2017. For a concrete application of this notion, see *Al Jadeed SAL & Ms Khayat* (n 20).

The UNGP have made their way into the General Comments of the committees monitoring the implementation of the ICCPR[55] and the ICESCR[56] The General Comments are not binding, but have great persuasive weight as interpretative instruments.[57] Like the Covenants, they are directed only at states, but as they determine the standards that states ought to apply domestically, including through enforcement on domestic actors, they can shape domestic law. That law may eventually form the basis for general principles of law or even customary international law that could arguably concern businesses directly. Some states have already incorporated due diligence obligations of businesses in legislation.[58] Hence, the status of the UNGP is susceptible to change. With this in mind, the remainder of this article examines the implications of the PRR Framework for businesses involved in settlements.

3 Respect – Avoiding Causation and Contribution to Human Rights Abuses

Settlements are the projects of occupying powers. The violations involved – whether of human rights, the right to self-determination or the prohibition on the transfer of civilian population to occupied territory – are not caused by businesses. However, businesses may become involved in the perpetration of these violations. This is often referred to as 'complicity', used in a broader sense than the criminal one.

[55] Human Rights Committee, General Comment No. 36 (2018) on Article 6 of the International Covenant on Civil and Political Rights, on the right to life, CCPR/C/GC/36 (20 October 2018) para 22.

[56] Committee on Economic, Social and Cultural Rights, General Comment No. 24 (2017) on State Obligations under the International Covenant on Economic, Social and Cultural Rights in the Context of Business Activities, E/C/12/GC/24 para 2.

[57] Zdzislaw Kedzia, 'United Nations Mechanisms to Promote and Protect Human Rights' in Janusz Symonides, *Human Rights: International Protection, Monitoring, Enforcement* (Ashgate and UNESCO 2003) 33–4. Also see David Kretzmer and Eckart Klein, 'The Human Rights Committee: Monitoring States Parties Reports 45 (2015)' Israel Yearbook on Human Rights 133, 159, referring to concluding observations on states' reports, on which General Comments were originally based, Christian Tomuschat, *Human Rights: Between Idealism and Realism* (3rd edn, Oxford University Press 2014) 234–5.

[58] David Gaukrodger, 'Business Responsibilities and Investment Treaties, Consultation Paper' (OECD Secretariat, 20 January 2020) 46, https://www.oecd.org/daf/inv/investment-policy/Consultation-Paper-on-business-responsibilities-and-investment-treaties.pdf. The UNGP are also gradually making their way into bilateral investment treaties, ibid 31.

UN Guiding Principle 13 states that the responsibility to respect human rights requires that business projects:

(a) Avoid causing or contributing to adverse human rights impacts through their own activities, and address such impacts when they occur;
(b) Seek to prevent or mitigate adverse human rights impacts that are directly linked to their operations, products or services by their business relationships, even if they have not contributed to those impacts.

The PRR Framework distinguishes types of complicity by the level of their proximity to the human rights abuse or violation.[59] It distinguishes direct complicity through contribution to abuse, when a business provides goods or services that it knows or ought to know will be used to carry out the abuse; from beneficial complicity, when a business benefits from human rights abuses even if it did not positively assist or cause them.[60]

3.1 Direct Complicity: Contributing to a Violation

The UNGP do not define or establish specific criteria for conduct that constitutes 'contribution'. The International Commission of Jurists suggests that the *legal* category of contribution consists of conduct which knowingly or foreseeably enables the occurrence of specific abuses, exacerbates specific abuses, or facilitates them.[61]

[59] UN Human Rights Council, 'Report of the Special Representative of the Secretary-General on the Issue of Human Rights and Transnational Corporations and Other Business Enterprises, John Ruggie: Clarifying the Concepts of "Sphere of Influence" and "Complicity"', UN Doc A/HRC/8/16 (15 May 2008) paras 54–70. Also see International Commission of Jurists, 'Corporate Complicity & Legal Accountability – Report of the International Commission of Jurists Expert Legal Panel on Corporate Complicity in International Crimes, vol. 1: Facing the Facts and Charting a Legal Path' (2008), 24Z https://www.icj.org/wp-content/uploads/2009/07/Corporate-complicity-legal-accountability-vol1-publication-2009-eng.pdf ('ICJ Report').

[60] GP 13(a) and 13(b) respectively; ICJ Report (n 59) 14–15; Andrew Clapham and Scott Jerbi, 'Categories of Corporate Complicity in Human Rights Abuses' (2000) 24 Hastings International & Comparative Law Review 339, 342. A third category is silent complicity, when a business operates in an environment where systematic or continuous human rights abuses occur that are not directly linked to it, and fails to intervene with the authorities to try to stop or prevent the abuses. Silent complicity is not addressed by the UNGP, which require businesses to take action only where the violation is *directly* linked to their activities.

[61] ICJ Report (n 59) 8–9, 24.

Businesses that contribute to human rights violations through the settlement project include construction companies that build settlements, and businesses that provide the settlements and their residents with electricity, water, gas and other basic utilities. Industrial parks have been built with the explicit intention of developing and reinforcing adjacent residential settlements.[62] Businesses based in parks or within the settlements thus facilitate the latter's continued existence. Businesses contribute to the continued existence of settlements regardless of where they themselves are based, when they provide goods and services related to the place of residence, such as transport and communication.[63]

An important type of contribution to the settlement project is financial.[64] Since not every relationship with a bad actor generates responsibility,[65] the proximity of the funding to violation of human rights is a matter for case-by-case analysis. A lender to a construction company that directly contributes to the establishment of a settlement assumes responsibility more directly than the lender of mortgages to individual homebuyers, who are beneficiaries of the violation; both are closer to the violation of rights than a bank which provides general financial services to settlers that are not related specifically to the settlements as mortgages are. Under the PRR Framework, due diligence requires commercial lenders to enquire about the object of their investment, including the identity of the borrower and its project. When the project is situated in a settlement the link is all too apparent. The situation may be more complex when a borrower is involved in multiple projects, only some of which are in the settlements. Lenders may nonetheless set conditions for granting loans, such as that the projects that they support not be connected with existing or future settlements.

These examples highlight that a link to territory is a criterion for proximity that is specifically relevant to settlements in occupied territory. This criterion seems to underpin the OHCHR's typology of businesses

62 Who Profits, 'Sodastream: A Case Study for Corporate Activity in Illegal Israeli Settlements' 23 (January 2011), https://whoprofits.org/wp-content/uploads/2018/06/old/WhoProfits-ProductioninSettlements-SodaStream.pdf.

63 It would exclude services that are provided to individuals irrespective of their place of residence, such as pension fund services: Crawford (n 22).

64 For details, see Human Rights Watch, 'Bankrolling Abuse: Israeli Banks in West Bank Settlements' (2018) www.hrw.org/report/2018/05/29/bankrolling-abuse/israeli-banks-west-bank-settlements.

65 Sabine Michalowski, 'No Complicity Liability for Funding Gross Human Rights Violations' (2012) 30 Berkeley Journal of International Law 451; ICJ Report (n 59) 16.

involved in the settlements that raise concern, which includes only activities that are directly related to the land. It refers to banking industry as that 'which helps to finance construction and infrastructure projects in settlements, provide loans and financial services to settlement councils, and provide mortgage loans to home buyers'.[66]

3.2 *Beneficial Complicity: Benefiting from Violations*

Business projects may be perceived as complicit in human rights violations when they benefit from them.[67] Industrial and agricultural businesses in the Israeli settlements and their industrial areas utilise land that is made available to them through restrictions on Palestinians' right to property and freedom of movement. Businesses based in industrial areas adjacent to settlements receive direct financial incentives from the government through rent subsidies, grants and tax benefits.[68] Providers of services such as transportation, regardless of where they are based, benefit from violations at least nominally, since they enjoy opportunities which would not exist if it were not for the violations.

As noted above, the latter group of businesses not only benefit from the settlements but also contribute to their continued existence. This overlap suggests that the distinction between contribution and benefit is of limited utility when it comes to businesses that operate in an environment that is in its essence a violation of human rights. It raises the question to what extent businesses can and should be held responsible for contributing to the perpetuation of such an environment.

3.3 *Perpetuation of Violations*

A central accusation levelled against the business sector, especially the industrial and agricultural sectors, is that by its very operation in the

[66] UN High Commissioner for Human Rights, 'UN Database of All Business Enterprises Involved in the Activities Detailed in Paragraph 96 of the Report of the Independent International Fact-Finding Mission to Investigate the Implications of the Israeli Settlements on the Civil, Political, Economic, Social and Cultural Rights of the Palestinian People throughout the Occupied Palestinian Territory, Including East Jerusalem: Report of the United Nations High Commissioner for Human Rights, UN Doc A/HRC/37/39 (1 February 2018) paras 3(f), 47.

[67] UNGP (n 44), Commentary to GP 17.

[68] B'Tselem (n 39) 43–4. For an industrial area advertising its advantages on these grounds, see https://tinyurl.com/ya6quqr3 (in Hebrew).

settlements it facilitates the perpetuation of the project.[69] In this context, the distinction between territory-related business activity and other activity appears less significant. The steady provision of goods and services allows settlers to continue residing in settlements and contributes to the perpetuation of the restrictions on rights no less than the physical maintenance of the settlements.

The question is whether businesses need to consider the impact of their conduct on the reversibility of the settlement project or, conversely, on its perpetuation. The notion of responsibility for perpetuation of the settlement project highlights a difference between legal accountability under human rights law and the responsibility of businesses under the PRR Framework: under international human rights law there is no collective responsibility. The critique regarding perpetuation of the regime is directed at an entire sector. Furthermore, under international human rights law, an actor's responsibility derives directly from its conduct, and not from the fact that its conduct, if legitimate in itself, enables another actor to violate rights.[70] The PRR Framework does not impose on businesses responsibility for the legal and social environment within which they operate. Due diligence requires businesses to address human rights risks across their value chains in light of their operating context,[71] but it does not require that they address the context itself.

The responsibility of businesses for perpetuating the legal environment in which they operate was addressed by the South Africa Truth and Reconciliation Commission. The Commission found that business was central to the economy that sustained the apartheid regime.[72] It noted conflicting views as to whether businesses have a social role beyond the conventional bounds of everyday business activity. One view condemned all business entities for having engaged in business under apartheid, while the other applauded them for such engagement, since such action provided jobs for millions of people, created infrastructure, unleashed democratising pressures (albeit unintentionally) and sustained

[69] Alessandro Tonutti, 'Feasting on the Occupation: Illegality of Settlement Produce and the Responsibility of EU Member States under International Law', 10, 13 (Al-Haq 2013), www.alhaq.org/publications/8075.html.

[70] In the context of state responsibility for violations of human rights, such complicity would be governed by the Articles on Responsibility of States for Internationally Wrongful Acts, with Commentaries (2011), UN Doc A/56/10, art 16.

[71] UNGP (n 44), Commentary to GP 17.

[72] Truth and Reconciliation Commission of South Africa (TRC), Report, vol 4, ch 2, para 161.

a base of economic activity that later provided a platform for economic growth in a democracy.[73] Although the Commission did not decide firmly between the two approaches, it expressed reservations with respect to the view that completely excluded moral considerations from business management. In its final findings it criticised certain industries for failing to respect specific labour rights and for failing to take responsibility for their involvement in designing apartheid rule.[74] It stopped short of holding that any single industry, or the business community as a whole, was responsible for sustaining the apartheid regime, or for enabling the perpetuation of human rights violations. In its recommendations the Commission endorsed the idea of a wealth tax to be levied on businesses in order to redress the unequal distribution of resources that apartheid has caused, as a 'welcome signal from corporate South Africa that it understands and accepts its own responsibility for the past and its commitment to stability and justice in the future'.[75] This recommendation can be said to have attributed some responsibility and blame to the entire business community, for its association with the regime.[76]

Criticism levelled against businesses operating in the Israeli settlements often resembles the criticism levelled against White businesses in apartheid South Africa, but the relevance of the Commission's findings to the context of the West Bank is far from clear. On one hand, today's business world is more inclined to regard social responsibility as a factor in business management. On the other hand, the South African Commission's recommendations were informed by its mandate, to conduct a post-conflict assessment of a way forward in a spirit of reconciliation. This is different from setting operative guidelines for a business operating during a conflict, with a view to vindicate a state's legal obligations. In addition, the Commission addressed the relationship of businesses with an apartheid regime whose very existence was grounded in illegality. As noted above, the Israeli presence in the West Bank is not in itself unlawful.[77] Not every interaction with it is tainted. Distinguishing settlement-related activities from others is not always

[73] ibid para 145. For endorsement of this argument by the Israeli Supreme Court, see *Yesh Din* (n 29) para 13.

[74] TRC (n 72) paras 164–7.

[75] ibid para 158.

[76] Nicoli Nattrass, 'The Truth and Reconciliation Commission on Business and Apartheid: A Critical Evaluation' (1999) 98 African Affairs 373.

[77] For a different view, see Orna Ben-Naftali, Aeyal M. Gross and Keren Michaeli, 'Illegal Occupation: Framing the Occupied Territories' (2005) 23 Berkeley Journal of International

easy, and thus cannot easily be the basis for categorical demands on the business community.

4 What Should Businesses Do?

Businesses are required to perform continuous due diligence processes to ensure that they do not become involved in human rights abuses.[78] When a business contributes to an adverse human rights impact, it should take the necessary steps to cease or prevent the impact, and use its leverage to mitigate any remaining impact to the greatest extent possible. Businesses should also use leverage when they do not contribute to an adverse human rights impact, but that impact is nevertheless directly linked to their operations, products or services by their business relationship with another entity. Among the factors that enter into the determination of the appropriate action in such situations are the business's leverage over the entity concerned, how crucial the relationship is to the project, the severity of the abuse, and whether terminating the relationship with the entity itself would have adverse human rights consequences. When the business lacks the leverage to prevent or mitigate adverse impacts, it should consider ending the relationship, taking into account credible assessments of potential adverse human rights impacts of doing so. The more severe the abuse, the more quickly the business will need to see change before it takes a decision on whether it should end the relationship.[79] In other words, a business cannot easily justify its continued benefit from an abuse on the ground that it cannot prevent or mitigate it.

These requirements were drafted with human rights abuses committed by private parties in mind. They are all the more pertinent when the abuses are committed by a state and constitute violations under law. Such is the case of businesses operating in the civilian settlements in occupied territory. The following sections consider some challenges to the application of the UNGP in that context, as they arise with regard to businesses operating in the Israeli settlements.

Law 551 ; but also Yaël Ronen, 'Illegal Occupation and Its Consequences' (2008) 41 Israel Law Review 201.

[78] UN Human Rights Council (n 59) paras 3, 4, 19–22.

[79] Leverage is the ability to effect change in the wrongful practices of an entity that causes harm if that harm is directly linked to the business activity. UNGP (n 44), Commentary to GP 19.

4.1 Leverage

The UNGP assume that businesses have the choice of operating without being complicit in a violation of rights. This may well be the case insofar as concerns large, multinational companies owned by Western corporations and operating in the Global South. For example, in states where employee protection is weak businesses can offer adequate salaries and working conditions to their employees beyond what local law guarantees. In addition, they may have significant leverage over the governments involved.

Business activity in settlements is a different ball game. First, it is inherently tainted by benefit from human rights violations even when as a business practice it is legitimate and would have raised no concern had it taken place elsewhere. Second, it is not clear what sort of leverage businesses are expected to exercise vis-à-vis the government. The PRR Framework suggests that businesses engage in dialogue with contracting governments to ensure that projects are carried out in a manner which does not violate human rights. For example, businesses in the extraction of natural resources sector can condition their investments on guarantees that the government provide alternative accommodation to communities that need to be displaced. Since the settlement project itself is unlawful, to demand that businesses exercise leverage means that they must pressure the government to abandon the settlement project. It is unrealistic to require businesses to negotiate 'mitigation of harm' by a political project that is inherently unlawful. It seems that the only means by which a business can ensure that it is untainted by involvement in human rights violations deriving from a settlement project is by removing itself from them in all manners. This may raise viability risks.

The UNGP do not provide a straightforward response to a situation in which the violation is severe, but so is the dependence of the business on it. Dependence implies great proximity and therefore a high level of responsibility, but also a high cost for the business. For businesses which depend for their existence on their very presence in the settlements, such as agricultural producers and tourism operators, removal means closing down with no certainty as to the future. This is not a hypothetical scenario. Many businesses that shut down when Israel disengaged from Gaza in 2005 could not re-establish themselves within Israel's borders because the costs were prohibitive.[80]

[80] According to a media report, these businesses relied on a cheap labour force and on income tax evasion. With regard to both, the benefit deriving from the location in the settlements was the lack of law enforcement, rather than different legal or economic

The lack of guidance in the UNGP for such a situation is not surprising, given their provenance, namely the interest in regulating the operation of strong transnational corporations in situations of weak rule of law.[81] Some indication of a lenient approach in the UNGP may be found in the fact that the UNGP do not categorically require businesses to end their business relationship as a last resort. The South African Truth and Reconciliation Commission took a similarly pragmatic approach when it chastised those who condemned all business people for having engaged in business under apartheid, for downplaying issues of realistic choice and differential power.[82] The UNGP do stipulate, however, that businesses should be prepared to accept the reputational, financial or legal consequences of their conduct.[83]

Businesses that are dependent for their existence on the settlements are probably for the most part Israeli-owned and based in the settlements. Under generally accepted rules on jurisdiction in civil law, in practice they are unlikely to be vulnerable to legal process, since they can be sued only in Israel, where the settlements would not be regarded as inherently violating human rights law. Businesses that are based in settlements or provide settlements or settlers with goods and services but are not inherently dependent on that location or clientele may be in a better position to remove themselves from the settlements. There have been instances where businesses scaled down or ended their activities in the settlements. In most cases these were foreign-based businesses and Israeli-based businesses under foreign ownership.[84] It seems that their overall financial and legal benefit outweighed the immediate financial loss.[85]

4.2 Legal Obligations under Domestic Law

The previous section concerns the leeway that businesses have in preventing and mitigating human rights abuses in terms of profitability and viability. A different concern may be legal constraints.

conditions. Meirav Arslosoroff, 'In Gush Katif they Wanted Compensation for Tax Evasion' Ha'aretz (20 January 2010) www.haaretz.co.il/misc/1.1185480 (in Hebrew).

81 Simons (n 50) 15.

82 TRC (n 72) para 146.

83 UNGP (n 44), Commentary to GP 19.

84 Gush Shalom, Settlements Products Wikia (ongoing project), http://settlement-products.wikia.com/wiki/Factories/Businesses_that_have_left_the_settlements.

85 Liesbeth Zegveld, 'Prosecution of Riwal for Involvement in Construction of Israeli Wall and Settlements Discontinued' Law in Action (14 May 2013) http://www.liesbethzegveld.com/en/selection-of-cases/prosecution-of-riwal-for-involvement-in-construction-of-israeli-wall-and-settlements-discontinued.

The UNGP do not entirely ignore the possibility that domestic law would limit the ability of businesses to honour the principles of internationally recognised human rights strictly. Businesses are nonetheless expected to be able to demonstrate their efforts in this regard,[86] for example by exercising leverage on the government to amend the law so as to comply with human rights standards. Ultimately, the UNGP are vague on the consequences of compliance with domestic law that violates international standards, other than warning that businesses should be aware that their conduct might reach the zone of legal risk.

Significantly for present purposes, the UNGP say nothing of the converse, namely the consequences of compliance with international human rights but in violation of domestic law.[87] The OHCHR 2018 report notes that some businesses operating in the Israeli settlements have indicated that they were acting in compliance with Israeli domestic law. The OHCHR's response, that the responsibility of businesses to respect human rights exists over and above compliance with domestic law,[88] is premised on businesses' ability to comply with both legal systems. However, operation in the settlements is not only permissible under Israeli law but in some instances is required under legal sanction. Specifically, the Prohibition on Discrimination in Products, Services and Entry into Places of Entertainment and Public Places Law (2000), as amended in 2017, provides that 'A person whose business is to provide products or public service ... will not discriminate in providing the product or private service ... on the basis of place of residence.'[89] This legislation, explicitly intended to prohibit refusals by businesses to serve Israeli settlements in the West Bank,[90] has already been successfully invoked.[91] Thus, conducting business in Israel entails a willingness to

[86] UNGP (n 44), Commentary to GP 23.

[87] For the avenues available to businesses required by domestic law to act in a manner that is contrary to international law in a different setting, see Yael Ronen, 'Big Brother's Little Helpers: The Right to Privacy and the Responsibility of Internet Service Providers' (2015) 31 Utrecht Journal of International and European Law 72.

[88] UN Database (n 12) paras 56–7.

[89] Prohibition on Discrimination in Products, Services and Entry into Places of Entertainment and Public Places 2000 s 3(a1) as amended.

[90] Statement of MK Shully Mualem-Refaeli, Knesset Records, 20th Knesset, 98th session (3 February 2016) 155–62. http://main.knesset.gov.il/Activity/plenum/Pages/SessionItem.aspx?itemID=575332.

[91] Expedited Civ 18-01-57974 *Fein* v. *Studio Keramica Ltd* (12 Feb 2019); Small Claims (J'lem) 16318-11-18 *Offir Cohen* v. *Pango Pay and Go Ltd* (20 October 2019).

conduct business in the settlements (or a risk of facing legal sanction for failing to do so).

Further complication concerns businesses incorporated or registered outside Israel. The preparatory work on the 2017 amendment does not suggest that foreign businesses were in the drafters' mind; however, there is nothing excluding such businesses from the law's ambit. They may face legal process in Israel if they refuse to give services in the settlements.[92] At the same time they may face legal process abroad if they do provide such services.[93] Businesses with a substantive link to another state that would substantiate its civil jurisdiction are at greater risk than businesses registered only in Israel. In order to avoid being caught in a bind, foreign-based businesses may need to choose between avoiding business in Israel, and being constantly vulnerable to legal process if they refuse to extend their business to the settlements.[94]

Domestic legislation that may sanction refusal to maintain business in the settlements exists elsewhere than in Israel. Some states have taken measures to counter the BDS movement that affect business in the settlements. For example, a New York Governor's executive order provides that state agencies and authorities deemed to be involved in BDS activities would lose public funding.[95] Since there is an overlap between the demands of the BDS campaign and compliance with the UNGP, a business that withdraws its presence from the settlements in line with the UNGP could be subject to penalty under the order.[96]

4.3 *Adverse Impacts of Terminating the Relationship*

The UNGP Commentary states that in determining whether to end a business relationship, the business must consider the severity of the

[92] A 2018 request for class action against Airbnb in a Jerusalem court was settled out of court with the defendant essentially amending its policy in line with the demand in the request for class action. Class Action (J'lem) 18-11-54132 *Maanit Rabinovich* v. *Airbnb* (18 July 2019).

[93] Quebec Court of Appeal, *Bil'in* v. *Green Park International and Green Mount International* 2010 QCCA 1455 (11 August 2010).

[94] For potential risks under the Prevention of Damage to the State of Israel through Boycott, 2011, see Human Rights Watch (n 64).

[95] New York Governor, 'Executive Order No 157 Instructing State Agencies and Authorities to Divest Public Funds Supporting BDS Campaign Against Israel' (5 June 2016) www.governor.ny.gov/sites/governor.ny.gov/files/atoms/files/EO_157_new.pdf.

[96] Marya Farah and Maha Abdallah, 'Security, Business and Human Rights in the Occupied Palestinian Territory' (2019) 4 Business and Human Rights Journal 7, 28.

adverse human rights impact of that relationship: the more severe the abuse, the greater the need to determine the fate of the relationship. In addition, businesses must consider whether terminating the relationship would have adverse human rights consequences.[97]

A central argument made to justify the continued presence of businesses in the Israeli settlements is that they provide employment to the Palestinian workforce. Removing businesses from the settlements, it is argued, would adversely impact employment opportunities for the local Palestinian population.[98] The question is whether this should change the calculus guiding the business. In the context of the UNGP's historical evolution, a similar argument was voiced that if businesses were required to pay minimum wages, they would have to dismiss many employees, who would remain without any income. As a matter of empirical fact, it is probably true that for many Palestinian employees in businesses in the settlements, the alternative might be, at least in the immediate future, unemployment or at least a decline in income. If that were not the case, Palestinians would hardly opt to work in the settlements in the first place.[99]

When emanating from the Israeli government, this argument is blatantly hypocritical, not least because the compulsion for Palestinians to work in Israeli businesses is caused in large measure by the consistent curtailing of the Palestinian economy by the Israeli government since the early days of the occupation.[100] The argument is also unacceptable when voiced by businesses. Illegal conduct cannot be justified on the grounds that it is the lesser evil. The moral imperative holds regardless of whether the standard is legally enforceable. Furthermore, the argument is misleading. First, it is based on a narrow view of the issue, limited to an immediate impact and disregarding wider and long-term ones. For example, withdrawal of business from the settlements would in the immediate term cut off the source of income to persons employed in them; but to the extent that it would eventually lead to removal of the settlements themselves, such withdrawal would enable access to economic resources that have been denied for many years, primarily

[97] UNGP (n 44), Commentary to GP 19.

[98] UN Database (n 12) para 51; Also see *Yesh Din* (n 29) para 13.

[99] Amir Paz-Fuchs and Yaël Ronen, 'Integrated or Segregated? Israeli-Palestinian Employment Relations in the Settlements' in Marco Allegra, Ariel Handel and Erez Maggor (eds), *Normalizing Occupation: The Politics of Everyday Life in the West Bank Settlements* (Indiana University Press 2017) 175.

[100] ibid 173–6.

agricultural land.[101] Second, the argument draws implicitly on the assumption that the business must maintain its profit margin or is at least entitled to maintain it. However, in the same way that paying minimum wages need not lead to mass dismissal if the business resigns itself to a small profit margin, removal of business from a settlement's industrial area need not necessarily mean dismissal of its Palestinian employees. The business may be able to continue employing them within Israel, albeit at a higher cost and lower profit margin.

Businesses also argue that if they remove themselves from the relationship, another player will take up their place; this would not only not remove the abuse, but might exacerbate it. However, the conduct of others cannot absolve an actor from its own responsibility.

5 Looking Ahead

This chapter considers implications of the PRR Framework for businesses operating in civilian settlements in occupied territory. Businesses should neither contribute directly to human rights violations nor benefit from them, and should use their leverage over other actors that are directly linked to them and who are involved in violations. As with any analysis based on international human rights standards, the article can offer only broad-brush guidance. The preceding sections suggest that businesses operating in the settlements can be viewed as benefiting from violations of human rights, since the settlement project is inextricably linked to such violations. Some businesses directly contribute to violations. Beyond that, determination of the obligations and leeway for action in specific cases can only be carried out on a case-by-case basis.

Despite its universal aspiration, the PRR Framework derives from a particular concern regarding state–business relations, namely the abuse by strong foreign businesses of their power over weak governments.[102] The Framework further assumes that human rights abuses can be isolated from legitimate commercial activity. These premises inform the Framework's guidance to businesses on how to discharge their due diligence responsibility. The unique context of settlement projects, for which the Israeli settlements serve as an example, challenges these premise.

[101] UN Database (n 12) paras 52–3. The report refers to the role of both the settlements and the occupation more generally in depressing the Palestinian economy.

[102] Scott Jerbi, 'Business and Human Rights at the UN: What Might Happen Next?' (2009) 31 Human Rights Quarterly 299, 301–3.

In light of the shortcomings of the PRR Framework in responding to this unique situation, perhaps it is appropriate to return to basic principles. The responsibility of businesses as a matter of international law arose in response to the limited reach of states' international human rights obligations and their political weakness. However, the obligations of states have expanded over the years. This includes the strengthening of states' obligations to protect against violations by third parties, and the growing acceptance that states have extraterritorial obligations.[103] It may be useful to demand of states that they take back the reins, as the first pillar of the PRR Framework requires.

[103] It has been suggested that through the duty to protect under the PRR Framework, the extraterritorial human rights obligations of states are expanding. Daniel Augenstein and David Kinley, 'When Human Rights "Responsibilities" Become "Duties": The Extra-Territorial Obligations of States that Bind Corporations' in Surya Deva and David Bilchitz (eds), *Human Rights Obligations of Business: Beyond the Corporate Responsibility to Respect?* (Cambridge University Press 2013) 271; ILA Study Group on Business and Human Rights, Final Report in the International Law Association, Report of the Seventy-Eighth Conference held in Sydney 19–24 August 2018 (16 November 2018) 1098, 1105.

7

Occupational Hazards: Gender and the Law of Occupation in Israel-Palestine

FIONNUALA NÍ AOLÁIN*

One glaring limitation in addressing the experiences of women in situations of armed conflict is the absence of a sustained analysis of the structural limits and capture of the law of occupation. This chapter addresses and bridges the gender gap in the law of occupation by addressing certain aspects of women's and girls' experiences in the Occupied Palestinian Territories. The chapter provides a brief historical contextualisation of the gender dimensions of belligerent occupation, addressing in particular the scope and gaps of the relevant treaty frameworks. It follows with an overview of certain gendered aspects to gendered lives under occupation, particularly focused on freedom of movement, family life, and gendered autonomy in long-term transformative occupations.

occupation, gender, human rights movement

One glaring limitation in addressing the experiences of women in situations of armed conflict is the absence of a sustained analysis of the structural limits and capture of the law of occupation. In almost all the major writing on the law of occupation, women and the relevance of gender analysis to understanding the limits of the law and the experience of living under occupation have been marginalised or entirely absent. David Kretzmer's scholarly writings made sizeable contributions to understanding and charting the legal, political and social effects of the Israeli occupation of the West Bank and Gaza.[1] In honouring David's

* This chapter acknowledges David Kretzmer's abiding personal and professional support over many decades. It also intrinsically acknowledges his long-standing support personally and professionally for women's rights and equality. The research underpinning this chapter was supported by the Political Settlement Research Project.

[1] David Kretzmer, *Israel and the West Bank: Legal Issues* (West Bank Data Base Project 1984); David Kretzmer, *The Occupation of Justice: The Supreme Court of Israel and the Occupied Territories* (State University of New York Press 2002); David Kretzmer, 'The

many contributions to that scholarly field, this chapter addresses and bridges the gender gap in the law of occupation by addressing certain aspects of women's and girls' experiences in the OPT.[2]

Gender considerations, and more particularly the experiences of women, have generally been at the margins of doctrinal and policy conversations concerning occupation, particularly in the legal realm.[3] If considered at all, women are generally 'added in' to the generic assessment of civilian protection.[4] More recently we have seen a move, in part

Advisory Opinion: The Light Treatment of International Humanitarian Law' (2005) 99 American Journal of International Law 88; David Kretzmer, 'Human Rights' (2005) 11 Israel Affairs 39; David Kretzmer, 'The Law of Belligerent Occupation in the Supreme Court of Israel' (2012) 94(85) International Review of the Red Cross 207; David Kretzmer, 'Terrorism and the International Law of Occupation' in Ben Saul (ed), *Research Handbook on International Law and Terrorism* (Edward Elgar 2014) 232.

2 Nomenclature of the Occupied Territories remains a highly contested legal and political space. I use the term based on its adoption in United Nations Security Resolutions and as applied by the Office of the High Commissioner for Human Rights: see 'Israeli Settlements in the Occupied Palestinian Territory, Including East Jerusalem, and Occupied Syrian Golan', 24 August 2016, UN Doc A/71/355, www.ohchr.org/EN/Countries/MENARegion/Pages/PSIndex.aspx.

3 In non-legal fields, including sociology and political science, one finds some attention paid to the experiences and subjectivities of occupation, but it remains marginal to human rights and international law analysis and practice. See, e.g., Simona Sharoni, *Gender and The Israeli-Palestinian Conflict: The Politics of Women's Resistance* (Syracuse University Press 1995).

4 Helen Kinsella, *The Image before the Weapon: A Critical History of the Distinction between Combatant and Civilian* (2011). This 'add women and stir' formula has a long history in international law. For example, in the context of the post-WWI negotiations, the 'Spanish Resolution', so-called because it was introduced by the Spanish delegation, was adopted by the 12th Assembly of the League of Nations on 24 September 1931. It read: 'The Assembly, convinced of the great value of the contribution of women to the work of peace and the good understanding between the nations, which is the principal aim of the League of Nations, requests the Council to examine the possibility of women cooperating more fully in the work of the League.' This presumed overlap between the feminine and the civilian has been the subject of stringent feminist analysis, including Helen Kinsella's exposure of how

> the practices of and referents for our current wars partially descend from, are governed by, the binary logics of, most immediately, Christianity, barbarism, innocence, guilt, and sex difference articulated in Grotius's text. These binaries are implicated in our contemporary distinction of 'combatant' and 'civilian', troubling any facile notion of what 'humanitarian' law is or what 'humanitarian' law does, and posing distinct challenges to theorizations of war and the laws taken to govern.

Helen Kinsella, 'Gendering Grotius: Sex and Sex Difference in the Laws of War' (2006) 34(2) Political Theory 161.

prefigured by the pressures of the UN Security Council-led Women, Peace and Security Agenda, to give recognition to gender/women as an 'analytical category' in conflict settings.[5] This gives some limited space to address women's needs as victims of violence or address presumed conundrums when women appear as perpetrators of violence, but does little to fundamentally engage with the overarching gender dynamics of occupation. In other disciplines, including criminology, feminists have paid attention to a wider array of harms experienced under occupation, including the 'occupation of the senses', addressing how the technologies of occupation manage 'language, sight, sound, time and space in the colony; the administration of who acts, who speaks, who gives birth and how, and who walks/moves/drives where and how; and what kind of language, music, smells, marches, colours, cultures and scenes are promoted and inscribed over the space, lives and bodies of the colonized'.[6] As I explore below, the rules related to occupation were not constructed with needs and experiences of women at the forefront, nor do they envisage what rules, structures, institutions and methods of intervention might follow as a result. This chapter operates from the premise that the gendered dimensions of occupation in general and the Israeli-Palestinian conflict in particular have substantially underreported and underrepresented the needs of women living under sustained occupation as well as the harms experienced by them.

The analysis in this chapter gives a brief historical contextualisation to the gender dimensions of belligerent occupation. Section 2 follows with a regulatory analysis, addressing the scope and gaps of the relevant treaty frameworks. Section 3 gives a general introduction to some of the key themes and approaches that are adopted by this analysis of gender and the law of occupation in the Israel-Palestinian context. Section 4 concludes the substantive analysis by honing in on certain illustrative examples that give context and depth to the broader claims. The conclusion points to the necessity of gendering the legal and political analysis

[5] The UN WPS Agenda was established by the adoption of United Nations Security Council Resolution 1325 in October 2000 with the goal inter alia of mainstreaming women's rights and security into the management, oversight and ending of conflict. See Nicola Pratt and Sophie Richter-Devroe, 'Critically Examining UNSCR 1325 on Women, Peace and Security' (2011) 13 International Feminist Journal of Politics 489, citing Nadje Al-Ali and Nicola Pratt (eds), *Women and War in the Middle East: Transnational Perspectives* (Zed Books 2009) 1–31.

[6] Nadera Shalhoub-Kevorkian, 'The Occupation of the Senses: The Prosthetic and Aesthetic of State Terror' (2017) 57 British Journal of Criminology 1279.

that intersects with occupation practices and procedures, underscoring the costs to women and girls from this intellectual and policy failure.

1 Historical Contextualisation

The core imperative of occupation law comes from the premise that belligerent occupiers maintain the 'status quo vis-à-vis the legislative and economic structure in the occupied territory [ensuring at the same time] humane treatment by all parties of the inhabitants during the period of occupation'.[7] Occupation is not an historical anomaly. Contemporary armed conflicts also demonstrate that temporary occupation often follows from hostilities between states.[8] Most classic definitions of occupation underscore the temporality of its status. Occupation is conceptually considered an aberration, a temporary state of affairs, a holding-position until the physical territory in question (and those inhabiting it) are returned to their original political status and territorial control reverts to the legitimate sovereign. Applicable bodies of legal norms are the Hague Regulations and the Fourth Geneva Convention as well as free-standing customary international law norms.[9] In long-term transformative occupations (as with other forms of extended territorial control), it is generally agreed that human rights law has parallel application with the law of armed conflict.[10]

[7] Eyal Benvenisti, *The International Law of Occupation* (2nd edn, Cambridge University Press 2012) 69.

[8] The obvious and recent examples include the occupations of Iraq and Afghanistan. Kaiyan Homi Kaikobad, 'Problems of Belligerent Occupation: The Scope of Powers Exercised by the Coalition Provisional Authority in Iraq, April/May 2003–June 2004' (2005) 54 International and Comparative Law Quarterly 253; R. Dobie Lagenkamp and Rex J. Zedalis, 'What Happens to the Iraqi Oil?: Thoughts on Some Significant, Unexamined International Legal Questions Regarding Occupation of Oil Fields' (2003) 14 European Journal of International Law 417.

[9] Hague Regulations Concerning the Laws and Customs of War on Land, annexed to Hague Convention Respecting the Laws and Customs of Land Warfare (entered into force 26 January 1910) 36 Stat. 2277. See Jean-Marie Henckaerts, 'Study on Customary International Humanitarian Law: A Contribution to the Understanding and Respect for the Rule of Law in Armed Conflict' (2005) 87 International Review of the Red Cross 175. Note that Article 43 of the Hague Convention required that the laws of the occupied country be respected unless the occupier was 'absolutely prevented' from doing so. There has been some subsidiary regulation of occupation by state administrations. This includes the 1949 Occupation Statute established by the three Western Allies in 1949. See Occupation Statute Defining the Powers to be Retained by the Occupation Authorities (entered into force 21 September 1949) 140 UNTS 202.

[10] On transformative occupation, see Adam Roberts, 'Transformative Military Occupation, Applying the Laws of War and Human Rights' (2006) 100(3) American

Many of our existent legal rules regarding occupation developed in parallel to and overlap with the norms governing trusteeship. Trusteeship was born in the nascent making of the post-WW1 collective security system, whereby the concept of 'mandate' was crafted to enable international oversight and control of Ottoman and German territories seized by the Allied powers.[11] Trusteeship held 'sovereignty in abeyance' pending the eventual evolution of the territories to full independence, with the characteristic that administration was to benefit the population and that it was subject to external oversight.[12] Understanding the masculine ordering and the patriarchy that infuse both systems gives us deeper insight into the centrality of a gendered order to the rulebook of occupation.

The principle *ex injuria jus non oritur*, or 'law does not arise from injustice', functions as a central concept within the law of occupation.[13] It is inherently linked to the obligations of occupiers to the territory and the civilian population they control, and affirms that unjust acts do not create law. The United States Report at the Hague Peace Conference explains, 'The law of *postliminium* was founded on the principle that the fact of war is not sufficient to destroy legitimate rights.'[14] This Roman

Journal of International Law 580; on parallel application of human rights and international humanitarian law in the context of occupation, see International Court of Justice, *Legal Consequences of the Construction of a Wall in the Occupied Palestinian Territory*, Advisory Opinion [2004] ICJ Rep 136.

11 Britain gained the mandate over Palestine, Iraq, Tanganyika and parts of Togo and Cameroon, France the mandate over Syria, Lebanon and the rest of Togo and Cameroon, Belgium over Rwanda and Burundi, South Africa over South West Africa, Australia over German New Guinea and (on behalf of the British Empire) Nauru, New Zealand over Western Samoa, and Japan the mandate for the former German islands north of the equator. Written texts were agreed dividing the mandates into three groups ('A', 'B' and 'C', distinguished supposedly by their 'civilisational' stage) and committing the mandatory power to various humanitarian ideals or administrative norms. The mandatory powers were given full governing authority, however, and oversight was kept to a minimum. See generally Alexandros Yannis, 'The Concept of Suspended Sovereignty in International Law and Its Implications in International Politics' (2001) 13 European Journal of International Law 1037.

12 *International Status of South West Africa*, Advisory Opinion [1950] ICJ Rep. 128, 143 (noting the language of Judge McNair).

13 In practice, one might argue that in transformative occupations its opposing principle is being advanced, *ex factis jus oritur* (the law arises from the facts). In parallel, where occupation results from the lawful use of force under international law, the framework of *jus post bellum* is usefully applied.

14 Benvenisti (n 7) 29.

law concept continues to hold sway, supporting the general proposition that free persons or objects taken in war will return to original state control (or status), with capture being a temporary state of affairs.[15]

These brief threads illustrate that, historically, the principle of sovereign equality has supported limitations on the exercise of power within occupied territories and ultimately permitted 'only the authority necessary for meeting the immediate needs of the occupation'.[16] This general rule is derived from 'the consolidation of three principles'. These are as follows:

> (1) 'all communities' need for a governing body;' (2) the need to 'enable the entity of that governing body to exercise public authority'; and (3) the principle that the 'entity that exercises public authority in an occupied territory must do so without dispossessing the actual sovereign completely and definitively'.[17]

Generally, only for the duration of the occupation, an occupant may change the laws in force in the country if one or more of these five ends require such changes to be made:

(1) The security of the occupying power and of its forces;
(2) The implementation of International Humanitarian Law and of International Human Rights Law (as far as the local legislation is contrary to such international law);
(3) The purpose of restoring and maintaining public order and civil life in the territory; and
(4) The purpose of enhancing civil life during long-lasting occupations; or
(5) Where explicitly so authorized under UN Security Council Resolutions.[18]

[15] Pomponius (Dig. 49. tit. 15. s. 14): 'There are two kinds of postliminium, for a man may either return himself or recover something.' Note that in this context, women were treated specifically. George Long notes that 'As to a wife, the matter was different: the husband did not recover his wife postliminium, but the marriage was renewed by consent.' William Smith and Anthon Charles, *Dictionary of Roman and Greek Antiquities* (J. Murray 1878).

[16] Benvenisti (n 7) 30.

[17] ibid 30, citing Pasquale Fiore, *Nuovo dritto internazionale pubblico* (2nd edn, vol. III, trans. Charles Antoine, 1885) 177.

[18] Marco Sassòli, 'Article 43 of the Hague Regulations and Peace Operations in the Twenty-First Century', *Program on Humanitarian Policy and Conflict Research at Harvard University*, 25–7 June 2004.

Reflecting on the core gender imperatives driving the law of occupation is to appreciate the centrality of territory and temporality in the construction of the legal rules. Thus, militaries (read generally men) who are aware of potentially losing power in the form of territorial control and political dominance to other men, are securing the external manifestations of that power (family, property and preservation of communal identity) in a form that enables their safe return at an unspecified future point. Occupation law was historically a compact between male military elites, a quid pro quo on masculine influence and a materialisation of complementary patriarchy that functioned to sustain the symbolic value of existent political form notwithstanding a temporary loss of territorial control during military hostilities. The reciprocity dimensions of occupation law reflect not only broader reciprocity frameworks in the law of armed conflict, but the specific benefits of maintaining political and military status quo arrangements notwithstanding the loss of territory during armed conflict.

2 Regulatory Framework

The 1907 Hague Convention sets out a series of rules on the methods and means of warfare and annexed to the Hague Convention IV are the Hague Regulations which include important parts of the Law of Occupation. Section III of the Regulations entitled 'Military Authority over the Territory of the Hostile State', is considered to constitute customary international law and forms the basis for our contemporary law of occupation. It includes the following provisions:

> Art. 46. Family honour and rights, the lives of persons, and private property, as well as religious convictions and practice, must be respected. Private property cannot be confiscated.[19]
>
> Art. 55. The occupying State shall be regarded only as administrator and usufructuary of public buildings, real estate, forests, and agricultural estates belonging to the hostile State, and situated in the occupied

[19] Other relevant provisions include Article 42 (stating that territory is considered occupied when it is actually placed under the authority of the hostile army); Article 43 (the authority of the legitimate power having in fact passed into the hands of the occupier, the latter shall take all the measures in his power to restore, and ensure, as far as possible, public order and safety, while respecting, unless absolutely prevented, the laws in force in the country); and Article 50 (no general penalty, pecuniary or otherwise, shall be inflicted upon the population on account of the acts of individuals for which they cannot be regarded as jointly and severally responsible).

> country. It must safeguard the capital of these properties, and administer them in accordance with the rules of usufruct.

Article 46 is the provision that most commentators view as being directly relevant to women's needs and protection under occupation.[20] The emphasis on family, the right to life, private property and religious tolerance comport to classical liberal assumptions about which values and rights have a hierarchical status during armed conflict and form the basis of responsibility for the occupying state.[21] The motif of paternal responsibility is sustained throughout.

In this scheme, a particular status is given to family honour, a concept that is tightly bound to the female body, reproduction and patriarchal order.[22] It is understood that the honour noted in the protective mantra is not the honour of the unequal or sexually violated female subject but rather the honour of the man or family to whom she is attached.[23] And it is obvious but worth re-emphasising that the most egregious harms imagined to occur to women are penetrative sexual harms, destroying their purity and chastity.[24]

Moreover, examining the other provisions of the Regulations through women's eyes and the lived experiences of women under occupation in highly patriarchal and stratified societies, it is possible to see the relevance of other provisions. These include general penalties (Article 46) in the context of house demolitions or respecting the laws in place in the territory under occupation (Article 43) with relevance to maintaining

[20] Rashida Manjoo and Calleigh McRaith, 'Gender-Based Violence and Justice in Conflict and Post-Conflict Areas' (2011) 44 Cornell International Law Journal 11, 19; Charlotte Lindsey, 'Women Facing War: ICRC Study on the Impact of Armed Conflict on Women', International Committee of the Red Cross (2011) 126.

[21] See, e.g., Kant and Bentham as examples of the application of classical liberal theory to international law and international relations. Note the interesting overlap with the Responsibility to Protect doctrine: Monica Hakimi, 'Towards a Legal Theory on the Responsibility to Protect' 2014 39(2) Yale Journal of International Law 247

[22] Joe Lunn, 'Male Identity and Martial Codes of Honor: A Comparison of the War Memoirs of Robert Graves, Ernst Jünger, and Kande Kamara' (2005) 69 Journal of Military History 713.

[23] Fionnuala Ní Aoláin, 'Sex-Based Violence and the Holocaust – A Reevaluation of Harms and Rights in International Law' (2000) 12 Yale Journal of Law and Feminism 43.

[24] The instrumentalism of this narrative is revealed by the use of female vulnerability narratives in the lead-up to the Second World War by government propaganda in the United Kingdom. See Nicoletta F. Gullace, 'Sexual Violence and Family Honor: British Propaganda and International Law during the First World War' (1997) 102(3) American Historical Review 714.

inequalities in divorce law, access to property and access to children.[25] All of these rules have blunt gender aspects upon forensic examination. How these provisions are interpreted, whether by military commanders or civilian courts, will affect women's experience under and access to law in the context of occupation.

When we shift gear and move to 1949, in the aftermath of the Holocaust and WWII, despite knowledge of the range and depth of sex-based harms experienced by women, the legal regulation of women's lives in the exposed context of occupation remains similarly constructed to that which emerged a half century earlier. Sexual violence aside, the legal imagination as to the types of harms that women might experience generally or disproportionately on account of their gender is notably constrained. Moreover, the limited references to women in the Conventions are overwhelmingly tied to the vulnerabilities of women as expectant or nursing mothers.[26] Geneva Convention IV is largely constructed from and in response to the Nazis' and other Axis regimes' concentration on selective practices of occupation during WWII. As literary narratives of occupation sites reveal, there were distinctly gendered actualities that followed occupation.[27] Little of that montage found expression in the law.

While the goal of Geneva IV was to better regulate the experiences of persons living under military occupation, the specific and distinct experiences of women are barely visible under the law. Article 27 of the Fourth Convention is the provision most often cited when we discuss the legal capture for harms experienced by women in the context of occupation.

> Art. 27. Protected persons are entitled, in all circumstances, to respect for their persons, their honour, their family rights, their religious convictions and practices, and their manners and customs. They shall at all times be humanely treated, and shall be protected especially against all acts of violence or threats thereof and against insults and public curiosity.

[25] This is an issue I have addressed at length elsewhere Fionnuala Ní Aoláin, 'Gendering the Law of Occupation: The Case of *Cyprus*' (2018) 27 Minnesota Journal of International Law 107 (2018).

[26] Judith G. Gardam and Michelle J. Jarvis, *Women, Armed Conflict and International Law* (Kluwer Law International 2001) 93.

[27] See, e.g., Kristen den Hartog and Tracy Kasaboski, *The Occupied Garden: A Family Memoir of War-Torn Holland* (Thomas Dunne 2009); Agnes Humbert, *Resistance: A Frenchwoman's Journal of the War* (trans. Barbara Mellor, Bloomsbury 2008); Curtis Whitfield Tong, *Child of War: A Memoir of World War II Internment in the Philippines* (University of Hawai'i Press 2011).

> Women shall be especially protected against any attack on their honour, in particular against rape, enforced prostitution, or any form of indecent assault.
>
> Without prejudice to the provisions relating to their state of health, age and sex, all protected persons shall be treated with the same consideration by the Party to the conflict in whose power they are, without any adverse distinction based, in particular, on race, religion or political opinion. However, the Parties to the conflict may take such measures of control and security in regard to protected persons as may be necessary as a result of the war.

The relevant legal framework is important on multiple grounds. First, awareness of the doctrinal limitations of the applicable law alert us to the gaps and silences surrounding the treatment of women and their fundamental lack of recognition under this regulatory framework. The lack of recognition translates into lacunae for women in recognition, accountability and enforcement when their rights are violated in situations of occupation. Second, the rule deficits are particularly relevant to the ending of conflict and occupation because a sizeable portion of transition is concerned with accountability for fundamental and systematic violations of law, when 'the law in these parts' is primarily based on the Fourth Geneva Convention (1949) we need to have a thorough grasp of what is permissible and what is not. This is the most direct route to claim-making on behalf of women during transitions from occupation. When there are no formal acknowledgments of obligations or harm, the accountability gaps are obvious. Finally, the inherent limitations in occupation law require us to be cognisant of human rights law applicability during occupation, which thereby function as 'gap-filler'.[28] In parallel, practitioners must increasingly take account of the application of international criminal law (ICL) as an overarching legal regime that

[28] ECtHR, *Aziz* v. *Cyprus*, App No 69949/01, 22 June 2005, paras 11, 28–9. This decision affirms that states cannot deny political rights and use occupation as an excuse to avoid their overarching human rights' obligations. See also ECtHR, *Prince Hans-Adam II of Liechtenstein* v. *Germany*, App No 42527/98, 27 June 2001, paras 45–8, 59, 68; I Ziemele, 'Case-Law of the European Court of Human Rights and Integrity of International Law' in R. H. Vinaixa and K. Wellens (eds), *L' influence des sources sur l'unité et la fragmentation du droit international* (Bruylant 2006) 199ff (outlining inter alia the ECHR's approach to occupation), 187–210. In respect of Israel, the International Court of Justice has found that 'the protections offered by human rights conventions does not cease in case of armed conflict, save through the effect of provisions for derogation of the kind to be found in Article 4 of the International Covenant on Civil and Political Rights': see *Legal Consequences of the Construction of a Wall in the Occupied Palestinian Territory*, Advisory Opinion [2004] ICJ Rep 136, paras 102–13.

intersects with the contemporary law of occupation. This overlap is made explicit by the inclusion in the Rome Statute creating the ICC of a war crimes provision that prohibits the transfer of civilian population into occupied territory.[29] This provision also lends itself to reflection on the gender-specific harms that have followed settlement establishment and protection for Palestinian women.[30] I explore this issue further below.

3 Gender and Transformative Occupation: Exploring the Complexity of Gendered Occupation in the Israel-Palestine context

> The Abu-Dahar Orchard.[31] This story is told as a small victory for Zouharia Abu-Dahar, the owner of a small property 1.5 square kilometres which consisted primarily of trees. She had been informed by the Israeli military commander in charge of the Occupied Palestinian Territories (OPT) in July 2004, that the trees on her property would be cut down entirely because they were situated in immediate proximity to the private residence of Shaul Mofaz, the newly appointed Israeli Defence Minister, whose house was right on the edge of the Green Line separating Israel from the OPT. Abu-Dahar took legal proceedings. Initially she was informed that the military order was 'incorrectly drafted'. The result a second decision mandating that along the property boundary a 'compromise' would be that only 60–70 per cent of her trees would be cut. An appeal to the Supreme Court ensued. Applying a proportionality test the Supreme Court found that only the dry bushes needed to be cut, the trees trimmed and the trunks of the trees left alone.

On the one hand this is a story that can be told as a victory and a validation of the legal constraints placed on belligerent occupiers. The orchard is saved by a resourceful mother and property owner. The Israeli High Court takes seriously the review of the home-based security of the Defense Minister for as long as he stays in office and finds a medium

[29] Under the War Crimes provisions, Article 8(b) (viii); the statute specifies that 'The transfer, directly or indirectly, by the Occupying Power of parts of its own civilian population into the territory it occupies, or the deportation or transfer of all or parts of the population of the occupied territory within or outside this territory' constitutes a war crime. Rome Statute of the International Criminal Court (entered into force 1 July 2002) 2187 UNTS 90 (ICC Statute).

[30] Women's Centre for Legal Aid and Counselling, 'Women's Voices: In the Shadow of the Settlements: A 2010 Report on Israel's Human Rights Violations against Palestinian Women' (2010).

[31] Drawn from the example given in Guy Davidov and Annon Reichman, 'Prolonged Armed Conflict and Diminished Deference to the Military: Lessons from Israel' (2010) 35 Law & Social Inquiry 919, 919–20.

way to satisfy both parties by applying a sophisticated balancing test. But that really only tells part of the story. As projects of feminist judgment from multiple countries tell us,[32] this is a muted judicial story, abstracted from the life and reality of the woman forced to seek a judicial remedy. Feminist method mandates that we focus on the omnipresent power in making the initial choice, a military voice that 'calls' out security needs every day in the Occupied Territories from the perspective of the occupier's security needs and not the security of the civilian whose life experiences occupation. The military demand profoundly implicates the life, quality and experiences of ordinary Palestinians. The globally insignificant battle over trees and bushes exposes a broader set of pressure points on the right to security, home, privacy and family life that are fully bounded in the *Abu-Dahar* decision. *Abu-Dahar* is unusual because the female protagonist wins a concession: she keeps her trees subject to the oversight of size, maintenance and requirement of the security demands of her military neighbour and occupier. Notably, in the Supreme Court decision this is not a case that hinges on rights per se – a clash of one set of rights over another. Rather the balance is one of security and rights, in a way that obscures and diminishes the totality of the rights quotient in play, and entirely disallows for the inherent power disparities of the woman defending her trees versus the rights of her neighbour who is both at the apex of the military hierarchy and the perceived subject of resulting personal risk.[33]

As other scholars have noted, many of the cases concerning the daily regulation of occupation in Israel-Palestine never get to court. The informal mediation increasingly encouraged by the Israeli Supreme Court to settle disputes between the military and the civilian population creates legal 'grey zones', where the absence of judicial review and the inherent imbalance of power between the military and the populace works to the advantage of the belligerent occupier, resulting in partial or poor remedies that give the illusion but not the substance of justice.[34] The imbalances may be greater when the informal mediation is taking

[32] Rosemary Hunter, Claire McGlynn and Erica Rackley (eds), *Feminist Judgments: From Theory to Practice* (Hart 2010).

[33] Commentators on the legalisation of the Israeli occupation have argued that the level of deference shown by the Israeli Supreme Court to military decisions has changed over time, and infer that substantive rule of law consciousness, specifically human rights law, is responsible. ibid.

[34] David Dyzenhaus, 'The Politics of Deference: Judicial Review and Democracy' in Michael Taggart (ed), *The Process of Administrative Law* (Hart 2006), 279.

place between women and military commanders given the omnipresent realities of culture, status and social norms in play. As such, human-rights-oriented judicial review is partial and as my interviews with leading human rights organisations in Israel consistently affirmed, it remained entirely unclear whether the resort to law operated to entrench and legitimate the occupation rather than challenge it.[35] In my preliminary review of the Israeli Supreme Court jurisprudence related to occupation, the phrases *gender*, *female* and *sex* were not found.[36] The term woman appears on occasion, including in the context of terrorist targeting (a failure to adhere to the principle of distinction affecting women and children),[37] the appropriateness of the placement of a portion of the wall and its effect on women and children,[38] and the protection of pregnant mothers.[39] However, there is no systematic attention to women's experiences under occupation, nor are the measures under review before the Israeli Supreme Court scrutinised from the perspective of gender harm, as part of a military necessity or proportionality test. In these circumstances, women face a triple bind. The relevant legal framework may not recognise the harms they experience under occupation; when women try to make the harms 'fit' recognised treaty and customary law categories, they lose the specifically gendered dimensions of the

[35] Interviews with B'Tselem: The Israeli Information Center for Human Rights in the Occupied Territories, and the Association for Civil Rights in Israel (ACRI), November 2011, Jerusalem. Fieldnotes on file with author. See also Kretzmer, *Occupation of Justice* (n 1).

[36] Israel Ministry of Foreign Affairs, *Judgments of the Israel Supreme Court: Fighting Terrorism within the Law* (2005). I note that my search was limited to English-language translated decisions, and that my review (including of Hebrew-only available decisions) is ongoing. I also note there is one reference to sex, in the context of a reference to Jewish law – Tosefta, Shabbat 16, 14 [21], (348) – but not directly to a female plantiff or subject of the administrative regime in the Occupied Territories.

[37] HCJ 201/09 *Physicians for Human Rights* v. *Prime Minister* 2009 PD 1 93, 105 (terrorists failed during the Second Intifada to distinguish between combatants and civilians, women, men or children).

[38] HCJ 1748/06, HCJ 1845/06, HCJ 1856/06, *Mayor of Ad-Dhahiriya et al.* v. *IDF Commander et al.* (14 December 2006) at 163–4, 178 (noting that an Israeli security barricade effectively denied passage to women with children). In this case, the Court held that the barricade was constructed for legitimate purposes, namely counter-terrorism, but was a disproportionate measure because it was not the 'least harmful measure that was capable of achieving the security purpose'.

[39] ibid. The Court considered fundamental protections of distinction, noting the duty to allow 'free passage of humanitarian medical supplies, as well as consignments of essential foodstuffs and clothing for children, pregnant women and mothers at the earliest opportunity, subject to several restrictions'.

experience as law neutralises its gendered content; and if recognition on these compromised terms is forthcoming, it may operate to entrench and sustain the meta-framework of occupation even as the appearance of partial remedy is provided.

One deeply challenging aspect of addressing the gender of occupation in the long-term OPT occupation is the prior obstacle of 'surfacing' occupation itself. As numerous scholars and policy-makers have noted in the Israeli-Palestinian context, the normalisation of occupation within the 'green' line means that civil society, as well as political and legal discourses in Israel, are primarily focused on a wide-spectrum analysis that prioritises broadly defined security threats, terrorism, settler expansion and military responses to enable containment. In this securitised space, there is a form of legal and political erasure of the facts and consequences for the civilian population of occupation.[40] This form of shifting means that it remains a challenge to address occupation per se much less to observe and account for the gendered consequences of occupation.

Based on a series of interviews in Israel during ongoing fieldwork (within the 1967 borders), it was notable that mainstream Israeli human rights organisations do not address or substantially include gender concerns or experiences in their reporting on conflict-/occupation-related human rights or humanitarian law violations.[41] Gendered experiences of occupation or gendered interfaces in the conflict zone were viewed as peripheral or marginal in the discourse of human rights/humanitarian law harms being addressed. In general, some scepticism was mooted as to how such violations could be incorporated and what the added value of this move would be.[42] There was a consistent thread in all conversations that gender violence was 'not part of this conflict zone'. In particular, with prompt from the interviewer (myself), the emphasis by interviewees on a lack of rape complainants through the various interfaces between Palestinian populations and Israeli soldiers was a position from which to negate the gender dimension to the occupation/conflict entirely.[43] In

[40] This maps onto Stanley Cohen's analysis of denial and its role in sustained human rights abuses on a systematic scale within a body politic. See Stanley Cohen, *States of Denial: Knowing about Atrocities and Suffering* (Polity Press 2000).

[41] Interviews with policy staff at B'Tselem and ACRI (n 35).

[42] ibid.

[43] The contrast lies with other high-profile occupations such as the Indonesian miltary occupation of East Timor in which Timorese women were the victims of sexual violence. A truth process (CAVR) established in 2001 found significant evidence that throughout

parallel, a series of interviews with domestic Israeli organisations whose mandate addresses intimate violence (primarily assault, rape, domestic violence) *within* the state of Israel revealed little 'seen' connection between rates, forms and patterns of intimate violence and the context of broader conflict/occupation in the jurisdiction.[44] Still, research in conflict jurisdictions elsewhere has demonstrated that the linkage between intimate violence, coercive control and other forms of sex-based harm is elevated and triggered by the broader conflict landscape as well as by specific triggering incidents.[45]

By contrast, in a series of interviews with Palestinian organisations, gendered experiences and gender harm were at the forefront of occupation analysis.[46] Women were viewed as bearing substantial burdens containing distinct gender dimensions.[47] In particular, the gendered impacts of stop and search on freedom of movement, family life, marriage, birth, death (particularly at checkpoints, crossings and airports) were viewed as deeply gendered experiences with specifically articulated gendered harms following. Nadera Shalhoub-Kevorkian has strikingly illustrated the way in which the dynamics of conflict and occupation have resulted in a 'frontline' role for Palestinian women in confrontation with the state of Israel as public space has been closed to, or contains

the years of occupation women 'were raped by Indonesian soldiers, were exposed to sexual discrimination and were frequently used as sexual slaves'. See Susanne Allden, 'Internationalising the Culture of Human Rights: Securing Women's Rights in Post Conflict East Timor' (2007) 8 Asia-Pacific Journal on Human Rights and the Law 1, 11.

44 Interviews with Rape Crisis Center staff in Tel Aviv and Jerusalem, 2011.

45 Monica McWilliams and Jessica Doyle, 'Violent Conflict, Political Settlement and Intimate Partner Violence: Lessons from Northern Ireland' PSRP Research Report 2017, www.politicalsettlements.org/wp-content/uploads/2017/11/201711_McWilliamsDoyle_ResearchReport_IntimatePartnerViolence.pdf.

46 See, e.g., Interviews with Al Haq: Defending Human Rights in Palestine since 1979 and the Women's Center for Legal Aid and Counselling (November 2017, Ramallah).

47 It is useful here to note the literature that broadly dismisses the effects or harms of occupation. Kontorovich argues, for example, that one sustained practice of the occupation settlements 'does not appear to have direct individual victims'. His analysis is located in the gravity assessment of the ICC statute (Article 17 (1) (d)), drawing selectively on the position papers of the ICC prosecutor and claiming that the primary criterion is the 'number of victims', particularly the number of deaths. Eugene Kontorovich, 'When Gravity Fails: Israeli Settlements and Admissibility at the ICC' (2014) 47 Israel Law Review 379, 387. His argument is part of a broader claim that the ICC would not have jurisdiction over the 'settlement enterprise' as such, and that the 'transfer' crime does not involve murder or direct physical violence. In his (controversial and empirically unfounded) view, according to 'many' authorities, the settlement activity may be 'purely consensual' (389).

detention and other challenges for, men.[48] This disconnect in the perceptions of a small though key sample of human rights and gender organisations exposes some of the difficulties that exist in bringing gender into any conversation addressing violations of the law of occupation as well as in creating a deeper and more nuanced understanding of women's lives under occupation.

4 Illustrative Examples of the Gendered Dimensions of Transformative Occupation

This short chapter can only canvass some of the gendered dimensions of living under belligerent occupation. That broader work has been canvassed elsewhere by this author,[49] and this final section sets out some of the relevant spheres of inquiry as well as providing a small number of concrete illustrations of gendered effects. In doing so, the analysis is driven by a life-span analysis to reveal the depth and complexity of women's lives under occupation. In short, this means examining the totality of women's lives from birth to grave to assess the specificity of occupation's harms at each pivotal point. I ask the following questions: What does it mean to be a girl child born into occupation, a female child living under occupation, a woman coming into adulthood under occupation, a woman seeking to marry and have a family under occupation, a woman giving birth under occupation, a woman raising children under occupation, a woman trying to work under occupation, a woman travelling from one place to another under occupation, a woman undertaking family and communal roles under occupation, a woman who is ill under occupation, a woman who dies under occupation? What does the law of occupation say to the life-cycle of a woman who can expect to be born and has lived or lives all of her adult life under occupation?

For the purposes of this chapter I focus on one specific but pervasive aspect of life for Palestinian women living under occupation, namely the

[48] Nadera Shalhoub-Kevorkian, *Security Theology, Surveillance and the Politics of Fear* (Cambridge University Press 2015); Moreover, given the significance of security to the legal ordering of occupation, it is not insignificant that Palestinian newborns have been labelled a 'demographic threat'; the regulation of birth for Palestinians under occupation has undergone a process of 'deep securitization'. Uriel Abulof, 'Deep Securitization and Israel's "Demographic Demon"' (2014) 8 International Political Sociology 396.

[49] Ní Aoláin (n 25) 107; Fionnuala Ní Aoláin, 'Gendering the Law of Occupation' PSRP Working Paper 2016, www.politicalsettlements.org/publications-database/gendering-occupation.

ongoing complexity of negotiating territory and space under occupation. There are of course other challenges, including most notably pervasive and systematic violence. As both Israeli and Palestinian human rights organisations have documented, a range of violent structures including but not limited to military and settler violence, threats and intimidation and a pervasive impunity for their action frame the ongoing day-to-day life of women in the Occupied Territories. However, the focus on spatial challenges of occupation demonstrates that these are multiple and have highly distinct gender implications. Specifically, at the macro level in Israel-Palestine, there is the territorial split between Gaza and the West Bank. Gaza was first occupied by Israel in 1967. Israel disengaged from Gaza in 2005, and the following year Hamas won a legislative victory over the PLO's Fatah, resulting in physical, political and economic isolation for the Strip's inhabitants.[50] International isolation heightened in the aftermath of Operations Cast Lead and Protective Edge, exacerbated by the continued intransigence of Fatah–Hamas reconciliation moves, deep security reliance between Israel and Egypt and regional instability, making this densely populated area highly unstable and the lived lives of those who inhabit it awful on multiple indicators.[51] Access between both geographies is cut off, with marked consequences for family and community connections, including marriage, death, birth, community and family integration, and inter-generational relationships.

In the West Bank, the security wall dominates the access arena, with particular and highly regulated checkpoints being the entry and exit spaces, where heightened scrutiny and the capacity of being subject to military questioning and detention impact in high-frequency ways on women's daily lives. There is a distinct female presence in these sites of access – movement into and out of the Occupied Territories – including both female Israeli soldiers and female Palestinian civilians passing

[50] Gisha – The Legal Center for Freedomn of Movement, 'The Gaza Cheat Sheet: Real Data on the Gaza Closure', 10 August 2016, www.gisha.org/UserFiles/File/publications/Info_Gaza_Eng.pdf.

[51] Gaza has one of the highest unemployment rates of any economy in the world (41.5 percent overall, 58 percent for youth); 80 per cent of the population rely on donor aid, 39 per cent are below the poverty line. Operation Protective Edge destroyed what there was of an agricultural sector, there are virtually no exports and the territory is sealed off from external movement in and internal movement out. See International Crisis Group, 'No Exit? Gaza and Israel between Wars', 26 August 2015, 7, www.crisisgroup.org/middle-east-north-africa/eastern-mediterranean/israelpalestine/no-exit-gaza-israel-between-wars.

through metal turnstile gates and driving past established concrete military posts. The masculinity of the space is also notable in the military presence that overshadows control of movement from one space to another.

Aside from the security wall, the OPT is spatially divided based on a formula of (temporary) agreement derived from the Oslo Accords. Under that Accord, an interim agreement designed to lead to Final Status negotiations, all West Bank land, excluding East Jerusalem, falls into one of three categories, Area A (currently 18 per cent), which is in theory under full PA security and civil control though there are frequent Israeli incursions; Area B (currently 21 per cent) under mixed PA/Israeli (mostly Israeli) control; and Area C (currently 61 per cent) under full Israeli control of security, civil affairs and building with the PA controlling the non-Israeli civilian population in civil matters (for example, family law) that do not impinge on Israeli competencies. These spatial geographies create a microcosm of regulation that creates multiple encounters with military and civilian regulation of individual lives (as well as settlers in multiple forms) for women. The spatial realities create regulatory disjunctions for the population as a whole,[52] but with specific effects on women's lives.

In the Israel-Palestine context there has been a dearth of research exploring the ways in which conflict-/occupation-specific harms have affected women, with some notable exceptions from non-governmental sources.[53] Moreover, as I have articulated elsewhere, the privileging of knowledge in human rights discourses imbued with hierarchies of harm, which notably elevates direct physical harms to the body as most egregious, means that the range of experiences women might define as harmful and abusive, and the responsibility of the state(s), are excluded from the conversations that predominate in identifying the 'relevant' human rights and humanitarian law violations that 'count' for scrutiny

[52] The most obvious of which is the highly complex terrain of administrative permits allowing (or not) access to parts of the Occupied Territories.

[53] Palestinian Women's Research and Documentation Center, 'Impacts and Challenges Facing Palestinian Families Regarding Residency in the Palestinian Territory: An Exploratory Study with a Gender Perspective' (July 2010); Women's Center for Legal Aid and Counselling, 'Women's Voices: In the Shadows of the Settlements' (2010); Fayhā' 'Abd al-Hādī, *'If I were Given the Choice . . .' : Palestinian Women's Stories of Daily Life during the Years 2000 to 2003 of the Second Intifada* (Women's Center for Legal Aid and Counselling 2007).

in the context of occupation.[54] This has meant that the consistent impediments to free movement will invariably have lower visibility and status than sexual or direct physical harms, even though the cumulative effects of closure, physical containment and estoppel in access to education, health and family may have staggering social, economic and physical effects on women. Because the law of occupation does not expressly protect freedom of movement, the parallel application of human rights norms in such situations is all the more weighty.

A reflection on the limitations placed on free movement within occupied territories underscores the gap between the harms that have visibility and status under the laws of occupation and those gendered harms that are rendered invisible to that body of legal norms. Here one can also take note of the increasing dependence on surveillance and securitisation allied with limitations on movement as the preferred modality of population control. As Shalhoub-Kevorkian cogently notes: 'The Israeli security and surveillance apparatus results in severe spatial restrictions for Palestinian Jerusalemites, limiting their access to family, social services, educational institutions and health facilities.'[55] The spatial limitations that have encroached and grown with the occupation in the OPT have distinct legal implications. While many occupation-related human rights violations have garnered international attention in the context of the occupation, most notably the use of torture or 'moderate physical pressure' ultimately decried by the Israeli Supreme Court as a violation of international treaty and customary law to which the state is bound,[56] other lesser-status violations have received less notice and less attention.

If the face of torture in the context of the occupation was the young male Palestinian, the female face of occupation is best captured by the long lines of women and children standing and waiting for processing each day at Qalandia checkpoint, one of the largest military checkpoints

[54] Ní Aoláin (n 49).

[55] Nadera Shalhoub-Kevorkian, 'E-Resistance and Technological In/Security in Everyday Life' (2012) 52 British Journal of Criminology 55, 56. 'Wherever you go, you discover there is a checkpoint. Their borders are in our homes, lives, bodies and relationships' (61).

[56] Though a December 2017 Supreme Court decision in the case of Assad Abu Gosh appears to walk back the trenchant repudiation of torture by exempting security agents from criminal investigation despite their undisputed use of 'coercive pressure' against a Palestinian detainee. See Elena Chachko, '"Pressure Techniques" and Oversight of Shin Bet Interrogations: Abu Gosh v. Attorney General' (*LAWFARE*, 22 December 2017), www.lawfareblog.com/pressure-techniques-and-oversight-shin-bet-interrogations-abu-gosh-v-attorney-general.

in the OPT, situated approximately ten minutes from the centre of Jerusalem. Between 23,000 and 26,000 Palestinians or residents of East Jerusalem pass through this checkpoint each day.[57] Having spent many days passing through this checkpoint while researching in the territory, I can attest to the seething mass of humanity, mostly in female form, that exits and enters its clutches. One could dwell on the humiliation, personal and communal, that accompanies undulating daily transfer from one territory to another, but for the purposes of this analysis my goal is to reflect on the complexity of female-centred harms that occur in these spaces.

There have been births (women giving birth at checkpoints as they seek access to medical care in Jerusalem from the OPT), deaths, the gendered verbal harassment of interface with young male and female soldiers who view and treat the other women as objects of threat, the experience of being treated as the othered 'other', the constant fear of indefinite detention without charge or trial, the taking of one's scant legal papers, the fear of being recruited as informers, and the insecurity of not knowing if you will get through. These cumulative harms are daily and constant – and framed by a legal and political narrative of security. One could engage in a separate analysis of security and liberty trade-offs, but as Gross has argued, the process of optimising trade-offs between 'security–liberty' are likely to be biased in ways that 'ought, at the very least, to be recognised and accounted for' and 'result in systematic undervaluation of one interest (liberty); and overvaluation of another (security)'.[58] What is invisible to the law of occupation is both the long-term effect of prolonged occupation and consistent daily limitation on the freedom of movement. A fundamental challenge for the feminist scholar as one accounts for how and where women experience the most consistent harms, is how the law should account for disparate gender impact. One specific recalibration that follows is to recognise and

[57] Miriam Berger, 'Israel's "Checkpoint Q": A Daily Hurdle for Palestinians', *World News* (26 April 2017), https://www.reuters.com/article/us-israel-palestinians-qalandiya-idUSKBN17S23D; Press Release, 'Middle East Situation Remains Critical, Special Committee on Palestinian Rights Told', UN Press Release GA/PAL/985 (21 June 2005); Helga Tawil-Souri, 'New Palestinian Centers: An Ethnography of the "Checkpoint Economy"' (2009) 12 International Journal of Cultural Studies 217, 224.

[58] Oren Gross, 'Security vs. Liberty: On Emotions and Cognition' in David Jenkins, Amanda Jacobsen and Anders Henriksen (eds), *The Long Decade: How 9/11 Changed the Law* (Oxford University Press 2014), 46–7.

reorder the status of harms (and thus legality of action) to the civilian population based on duration and undue burdens on women.

5 Conclusion

An important gendered point of conclusion is that, despite the disparate characterisations between the occupier and occupied in the Israeli-Palestinian context – one liberal democratic regime poised against a less liberal and emergent regime whose democratic qualities are suspect – the point of convergence between these two entities for women under occupation is their complementary patriarchy, the sense in which both cede proprietary value to religious doctrine in the regulation of women's lives, and a common lack of liberal thinking when restrictions on women are at issue. There is also the overarching presence and influence of external international male elites to account for in the mix. Here my central contention is that occupation law can serve the patriarchal interest of male elites and the interest convergence of both is unexpected but real. Complementary patriarchy is evident in the deference to 'family rights', 'honour' and 'manners and customs', which, while seemingly neutral and deferential concepts, notoriously work against women's interests.[59] Such cultural arguments are not raised as a barrier to protect men's dignity interests in the context of occupation. Although occupiers will stretch interpretation of prior legal norms to the benefit of the protected population and will manipulate legal norms to their own benefit, it remains consistent that interpretation does not bend to accommodate the needs and interests of protected female populations.

Most obvious in any assessment of occupation is a sustained invisibility of women's lived lives in their myriad roles and identities under occupation. The double layers to this invisibility have internal and external dimensions – connected both to the experience of communities under occupation, the masculinity of regulation, and of perceived threat, as well as to the lower status of women within their own communities.

[59] See Gardam and Jarvis (n 26), 93, 107–10, and see Jasen's study of how women are subjected to interlocking ideologies of gender, colonialism and race and how dominant beliefs and hegemonic ways of thinking are capable of affecting women's experiences of childbirth in material ways. Thus, 'self-sufficiency has been eroded by a process of colonization which introduced new health risks, and by a civilizing mission which undermined old knowledge'. Patricia Jasen, 'Race, Culture and the Colonization of Childbirth in Northern Canada' (1997) 10(3) Social History of Medicine 383, 399.

Surfacing women in multifaceted ways in the way of occupation is an essential aspect of this work.

In conclusion, it would be remiss to close without affirming the agency and resistance practised by women living under occupation. That resistance is both manifest and subversive. It is revealed in birthing choices, mothering skills and manoeuvring, the continued and defining presence of women in public space, in women's movement through and within territory, in community engagement, in solidarity, in challenging – within their communities and directly – the occupation regime. It manifests in the everydayness of women's lives under belligerent occupation where normality and predictability have long been suspended. Paying attention to the everyday has been a fruitful site for feminist scholars to reveal the complexity, beauty and determination of women's lives. There is much work still to be done in the context of the OPT to reveal the fullness of this reality. This chapter is one step in that direction.

8

Rule of Law *De Jure* and/or *De Facto?*

Shamgar and the International Law of Belligerent Occupation

YUVAL SHANY*

The chapter revisits some of the main contributions by Meir Shamgar, who served between 1961 and 1995 as Israel's Military Advocate General, Attorney General, Judge and President of the Supreme Court, to the development of Israeli jurisprudence relating to the interpretation and application of international law in general, and the law of belligerent occupation in particular. Arguably, the legal structures constructed by Shamgar proved to be resilient because they were based on his deep understanding of international law and commitment to basic legal values. Among the topics discussed are Shamgar's contribution to subjecting Israel's activities in the West Bank and Gaza Strip to rule of law concepts, his nuanced position on the application of the Fourth Geneva Convention, his support for a flexible interpretation of the law of belligerent occupation and the balancing he performed between Israeli security interests and the needs and interests of the Palestinian inhabitants. While this chapter focuses on the work of one exceptional Israeli jurist, it offers broader insights about Israel's approach to international law and the law applicable to the occupied territories, and about the relationship between international law as a constraint upon political power and as a cloak for the exercise of such power.

law of belligerent occupation, Israel, Palestine, Supreme Court, Fourth Geneva Convention, Meir Shamgar

* This chapter is based on a lecture given at an annual Ministry of Justice international law conference in Tel Aviv (January 2020), which was dedicated to the memory of President Shamgar. Among the speakers in the conference was Prof. David Kretzmer who litigated the *Afu* case before a bench of the Supreme Court headed by President Shamgar. Thanks are due to Dr Gilad Noam and Noa Geva for their assistance in collecting the materials on which the lecture and the chapter were based. The author's positions on the approach of Shamgar to the international law of belligerent occupation have been shaped, to a large extent, by the scholarship of Prof. Kretzmer on the topic, and this chapter is dedicated to him.

Introduction

Israeli courts had relied on international law before Meir Shamgar (1925–2019) became a Supreme Court judge in 1975, and continued to rely on international law after he retired in 1995. Still, no Israeli judge has had an influence like Shamgar on the legal doctrine governing the application of international law by Israeli courts, and no Israeli jurist has had an impact like Shamgar on the specific question of the interpretation and application of law of belligerent occupation to the West Bank and Gaza Strip, and on the extension of the jurisdiction of the Israeli Supreme Court to claims originating from these territories. Such influence and impact were no doubt facilitated by Shamgar's unique career path, which placed him in the years 1961–95 in key decision-making positions relating to the application of international law in the occupied territories: Military Advocate General (MAG)(1961–8),[1] Attorney-General (AG)(1968–75), Supreme Court judge (1975–95) and President of the Supreme Court (1983–95).

Still, the lasting effect of Shamgar's decisions on international law, and the analytical concepts and legal conclusions he developed through these decisions, cannot be explained merely by his being in the right place at the right time. The legal structures he constructed were resilient because they were based on Shamgar's deep understanding of international law in the post-World War Two era, and because they were shaped in light of the basic legal values in which Shamgar believed throughout his life: rule of law, procedural fairness and common decency.[2] This combination of knowledge and principles rendered his decisions doctrinally robust and legitimate (in the eyes of many), and helped sustain their longevity.

What's more, Shamgar's approach to the interpretation and application of international law in general, and of the law of belligerent occupation in particular, was consistent with an ideological and political position broadly held in Israel between 1967 and 1993 (i.e., between the Six Day War and the Oslo Accords), with regard to the territories it occupied in the 1967 War. According to this position, the West Bank and Gaza Strip are part of historical *Eretz Israel* (Land of Israel), over which the state of Israel has legitimate historical claims, as well as legal rights.[3]

[1] In the last year to his service as MAG, Shamgar also held, in parallel, the position of Ministry of Defence legal advisor.

[2] Shamgar's attachment to such principles can be read between the lines of his 2015 autobiography. See, e.g., Meir Shamgar, *An Autobiography* (Yediot 2015) 25, 181, 327, 656.

[3] In fact, Shamgar was politically affiliated in his young days with the Etzel (or Irgun) – a militant branch of Revisionist Zionism that fought for Jewish statehood against the British

As a result, these territories are not occupied in the full sense of the word,[4] but rather administered under the laws of belligerent occupation, until a political settlement of the Israeli-Palestinian conflict is reached. Until that time arrives, Shamgar – like many others in the liberal centre-right political camp in Israel – seemed to believe in the moral imperative of treating Palestinian civilians residing in the territory fairly, and in the need to abide by the state of Israel's obligations under international law. The legal construct Shamgar developed as an AG and a judge reflected his own moral convictions, but also the ambivalence of many Israeli decision-makers about the status of the territories: only some parts of the law of belligerent occupation applied *de jure* to the situation in the West Bank and Gaza Strip; other norms, which could be plausibly construed as inapplicable, were not applied as a matter of law, but applied *de facto* as a matter of policy. Israeli administrative law – including its principles of 'natural justice' (e.g. the right of individuals to a hearing prior to administrative measures which may adversely affect their rights)[5] – provided another set of assurances against arbitrary use of government power, thereby complementing the protections afforded by the law of belligerent occupation.

Arguably, a jurist with less attachment to considerations of procedural fairness and international legality might have advanced a less elaborate legal framework, which would have given the government of Israel more of a carte blanche to promote its political agenda in the West Bank and Gaza Strip; at the same time, an Israeli less attached to the historical rights of the Jewish people over *Eretz Israel* might have been more inclined to dismiss claims concerning the *sui generis* situation of the West Bank and Gaza Strip.[6] By contrast, the legal paradigm developed by

Mandate. He was detained by the British authorities in Palestine in 1944 and was held until 1948 in prison camps in East Africa.

[4] In his autobiography, Shamgar wrote: 'At the national level I see a substantial difference. The British were a foreign government here. I believed they betrayed the commitment they gave in the Declaration of Lord Balfour, and the State of Israel was established lawfully, out of the historical right of the people of Israel in its land, according to rules of international law. In 1967 we did not invite Arab states to attack us . . . as a result, blame for the war during which we conquered territories lies on their shoulders . . . Ultimately, this is a conflict between two peoples of territory, and the Palestinians oppose our very presence here' (unofficial translation). Shamgar (n 2) 255–6.

[5] See, e.g., Colin S. Diver, 'Israeli Administrative Law from an American Perspective' (1997) 4 Mishpat Umimishal I, XI.

[6] One may draw an interesting contrast between Shamgar's ambivalent approach to the status of the Occupied Territories in the post-1967 period, and the approach taken by the legal advisor to the Israeli Foreign Ministry at the time, Theodor Meron, who wrote in 1967–8 two significant legal opinions premised on the formal application of the Fourth

Shamgar – the Shamgar paradigm (whose main elements are discussed below) – allowed the Israeli government to keep the question of sovereignty over the West Bank and Gaza Strip in a situation of abeyance, while maintaining considerable room for advancing policies with long-term implications for the status quo on the ground. Interestingly enough, the lifespan of the Shamgar paradigm appears to have been pegged to the period of political indecision in Israel about the status of the Occupied Territories, which characterised the first quarter of a century after 1967. Once the situation on the ground started to change considerably, with the Intifada, the Oslo Accords and the sharp rise in settlement activity, the Shamgar paradigm lost much of its relevance, although, as a formal matter, it continued to apply.

This chapter revisits some of the main contributions by Meir Shamgar to the development of Israeli jurisprudence relating to the interpretation and application of international law in general, and the law of belligerent occupation in particular. Among the topics discussed are Shamgar's contribution to subjecting Israel's activities in the West Bank and Gaza Strip to rule-of-law concepts, his nuanced position on the application of the Fourth Geneva Convention[7] to the Occupied Territories, his support for the elastic interpretation of the law of belligerent occupation and his approach to balancing between Israeli security interests and the needs and interests of the local Palestinian inhabitants. While this chapter focuses on the work of one exceptional Israeli jurist, broader insights can be drawn from the discussion below about Israel's approach to international law and to the law applicable to the Occupied Territories, and perhaps also about the relationship between international law as a constraint upon political power and as a cloak for the exercise of such power.

1 Rule of Law

Few legal decisions have had as many dramatic consequences in the legal history of Israel as the one decision taken by Shamgar, shortly after beginning to serve as AG. This was his decision not to oppose the

Geneva Convention to the Occupied Territories. See Theodor Meron, 'The West Bank and International Humanitarian Law on the Eve of the Fiftieth Anniversary of the Six-Day War' (2017) 111 American Journal of International Law 357, 358–9.

7 Geneva Convention (IV) Relative to the Protection of Civilian Persons in Time of War (entered into force 21 October 1950) 75 UNTS 287 (GC IV).

submission of petitions by West Bank and Gaza Strip Palestinians to the Israeli Supreme Court, sitting as the High Court of Justice (i.e. a first and last instance administrative court). In his autobiography, Shamgar presents his decision in the following words:

> The ideology underlying this approach provided that effective judicial supervision over military conduct should be established, and that this is only possible by granting the possibility to a person in the administered area to seize a civilian court, exercising superior judicial review over the application of administrative law norms. Even from the distance of years it is hard to overestimate the importance of this decision . . . Israel became the first and only state that allowed residents of an administered territory to approach its legal instances as the state responsible for military governance, even to its most supreme instance.[8]

This decision appears to reflect Shamgar's world view, that is, that Israel must conduct itself as a rule-of-law state, that state officials, including the military when operating in occupied territories, must abide by the applicable law, and that judicial review by independent courts is an essential condition for such legal structures to hold.[9] This decision resulted in many thousands of cases being brought to the Court by Palestinians, challenging the legality of numerous measures taken by the Israeli authorities in the West Bank and Gaza Strip, rendering the Occupied Territories the most judicially scrutinised occupation in history.

The opening of the doors of the Israeli Supreme Court to Palestinian applicants has been described in some of the literature as providing them with a false hope, since they lost in most cases litigated in court;[10] according to this narrative, judicial review mostly served as a legal facade intended to legitimise the Israeli occupation, and may have been one of the secrets of its exceptional longevity.[11] At the same time, even critics of

[8] Shamgar (n 2) 304–5 (unofficial translation).

[9] Some commentators attributed Shamgar's attachment to acting in a restrained manner and to taking legal obligations seriously to his childhood in pre-World War Two Danzig. See, e.g., Arnon Segal, 'Judge Shamgar: "Every Act of Torture is Unlawful"', *Makor Rishon* , 2 January 2016, www.makorrishon.co.il/magazine/178407 (in Hebrew); Diana Bahur Nir, 'My Father Sent Our Tax Money to the Nazi Town We Escaped From: "I Don't Want Someone to Say that Jews Run Away and Don't Pay"', *Calcalist*, 10 October 2019, www.calcalist.co.il/local/articles/0,7340,L-3707369,00.html (in Hebrew).

[10] Ronen Shamir, 'Landmark Cases and the Reproduction of Legitimacy: The Case of Israel's High Court of Justice' (1990) 24 Law & Society Review 781.

[11] See, e.g., David Kretzmer, *The Occupation of Justice: The Supreme Court of Israel and the Occupied Territories* (State University of New York Press 2002) 2.

the Court accepted that awareness by military authorities of the fact that every measure they would take in the West Bank and the Gaza Strip would be reviewed by the Court often operated as a restraining factor, and required them to regularly evaluate the legal implications of their conduct.[12] This, in turn, rendered the law of belligerent occupation and Israeli administrative law meaningful legal criteria for the assessment of governmental measures undertaken in the Occupied Territories.

Another important consequence of Shamgar's decision not to contest petitions to the Court by Palestinians was a sharp increase in the number of cases dealt with by the Israeli Supreme Court that required deciding upon questions of international law. Up until 1967, the engagement of Israeli courts with international law was limited in scope and related mostly to technical legal issues which were not regulated by domestic statute,[13] such as jurisdiction over crimes committed at sea onboard Israeli vessels,[14] consular immunity[15] and the extraterritorial reach of property seizure orders.[16] However, after 1967, the Supreme Court started dealing extensively with international law in thousands of cases relating to the Occupied Territories, many of which involved difficult legal questions and sensitive political issues. While the Supreme Court developed particular expertise in the law of belligerent occupation, it also had many new opportunities to address general international law issues (such as the rules of treaty interpretation)[17] and international human rights law.[18] It is no accident that the leading judgment in the history of the Supreme Court about the status of international law in Israeli law was written (by Shamgar) in connection with the application of the Fourth Geneva Convention by Israeli courts.[19]

One specific case which illustrates the strong commitment by Shamgar to the rule of law and its relationship to rules of international law is the *Tsemel* case, which dealt with the grounds for detention and detention

[12] See, e.g., David Kretzmer, 'The Law of Belligerent Occupation in the Supreme Court of Israel' (2012) 94 International Review of the Red Cross 207, 235.

[13] One glaring exception has been the landmark *Eichmann* case, which established the principle of universal jurisdiction. CrimA 336/61 *Eichmann* v. *AG* 1962 ILR 37 277.

[14] CrimA 174/54 *Shtempfer* v. *AG* 1956 10 PD 5.

[15] CA 208/52 (Jer.) *Successors of Shevavo* v. *Halen* 1952–3 PM 8 455.

[16] HCJ 279/51 *Amsterdam* v. *Minister of Finance* 1952 PD 6(1) 945.

[17] See, e.g., HCJ 785/87 *Afu* v. *IDF West Bank Commander* 1988 PD 42(2) 4.

[18] See, e.g., HCJ 13/86 *Shahin* v. *IDF Commander in Judea and Samaria* 1987 PD 41(1) 197.

[19] *Afu* (n 17).

conditions in a prison camp operated by the IDF in South Lebanon.[20] Unlike in the West Bank and the Gaza Strip, Israel has never established a military or civil administration apparatus to govern the parts of South Lebanon it controlled between 1982 and 2000. Shamgar rejected the state's arguments that its military operations in South Lebanon, including military detention, were shielded from judicial review by reason of the act-of-state doctrine. Instead, he held that, unlike questions of battlefield conduct, questions relating to the lawfulness and conditions of military detention are justiciable, even if the detention takes place outside Israeli territory.[21] Shamgar also held that the law of belligerent occupation applies in areas of South Lebanon under Israel's effective control[22] – understood as areas in relation to which Israel is in a position to exercise authority *in lieu* of the lawful sovereign – notwithstanding the fact that no Israeli administrative infrastructure was actually established in occupied South Lebanon.[23]

[20] HCJ 102/82 *Tsemel* v. *Minister of Defence* 1983 PD 37(3) 365. Another interesting decision rendered by Shamgar in relation to the situation in South Lebanon is HCJ 574/82 *Al Nawar* v. *Minister of Defence* 1985 PD 39(3) 449. The case dealt with the designation of property seized in South Lebanon as public or private for the purpose of assessing the legality of its confiscation. Shamgar rejected the state's objection to the justiciability of the claim, but went on to apply Article 53 of the Hague Regulations to decide that private property put to use by a terror organisation should be redesignated as public property. He further acknowledged the relevance to the case of the Fourth Geneva Convention and the Hague Convention for the Protection of Cultural Property in the Event of Armed Conflict.

[21] *Tsemel* (n 20) 379.

[22] In fact, Shamgar's position in the *Tsemel* case regarding the applicability of the Fourth Geneva Convention in court proceedings reviewing Israeli activities in South Lebanon is more progressive than the position he himself took with respect to the application of the Convention in court proceedings reviewing Israeli measures in the West Bank and Gaza Strip. See *Afu* (n 17) 47. This perhaps suggests that, for Shamgar, the main difficulty related to the application of the Fourth Geneva Convention in Israeli domestic courts was its sovereignty implications (i.e. that the territory belonged to another High Contracting Party before being occupied by Israel) and not the non-customary status of the provisions of the Convention (which under Israel's dualistic system would prevent direct reliance on its provisions by domestic courts in all geographical contexts). In the South Lebanese context, involving an area with regard to which Israel made no sovereignty claim and had recognised another High Contracting Party (Lebanon) as having sovereign title, Shamgar did not experience any difficulties in relying on the Fourth Geneva Convention. It may be noted, however, in this connection, that the state did not oppose explicitly such application and asserted during the hearings in the *Tsemel* case that it strives to meet the humanitarian standards set out in the GC IV relating to conditions of detention. *Tsemel* (n 20) 368.

[23] ibid 373.

The upshot of the *Tsemel* decision is that the military does not operate in occupied territory in a legal vacuum, and remains subject to the law of belligerent occupation, even when the state refrains from administering the occupied area as such. In fact, one may regard the *Tsemel* decision as offering a more progressive threshold for the applicability of the law of belligerent occupation than what was provided more than twenty years later by the ICJ in *Congo* v. *Uganda*, where the Court leaned towards construing effective control as requiring the *de facto* exercise of governmental authority.[24]

2 Application of the Fourth Geneva Convention in the West Bank and Gaza Strip

As already indicated, Shamgar was the architect of the legal position developed by Israel concerning the *de jure* inapplicability of the Fourth Geneva Convention to the occupation of the West Bank and Gaza Strip. In a speech given in Tel Aviv University in 1971 during his tenure as AG, Shamgar presented the approach taken by the Israeli government, pursuant to his legal advice, in the following terms:

> In my view, *de lege lata*, the automatic applicability of the Fourth Convention to the territories administered by Israel is at least extremely doubtful, to use an understatement, and automatic application would raise complicated juridical and political problems.[25]

In developing this position,[26] Shamgar was clearly influenced by the writings of Prof. Yehuda Blum from the Hebrew University, who developed the

[24] *Armed Activities on the Territory of the Congo (Democratic Republic of Congo* v. *Uganda)*, Judgment [2005] ICJ Rep 168, 230 ('In order to reach a conclusion as to whether a State, the military forces of which are present on the territory of another State as a result of an intervention, is an "occupying Power" in the meaning of the term as understood in the jus in bello, the Court must examine whether there is sufficient evidence to demonstrate that the said authority was in fact established and exercised by the intervening State in the areas in question. In the present case the Court will need to satisfy itself that the Ugandan armed forces in the DRC were not only stationed in particular locations but also that they had substituted their own authority for that of the Congolese Government').

[25] Meir Shamgar, 'The Observance of International Law in the Administered Territories' (1971) 1 Israel Yearbook on Human Rights 262, 263.

[26] It is interesting to note that the initial orders promulgated by the IDF in the West Bank and Gaza Strip in June 1967 did allude to GC IV as a source of law governing the exercise of military authority in the area. However, decrees issued from August 1967 onwards stopped making any allusion to GC IV. This may reflect some internal disagreement in

missing reversioner theory.[27] According to this theory, the serious flaws in Jordan's claim of legal title over the West Bank (which it had conquered in 1948 in an aggressive war), and the absence of any sovereignty claim by Egypt in connection with the Gaza Strip, implied that following the termination of the British Mandate over Palestine in 1948, no state had a valid sovereign title over these areas prior to their occupation by Israel in 1967 (in what Israel considered to be a legitimate war of self-defence). This implied that Israel had a stronger claim of title over these territories than either Jordan and Egypt. The claim about the lack of a valid Jordanian and Egyptian title also implied that Article 2(2) of the Fourth Geneva Convention, which alluded to the occupation by one High Contracting Party of the territory of another High Contracting Party, was inapplicable, resulting allegedly in the inapplicability of all provisions of the Convention relevant to situations of belligerent occupation.[28] This is why Shamgar believed that acceptance of the application of the Fourth Geneva Convention would generate 'legal and political problems', and might undercut Israel's legal claims to title over the West Bank and Gaza Strip, should it decide to annex them at a later point in time (as it did in 1967 with respect to East Jerusalem).

At the same time, Shamgar stated in his 1971 speech that the policy of the government of Israel would be to apply *de facto* the humanitarian provisions of the Fourth Geneva Convention in the West Bank and Gaza Strip:

> The territorial position is thus *sui generis*, and the Israeli Government tried therefore to distinguish between theoretical juridical and political problems on the one hand, and the observance of the humanitarian provisions of the Fourth Geneva Convention on the other hand. Accordingly, the Government of Israel distinguished between the legal problem of the applicability of the Fourth Convention to the territories under consideration which, as stated, does not in my opinion apply to

government circles about the Convention's applicability. For a discussion, see Kretzmer (n 11) 32–3.

27 Yehuda Z. Blum, 'The Missing Reversioner: Reflections on the Status of Judea and Samaria' (1968) 3 Israel Law Review 279. On the possible influence of this piece on Israeli policy, see Eyal Benvenisti, 'An Article that Changed the Course of History?' (2017) 50 Israel Law Review 269. But see Yehuda Z. Blum, 'The Status of Judea and Samaria Revisited: A Response to Eyal Benvenisti' (2018) 51 Israel Law Review 165.

28 For a critique of the legal conclusion relating inapplicability of GC IV, see, e.g., Meron (n 6) 361–4. See also *Legal Consequences of the Construction of a Wall in the Occupied Palestinian Territory*, Advisory Opinion [2004] ICJ Rep 136, [174–7].

> these territories, and decided to act *de facto* in accordance with the humanitarian provisions of the Convention.

In actuality, the approach taken by Shamgar in connection with the *de jure* and *de facto* application of the Fourth Geneva Convention offered more than just a distinction between those aspects of the Convention that affected Israel's potential sovereignty claim and the humanitarian provisions of the Convention. It also hinged the application of the Fourth Geneva Convention not on law, but rather on policy – arguably providing the Israeli government some discretion as to whether or not to legally implement the said provisions. Finally, the qualification of certain provisions of the Fourth Geneva Convention as humanitarian in nature left considerable room for interpretation as to their precise contents.[29]

It has already been observed by some commentators that the position laid down by Shamgar suffered from doctrinal inconsistencies, and that similar legal and political concerns to the ones raised vis-à-vis the Fourth Geneva Convention could also have been raised against the 1907 Hague Regulations, which distinguish between the occupier and the legitimate sovereign (implying that the former cannot be regarded as the latter), but which Israeli courts nonetheless applied regularly.[30] In fact, Benvenisti had noted the oddness of the outcome by which Israel rejected on sovereignty grounds the Fourth Geneva Convention, which is predominantly focused on protecting civilians, but accepted the application of the 1907 Hague Regulations, which include fewer humanitarian protections and more significant protections for the rights and interests of the ousted sovereign.[31] In the same vein, the distinction offered by Shamgar and other judges between the customary law status of the 1907 Hague Regulations and the alleged non-customary status of the Fourth Geneva

[29] For example, it has been maintained by Israeli courts over the years that the humanitarian provisions of the Convention have to be construed in light of the state's security interest in effectively fighting terror. See, e.g., HCJ 8091/15 *The Centre for Protection of the Individual* v. *Minister of Defence* (unpublished, 31 December 2014) para 22 (per Rubinstein).

[30] See, e.g., Roy Ariav, 'The Article by AG Shamgar on the Law Applicable in Judea, Samaria and the Gaza Strip – 1971', in Ministry of Justice, *Legal Roots* (2019) (in Hebrew), www.gov.il/he/Departments/publications/reports/roots_1971. It may be noted that the state decided not to challenge the application of the 1907 Hague Regulations before Israeli courts. See, e.g., HCJ 302/72 *Abu Hilu* v. *Gov't of Israel* 1973 PD 27(2)169. Only in 1988 did the Court confirm the *de jure* applicability of the 1907 Hague Regulations – *Afu* (n 17) 50. Eyal Benvenisti, *The International Law of Occupation* (2nd edn, Oxford University Press 2012) 208.

[31] Benvenisti (n 30) 207.

Convention, which served as another explanation for a court in a dualist country to rely on the former but not on the latter instrument,[32] has also been criticised for its failure to consider post-1949 developments in customary international law.[33] Doubts were also expressed about the suitability of dualism-based distinctions for determining the application of international treaties in occupied territories governed by international law rather than by the domestic law of the occupier.[34]

But it would be wrong, in my view, to evaluate the Shamgar paradigm solely through the prism of the doctrinal validity of each of its elements. The paradigm comprised a body of law which contained the few hard and fast rules found in the 1907 Hague Regulations (such as the prohibition against confiscation of private property),[35] a number of open-ended principles derived from the same Regulations, which left ample room for interpretation (such as the need to respect 'unless absolutely prevented' the laws in force in the occupied territory),[36] principles of Israeli administrative law (which is largely case law-based), and vaguely defined 'humanitarian provisions' of the Fourth Geneva Convention that appeared to apply as a matter of policy.[37] Such a framework contained some important rule-of-law guarantees, designed to prevent serious cases of abuse and arbitrariness, while leaving the government considerable flexibility to advance its military and political goals in the West Bank and the Gaza Strip, as they evolved over time (including, at times, economic integration between Israel and the Occupied Territories, harsh counter-terrorism measures and the construction of Israeli settlements inside these areas).

[32] *Afu* (n 17) 39, 47.

[33] See, e.g., Yutaka Arai-Takahashi, *The Law of Occupation: Continuity and Change of International Humanitarian Law, and Its Interaction with International Human Rights Law* (Martinus Nijhoff 2009) 336–7.

[34] Unlike in ordinary administrative law cases, where government agencies derive their authority from the domestic law, the basis for any exercise of governmental authority in occupied territories is international law. Hence, one could have argued that international law directly delineates the powers and authority of Israeli military officials. See, e.g., Kretzmer (n 11) 32.

[35] Hague Convention (IV) respecting the Laws and Customs of War on Land and its annex: Regulation concerning the Laws and Customs of War on Land, Martens Nouveau Recueil (ser 3) 461 (entered into force 26 January 1910) (Hague Regulations), art 46.

[36] ibid art 43.

[37] Only in 2002 did the Supreme Court hold that it would consider the state bound to apply the humanitarian provisions of GC IV by virtue of the public declaration of AG Shamgar. HCJ 7015/02 *Ajuri* v. *IDF West Bank Commander* 2002 PD 56(6) 352.

The resilience of the paradigm, and perhaps also Shamgar's interest in developing it in the first place, can be explained in that it offered a relatively good fit to a complex situation of belligerent occupation: the area occupied by Israel in 1967 had no clear chain of sovereignty, but emerged from the process of decolonisation (i.e. the end of the British Mandate over Palestine) into occupation; furthermore, Israel, the occupier, had strong historical links to the area, and a plausible legal claim over it. Shamgar's paradigm, which resulted in a 'thin' application of the law of belligerent occupation, bought Israel time – about a quarter of a century, to be more precise – to explore different policy options vis-à-vis the West Bank and Gaza Strip, while ostensibly remaining within the ambit of the law of belligerent occupation, subjecting throughout this time the relevant government activity in the area to judicial review.

It is perhaps ironic that shortly after Shamgar's famous decision in the *Afu* case (1988), which comprehensively and vigorously defended the 'thin' application of the law of belligerent occupation,[38] the Shamgar paradigm started unravelling. Whereas in 1967 – eighteen years after the conclusion of the Fourth Geneva Convention – it was still plausible to maintain that certain of its key provisions were not customary in nature, this was hardly the case in the late 1980s, when the Convention attained near universal ratification.[39] Furthermore, the legal applicability of the Fourth Geneva Convention, including its applicability to the West Bank and Gaza Strip, had been extensively discussed by the early 1990s before international organisations[40] and by international experts,[41] in a manner

[38] *Afu* (n 17). At the heart of the *Afu* case stood the question of the legality of deportations of suspected terrorists from the Occupied Territories, notwithstanding the sweeping prohibition found in art 49(1) of GC IV (n 7). Shamgar took the position that following a literal reading of the provision would lead to absurd results, and that the provision has to be read against the specific historical context of World War Two-era deportations. As a result, he was of the view that deportations of terror suspects, substituting criminal proceedings, were not prohibited. He also reaffirmed the inability of the Court to rely on Article 49 when exercising judicial review by virtue of its alleged non-customary status and Israel's dualist legal system.

[39] All UN members are parties to the Geneva Convention (see International Committee of the Red Cross, 'Treaties, States Parties and Commentaries', https://ihl-databases.icrc.org/applic/ihl/ihl.nsf/States.xsp?xp_treatySelected=380&xp_viewStates=XPages_NORMStatesParties). Almost all states that were members of the UN in 1990 ratified the Convention before that date.

[40] See, e.g., UNSC Res 446(1970), UN Doc S/RES/446 (1979); UNSC Res 681, UN Doc S/RES/681(1990).

[41] See, e.g., ICRC, 'Conference of the High Contracting Parties of the Declaration to the Fourth Geneva Convention', Statement of the ICRC, 5 December 2001, para 2, www.icrc

that demonstrated a broad and consistent rejection of the Israeli position. Furthermore, actual practices in the Occupied Territories, especially the sharp rise in settlement activities after Likud came into power in Israel in 1977 and the harsh security measures adopted in the wake of the First Intifada (1987–91), including an increased resort to punitive house demolitions and deportations, became harder and harder to justify even under a 'thin' reading of the law of belligerent occupation.[42]

A related reason for the decline of the Shamgar paradigm in the 1990s has been changes in the Israeli position with regard to the status of the West Bank and Gaza Strip as occupied territory. The establishment of a Palestinian Authority in the West Bank, pursuant to the Oslo Accords (1993–5), the introduction of the West Bank separation barrier (2002–6) and the Israeli withdrawal from the Gaza Strip in 2005, have been part of a political separation agenda, which gave rise to claims of loss of Israeli effective control over parts of the area.[43] At the same time, political calls for *de jure* annexation of West Bank areas remaining under direct Israeli rule have increased and coincided with a deepening of Israeli control of these parts, resulting in a process of *de facto* annexation.[44] Both developments – partial separation and *de facto* annexation – are, however, incompatible with a belligerent occupation paradigm premised on effective control and respect of the existing status quo. Still, it is important to note that despite its decreasing relevance to realities on the ground, the Shamgar paradigm remains the legal point of departure for analysing the lawfulness of measures taken by Israel in the West Bank, and that Shamgar's legacy of elastic interpretation still has much influence on the approach of the Israeli judiciary to the law of belligerent occupation.[45]

.org/en/doc/resources/documents/article/other/5fldpj.htm#2; Ardi Imseis, 'On the Fourth Geneva Convention and the Occupied Palestinian Territory' (2003) 44 Harvard International Law Journal 65, 95.

42 It is interesting to note that the 1993 Supreme Court judgment on the legality of the deportation to Lebanon of 415 Hamas activists was based almost exclusively on Israeli administrative law, staying away from a discussion of the international lawfulness of this collective deportation measure. HCJ 5973/92 *Association for Civil Rights in Israel* v. *Minister of Defence* 1993 PD 47(1) 267.

43 See, e.g., HCJ 9132/07 *Bassiouni* v. *Prime Minister of Israel*, judgment of 30 January 2008; Eyal Benvenisti, 'Responsibility for the Protection of Human Rights under the Interim Israeli-Palestinian Agreements' (1994) 28 Israel Law Review 297.

44 See *Wall* (n 28) 184.

45 See, e.g., HCJ 2164/09 *Yesh Din* v. *IDF West Bank Commander* (published on Nevo, 26 December 2011) (construing Israel's mineral extraction policies in the West Bank as part of a dynamic obligation to develop the area).

3 Elastic Interpretation of the Law of Belligerent Occupation

Shamgar wrote dozens of legal decisions on the interpretation and application of the 1907 Regulations, many of which refer also to the Fourth Geneva Convention (notwithstanding the doubts about its applicability), and some also refer to international human rights law (whose applicability to occupied territories Shamgar rejected as not supported by contemporary state practice).[46] These decisions provide a valuable perspective into Shamgar's great efforts to reconcile considerations of legality and pragmatism, which often translated themselves into applying international law, but giving it an elastic interpretation which takes account of *de facto* developments on the ground and the unique history of the Occupied Territories. In this regard, Shamgar acquired over the years a vast knowledge about the law of belligerent occupation, and this high level of expertise often served him well in identifying breaking points, beyond which the law could not be bent to accommodate reality.

Several decisions by Shamgar dealt with intricate questions about property rights and zoning and planning in the West Bank, which required a sophisticated analysis of the interplay between the law of belligerent occupation and pre-1967 Jordanian law (which Israel kept in place, as required by Article 43 of the Hague Regulations), and resulted in Israel exercising considerable sovereign powers over property matters. For example, in the *Nazer* case, he established principles for settling disputes over the private or public nature of contested property (in light of Israel's obligations under Article 55 of the Hague Regulations to safeguard public property), and introduced a legal duty to approach an appeals commission established by the Israeli military authorities before bringing conflicts over property rights to the attention of Israeli courts.[47] In the *Dudin* case, he accepted the authority of the IDF to establish planning and zoning committees, as part of the duty of the military under Article 43 of the Hague Regulations to restore and ensure public order and civil life (*l'ordre et la vie publics*).[48] In the *Juha* case, Shamgar developed the distinction between property confiscation and requisition, setting an expectation that any temporary utilisation of private property would be limited in time and properly compensated for in accordance

[46] See, e.g., HCJ 87/85 *Arjub* v. *IDF Judea and Samaria Military Commander* 1988 PD 42(1) 353, 363–4; HCJ 13/86 *Shahin* (n 18) 209–12.

[47] HCJ 285/81 *Nazer* v. *IDF Commander in Judea and Samaria* 1982 PD 37(1) 701.

[48] HCJ 4154/91 *Dudin* v. *IDF West Bank Commander* 1991 PD 46(1) 89.

with Article 52 of the Hague Regulations.[49] In the *Timraz* case, he added the notion that the compensation due should also capture irreparable damage caused to the property seized.[50] Finally, in the *Agrayev* case, Shamgar allowed Israeli authorities to assume power previously held by the Jordanian Custodian for Enemy Property, with a view to requalifying certain private property as public property.[51]

The cumulative effect of these (seemingly technical) decisions has been the development of a sophisticated administrative and legal framework for exercising governmental power in the Occupied Territories in the field of property law in ways that are orderly and predictable. In other words, it established a *de jure* and *de facto* rule of law in this sensitive field of the law of belligerent occupation. At the same time, the framework developed by Shamgar resulted in affording the Israeli authorities considerable discretion in applying their legal powers under the law of belligerent occupation, as it allowed them to replace a host of local institutions and to promote through pre-1967 local law and post-1967 military law the public interest as understood by Israel. While it may be alleged that such normative flexibility is inevitable in situations of long-term occupation,[52] its upshot was that Israeli decision-makers could work around some key limitations of the law of belligerent occupation in ways that might have gone beyond what Shamgar envisioned: for example, the prohibition against confiscation of private property was circumvented through the use of open-ended requisition or seizure orders,[53] and the designation of land as public property allowed establishing Israeli settlements on them, in circumvention of the Supreme Court's prohibition on constructing civilian settlements on private land without a clear security justification.[54]

One key judgment issued by Shamgar which focused on the need to adapt the law of belligerent occupation to the particular challenges of

49 HCJ 290/89 *Juha* v. *IDF Commander in Judea and Samaria* 1989 PD 43(2) 116.

50 HCJ 24/91 *Timraz* v. *IDF Commander in the Gaza Strip* 1991 PD 45(2) 325.

51 HCJ 277/84 *Agrayev* v. *Appels Committee under Governmental Property Order, Judea and Samaria Area* 1986 PD 40(2) 57.

52 For a discussion, see Adam Roberts, 'Prolonged Military Occupation: The Israeli-Occupied Territories since 1967' (1990) 84 American Journal of International Law 44, 96–8.

53 See, e.g., Kretzmer (n 11) 83.

54 In its landmark judgment in *Dawikat* (HCJ 390/79 *Dawikat* v. *Gov't of Israel* 1979 PD 34 (1) 1), the Supreme Court banned the establishment of Israeli settlements on private Palestinian land, since private property could only be infringed for reasons related to Israel's security needs or for the needs and interest of the local population in the territory under belligerent occupation.

long-term occupation was written in the *Abu Itta* case, dealing with plans by the Israeli government to harmonise certain tax arrangements in Israel and the occupied territories.[55] The judgment – spanning over 128 pages – provides a masterly survey of different sources of the law of belligerent occupation dealing with the exercise of taxation power by the occupier. After finding that no specific international law rule prohibited necessary reforms of the local tax code, and after discussing the potential applicability to the situation of the Martens Clause[56] and of the possible treatment of legal *lacunae* as permissions by implication,[57] Shamgar concluded that the planned measure could be justified under Article 43 of the Hague Regulations. Arguably, the long duration of the occupation permits changes in pre-existing legislation designed to benefit the local population. In the circumstances of the case, he accepted the position that tax harmonisation that would allow free movement of people and goods between Israel and the Occupied Territories has benefits for the local economy.[58] Here too, flexibility in deviating from the legal *status quo ex ante* had a plausible pragmatic justification; however, the economic integration policy it facilitated has been harnessed in the service of a long-term policy of 'creeping annexation' of large parts of the West Bank – arguably, an outcome that was hardly beneficial for the local Palestinian population.

One particularly controversial set of decisions issued by Shamgar addressed the possibility of reliance by the Israeli authorities on domestic Jordanian legislation to justify harsh security measures, even when such domestic legislation appeared to stand in tension with the international law

[55] HCJ 69/81 *Abu Itta* v. *IDF Commander in Judea and Samaria* 1983 PD 37(2) 197.

[56] ibid 282–3. See Hague Convention IV (n 35) preamble ('Until a more complete code of the laws of war has been issued, the High Contracting Parties deem it expedient to declare that, in cases not included in the Regulations adopted by them, the inhabitants and the belligerents remain under the protection and the rule of the principles of the law of nations, as they result from the usages established among civilized peoples, from the laws of humanity, and the dictates of the public conscience. They declare that it is in this sense especially that Articles 1 and 2 of the Regulations adopted must be understood').

[57] ibid 240–1. Shamgar cites Kelsen in support for the proposition that in the event of a legal *lacuna* states maintain freedom of action.

[58] ibid 313–14. Shamgar mentions in this regard (but does not fully endorse) the position of Prof. Yoram Dinstein, according to which a useful rule of thumb to be used in order to evaluate the benevolent motives of the occupier in introducing legal reforms in occupied territories is whether the same reform measures were introduced in the occupier's own legal system.

of belligerent occupation. Specifically, Shamgar allowed for the invocation of Regulations 112 and 119 of the 1945 Defence (Emergency Regulations) (enacted by the British Mandate authorities in Palestine and retained in force after 1948 by the Jordanian authorities), authorising deportations and punitive house demolitions, notwithstanding their incompatibility with the Fourth Geneva Convention.[59] This has resulted in further erosion of the protections afforded to Palestinians in the West Bank and Gaza Strip by the laws of belligerent occupation, including the ambiguous 'humanitarian provisions' of the Fourth Geneva Convention. It also resulted in more power granted to Israeli military authorities to apply exceptionally oppressive measures. Note, however, that Shamgar also opposed some excessive features of applicable Jordanian legislation, and that in 1968, during his term as MAG, legislation was passed to remove the death penalty from Jordanian criminal law applicable in civilian courts in the West Bank and Gaza Strip[60] (almost in parallel, in 1967, the Israeli government instructed the military prosecution not to seek the death penalty in criminal cases before military courts).[61] Even such commendable measures of restraint, however, have been introduced through a policy decision, and not due to acceptance of any legal restriction imposed by international law on Israel's ability to rely on the pre-1967 law in the occupied territories.

4 Balancing Security Interests and Individual Rights

A final area briefly surveyed in this chapter is Shamgar's approach to balancing between security interests and individual rights in the course of interpretation and application of the law of belligerent occupation. Here too, one can find in the decisions he issued considerations of legality and pragmatism. Furthermore, although Shamgar was known to be a security-minded judge (an outcome probably explained by his military background),[62] he was also sensitive to the need to treat individuals

[59] See HCJ 51/85 *Nazal* v. *IDF Commander in Judea and Samaria* 1985 PD 39(3) 645; HCJ 897/86 *Jabber* v. *IDF Central Command Chief* 1987 PD 41(2) 522.

[60] Military Order on Local Courts (Death Penalty) No. 268 of 24 July 1968, 14 Proclamations, Orders and Appointments by Judea and Samaria Command 537 (1968).

[61] See Ron Dudai, 'Restraint, Reaction, and Penal Fantasies: Notes on the Death Penalty in Israel, 1967–2016' (2018) 43 Law and Social Inquiry 862, 867.

[62] See, e.g., HCJ 270/88 *LSM – Law in the Service of Men* v. *IDF Commander in the West Bank* 1988 PD 42(3) 260 (security may justify limiting access to telephone communication to permit holders).

fairly, especially individuals deprived of their liberty (a tendency perhaps explained by his personal experience of imprisonment before 1948).

One set of cases decided by Shamgar that involve harsh security measures are cases of deportation from the West Bank and Gaza Strip of individuals posing a security risk. The *Afu* case and the controversy surrounding the decision to deport the petitioners, notwithstanding the specific language of Article 49 of the Fourth Geneva Convention, has already been mentioned above. Other deportation decisions Shamgar issued in cases involving suspected terrorists who infiltrated the West Bank after 1967 appear to be less problematic from a law of belligerent occupation perspective,[63] yet also reveal an approach placing limited premium on the legal right of individuals to remain in the Occupied Territories. Ultimately, it appears that for Shamgar, the decision to deport an individual posing a security risk, as an alternative to a criminal prosecution that could have resulted in a harsh sentence, did not constitute a disproportionate measure.[64] He thus opposed reading Article 49 as containing an absolute ban on deportation that would prevent the Court from engaging in a balancing of interests even in cases involving individuals heavily involved in hostile militant activity.

Another set of cases reflective of a narrow approach towards a right of presence in the Occupied Territories dealt with the question of family reunifications. In the leading case on the matter, the *Shahin* case, the petitioners invoked the right to family reunification under international human rights law in order to support applications by non-residents of the West Bank and the Gaza Strip to enter the area to reunite with their spouses – a claim which Shamgar rejected as a matter of international law applicable to occupied territories.[65] Furthermore, he sided with the state in upholding the policy of refusal of all requests that do not raise exceptional humanitarian considerations.[66] Shamgar also upheld in

63 HCJ 159/84 *Shahin* v. *IDF Commander in the Gaza Strip* 1985 PD 39(1) 309; HCJ 454/85 *Qasrawi* v. *Minister of Defence* 1985 PD 39(3) 401.

64 Shamgar comments wryly in *Afu* that according to the petitioners even a decision to deport spies or saboteurs who are present in occupied territories, instead of trying and sentencing them to death, would have been a grave breach of GC IV. *Afu* (n 17) 30.

65 *Shahin* (n 18) 215. Shamgar was of the view that human rights treaties, such as the International Covenant on Civil and Political Rights, did not apply to the situation at hand since Israel had not ratified it at the time, because they were not meant to apply in conflict situations as illustrated by the respective derogation clause. See also HCJ 263/85 *Awad* v. *Civil Administration Commander – Ramallah Region* 1985 PD 40(2) 281 (family reunification is an act of charity not a matter of right).

66 *Shahin* (n 18) 215.

another case the policy of refusing family visits by individuals whose family reunification applications were pending, in order not to facilitate personal developments (such as family expansion) that could prejudge the application.[67] The rigidity of the approach followed in these family reunification cases appears to derive, inter alia, from a sense that the protections afforded by the law of belligerent occupation to residents of the occupied area did not include a right to facilitate the migration into the area of foreign spouses. These decisions anticipate litigation in Israel in the early twenty-first century concerning the security implications of family reunification, which also adopted a restrictive approach to immigration to Israel proper in connection with the realisation of family rights.[68]

By contrast, in cases involving the rights of security detainees and criminal defendants, Shamgar demonstrated considerable sensitivity to the procedural rights of individuals affected by liberty-restricting legal measures. For example, in the *Abu Bakker* case, he insisted that military authorities must not merely carry the burden of justifying the initial exercise of administrative detention powers, but that they must also establish the need for extending the initial detention period.[69] In the *Arjub* case, he held that international law does not require military courts to offer an appeal in criminal cases, but opined that in the context of a long-term occupation, the military should nonetheless proceed to establish such a procedure.[70] Shamgar also opined that there is no contradiction between proper legal proceedings and the need to effectively fight terrorism.[71] In another humanitarian context, relating to the right of access of Palestinian residents to medical services, Shamgar urged for the specification of clear procedures for the movement of physicians and patients in times of curfews.[72] Such cases clearly stand for the proposition that security needs can be effectively realised within a legal framework that ensures procedural fairness and decent treatment.

[67] HCJ 683/85 *Mashta'a* v. *IDF Commander in the Gaza Strip – Civil Administration* 1986 PD 40(1) 309.

[68] See HCJ 7052/03 *Adalah* v. *Minister of the Interior* 2006 PD 61(2) 202; HCJ 466/07 *Galon* v. *AG* 2012 PD 65(2) 44.

[69] HCJ 466/86 *Abu Bakker* v. *Military Court Judge in Nablus* 1986 PD 40(3) 649.

[70] *Arjub* (n 46).

[71] ibid 378.

[72] HCJ 477/91 *Association of Israeli-Palestinian Physicians for Human Rights* v. *Minister of Defence* 1991 PD 45(2) 832.

5 Conclusion

Meir Shamgar was the architect of the international law of belligerent occupation, as interpreted and applied in Israel. The paradigm he developed offered *de jure* application of only some of the relevant international norms (subject to elastic interpretation), and provided important guarantees for procedural fairness, *de facto* protection of certain needs and interests and broad access by Palestinians to judicial review. It dramatically shaped the manner in which Israel administered the West Bank and Gaza Strip between 1967 and 1993, and retains some influence even today – despite the significant changes on the ground and in the attitude of recent Israeli governments towards the status of the Occupied Territories, including movements in the direction of political separation and *de jure* and *de facto* annexation.

At an abstract level, Shamgar was, and still is, the Israeli judge most identified with the notion that the rule of law serves as the basis for legitimate governmental power – a notion which included, according to Shamgar, adherence to rules of international law when exercising military government power. Although Shamgar was not reticent about attempting to shape and influence the contents of international law and to adjust it to the particular conditions existing in the Occupied Territories, he never considered ignoring it altogether, or allowing the violation of what he considered to be binding and *de jure* applicable rules of law. Whereas the contours of the legal framework were somewhat elastic, not remaining inside it was never an option.

9

Political Liberalism in a Jewish and Democratic State

GILA STOPLER

The chapter claims that Political Liberalism (PL) is unsuitable to the Israeli situation. PL envisions a liberal constitutional structure that protects the rights of free and equal citizens and serves as an ideational basis for a reasonable overlapping consensus. My internal critique of PL is that its loose definition of reasonable comprehensive doctrines, together with the ideas of overlapping consensus, impartiality and public reason, curtail PL's ability to maintain a liberal constitutional structure that adequately protects rights. Essentially, PL's reliance on the willingness of illiberal groups to embrace it renders it ineffective where such groups wield a more than negligible political power. Israel is such a setting. A second reason for PL's unsuitability for Israel is that Israel's constitutional structure includes fundamental deviations from liberal constitutional principles, both in the area of religion–state relations and in the area of ethnic (Jewish–Arab) relations. Consequently, application of PL in Israel must be preceded by a fundamental change in Israel's constitutional structure. Otherwise the application of a form of PL adjusted to its current constitutional structure would result in the continued violation of the rights of ethnic and religious minorities and of women, and lead to the instability of Israeli democracy.

Political Liberalism, reasonable comprehensive doctrines, public reason, Jewish and democratic, semi-liberal, religion, traditionalists, human rights, women's rights, ethnic minority

1 Introduction

In his 1993 book *Political Liberalism*, John Rawls introduced a new variant of liberalism – Political Liberalism – suggesting that it, rather than comprehensive liberalism, was the appropriate political theory for modern heterogeneous democratic societies in which a pluralism of incompatible yet reasonable comprehensive religious, philosophical and moral doctrines exists.[1] The purpose of Political Liberalism was to lay out the framework for a constitutional democratic regime that enabled citizens to embrace these reasonable and incompatible comprehensive doctrines while living together and maintaining over time a stable and just society of free and equal citizens.[2] Accordingly, Rawls sought to introduce a political structure within which 'deeply opposed though reasonable comprehensive doctrines may live together and all affirm the political conception of a constitutional regime'.[3] Embracing Rawls's influential theory, Israeli writers such as Mautner have suggested that Political Liberalism is an appropriate political scheme for Israel's deeply divided society. According to Mautner, the application of Political Liberalism to Israel would allow secular Jews and religious Jews as well as Jews and Arabs to live together in Israel despite their vastly different comprehensive doctrines and maintain a stable Israeli society that properly protects the rights of all its citizens.[4] In this chapter I want to question this assumption.

My critique of the possible application of Political Liberalism to the Israeli situation will be twofold. My first critique will be internal to the theory of Political Liberalism and will claim that through the use of concepts such as reasonable comprehensive doctrines, reasonable overlapping consensus, impartiality and the idea of public reason, Political Liberalism enables and countenances restrictions on individual rights which should not be tolerated. Thus, in Section 2 I will briefly introduce the basic principles of Rawls's Political Liberalism, focusing on the concepts mentioned above, and critique the way in which Political Liberalism finds comprehensive doctrines that violate rights to be reasonable and shields illiberal doctrines, especially religious ones, from criticism, thereby providing insufficient protection for the rights of citizens as free and equal. Essentially, I will claim that Political Liberalism's reliance on the willingness of illiberal groups to embrace it renders it ineffective in settings

1 John Rawls, *Political Liberalism* (Columbia University Press 1993) xviii. According to Rawls, comprehensive doctrines apply not only to the political organisation of society but also include conceptions as to what is of value in human life, ideals of personal character, friendship, familial and associational relationships and other aspects that inform our conduct, and even our life as a whole (13).

2 ibid xviii, xx.

3 ibid xx.

4 Menachem Mautner, *Law and the Culture of Israel* (Oxford University Press 2011) 201–4.

in which such illiberal groups wield anything more than negligible political power. Israel is such a setting.

My second critique will be external to the theory and directed at its application to the Israeli context. Political Liberalism is premised on the existence of a liberal constitutional structure that serves both as a basis for the constitutional protection of the rights of citizens as free and equal and as an ideational basis from which the reasonableness of comprehensive doctrines and the overlapping consensus, as well as public reason, are derived. I will claim that contrary to common perceptions Israel's constitutional structure cannot be considered liberal and should be understood as semi-liberal, as it includes fundamental deviations from liberal constitutional principles, both in the area of religion–state relations and in the area of ethnic (Jewish–Arab) relations. Consequently, an application of Political Liberalism in Israel must be preceded by a fundamental change in Israel's constitutional structure and principles. In Section 3 I will explain why I regard Israeli constitutionalism as semi-liberal and claim that the application of a form of Political Liberalism to Israeli constitutionalism would result in the continued violation of the rights of ethnic and religious minorities and of women and to its legitimation, and further jeopardise Israeli democracy. I will show that when applied in the Israeli semi-liberal context the internal defects of Political Liberalism and its inability to maintain a just society that protects the rights of all its citizens are intensified. Moreover, the constitutional understanding of reasonableness expands to include clear violations of rights that become part of the accepted political conception of justice.

2 Political Liberalism and the Protection of Rights of Free and Equal Citizens

2.1 An Overview of the Relevant Concepts of Political Liberalism

The point of departure of Rawls's Political Liberalism is that modern democratic societies are characterised by a pluralism of incompatible yet reasonable comprehensive religious, philosophical and moral doctrines, each of which is affirmed by some, but not all, citizens. The purpose of Political Liberalism is to lay out the framework for a constitutional democratic regime that will enable citizens to embrace these reasonable and incompatible comprehensive doctrines while living together and maintaining over time a stable and just society of free and equal citizens.[5] Rawls emphasises that Political Liberalism should not be regarded as part of an Enlightenment project since Political Liberalism takes as a given the existence of an array of different reasonable comprehensive doctrines, religious and non-religious, liberal and illiberal, and is not meant to replace or challenge them.[6] Rather, the idea is to formulate a liberal political conception that religious and illiberal doctrines might be able to endorse.[7]

In a constitutional democratic regime guided by Political Liberalism citizens are expected to simultaneously affirm both their personal comprehensive doctrine, which is only shared by some, and a general political conception that is shared by everyone. This duality in turn results in the distinction between a public basis of justification (public reason) that should be generally acceptable to citizens and that applies to fundamental political questions, and the non-public bases of justification that are grounded in the various existing reasonable comprehensive doctrines and are likely acceptable only to those who affirm them.[8] The idea of public reason entails that decisions regarding constitutional essentials and questions of basic justice need to be justified in ways that all citizens as free and equal are able to endorse in light of their own reason. Reasons for such decisions must fall under the political values expressed by a political liberal conception of justice, and cannot be derived solely from comprehensive religious and philosophical doctrines.[9] While in the past Rawls has expressed the view that non-public reasons could not be brought into public debate at all, he later relaxed this restriction to allow non-public reasons to be brought into the debate as long as in due course public reasons are offered in support of the same views.[10] Jürgen Habermas has further relaxed this requirement which he termed the 'institutional translation proviso' and has charged secular citizens with the duty to open their minds to the religious reasons offered and 'enter into dialogues from which religious reasons then might well emerge in the transformed guise of generally accessible arguments'.[11]

[5] Rawls (n 1) xviii, xx.
[6] ibid xviii, xx, xl.
[7] ibid xlvii.
[8] ibid xxi.
[9] John Rawls, *Justice as Fairness: A Restatement* (Universal 2004) 90–1.
[10] ibid.
[11] Jürgen Habermas, 'Religion in the Public Sphere' (2006) 14 European Journal of Philosophy 1, 10–11.

An important feature of Political Liberalism that follows from the distinction between a pluralism of reasonable comprehensive doctrines and a general liberal political conception, as well as from the idea of public reason, is Political Liberalism's impartiality towards reasonable comprehensive doctrines. The essence of such impartiality is that Political Liberalism does not attack, criticise or reject any reasonable comprehensive doctrine or the views expressed in it.[12] This is because the judgments rendered by these doctrines are not and need not be based on public reason and can therefore only be evaluated from within the doctrines themselves and not from within the liberal political conception of justice.[13]

Rawls' definition of reasonable comprehensive doctrines is deliberately wide and loose. Thus, in order to count as reasonable a doctrine needs to be a more or less coherent and consistent exercise of theoretical as well as practical reason and it needs to draw on a tradition of thought and be stable over time, but still open to change for reasons that it views as good and sufficient.[14] In addition, a reasonable comprehensive doctrine must endorse some form of liberty of conscience and freedom of thought.[15] Accordingly, religious doctrines with an account of free faith are understood, in principle, to be reasonable comprehensive doctrines. Rawls assumes that 'except for certain kinds of fundamentalism, all the main historical religions admit of such an account and thus may be seen as reasonable comprehensive doctrines'.[16]

Rawls believes that although in a democratic society citizens always have conflicting comprehensive views, they are able to achieve a reasonable overlapping consensus over a shared liberal political conception of justice, even if they affirm this conception, at least in part, for different reasons. A reasonable overlapping consensus means that 'the political conception is supported by the reasonable though opposing religious, philosophical, and moral doctrines that gain a significant body of adherents and endure over time from one generation to the next'.[17]

To conclude and summarise this short overview, Political Liberalism's main goal is to allow a variety of deeply opposed comprehensive doctrines

[12] Rawls (n 1) xxi–xxii.
[13] ibid.
[14] ibid 59.
[15] ibid 60–1.
[16] ibid 170.
[17] Rawls (n 9) 32.

to co-exist side by side within a stable and enduring liberal political framework. In order to achieve this goal, Political Liberalism relies on the idea of public reason, which supposedly shields society from the adverse effects of illiberal comprehensive doctrines privately shared by many citizens; it employs a loose understanding of what makes comprehensive doctrines reasonable and refuses to judge or criticise the contents of such doctrines; and it assumes that a democratic society that has worked reasonably well over time achieves a reasonable overlapping consensus over a liberal political conception of justice suitable for a constitutional regime. In the next subsection I will argue that it is questionable whether the structure of Political Liberalism which is so accommodating of illiberal comprehensive doctrines can actually guarantee a liberal constitutional democratic regime that can maintain over time a stable and just society of free and equal citizens.

2.2 Political Liberalism and the Protection of the Rights of Free and Equal Citizens

Rawls assumes that within modern democratic societies that are characterised by a pluralism of incompatible yet reasonable comprehensive religious, philosophical and moral doctrines, it is possible to maintain a constitutional democratic regime that enables citizens to embrace these reasonable and incompatible doctrines while living together and maintaining over time a stable and just society of free and equal citizens. This, he explains, can be done by reaching a reasonable overlapping consensus around a reasonable political conception of justice.[18] However, Rawls concedes that his theory of Political Liberalism cannot prove, and does not even attempt to prove, that the reasonable overlapping consensus on which the successful realisation of the theory is predicated will indeed form around a reasonable liberal political conception of justice. Thus, he explains, the most Political Liberalism does 'is to present a freestanding liberal political conception that does not oppose comprehensive doctrines on their own ground and does not preclude the possibility of an overlapping consensus for the right reasons'.[19]

It may be that Political Liberalism does not preclude the possibility for an overlapping consensus to form around a reasonable liberal political conception of the good and to maintain over time a stable and just

[18] Rawls (n 1) xlviii.
[19] ibid.

society of free and equal citizens. However, it also does not preclude the reverse. As Rawls concedes: 'an overlapping consensus of reasonable doctrines may not be possible under many historical conditions, as the efforts to achieve it may be overwhelmed by unreasonable and even irrational (and sometimes mad) comprehensive doctrines'.[20] I would argue that the way Political Liberalism conceptualises its core ideas of reasonable comprehensive doctrines, reasonable overlapping consensus and public reason, makes it likely that not only in historical but also in many contemporary settings the application of principles of Political Liberalism will not realise the ambition of achieving an overlapping consensus that maintains a just society of free and equal citizens. One reason for this is Rawls' expansive definition of reasonable comprehensive doctrines, which includes even comprehensive doctrines that advocate extensive violations of rights. The only comprehensive doctrines that Rawls finds unreasonable are doctrines that do not endorse some form of liberty of conscience and freedom of thought; doctrines that support egregious violations of rights such as slavery in ancient Athens or in the antebellum South; and doctrines that espouse certain kinds of religious fundamentalism.[21] All other comprehensive doctrines, including illiberal doctrines, both religious and non-religious, that advocate gender, sexual orientation, racial and religious discrimination, would still count as reasonable as long as they are willing to accept the political conception of citizens as free and equal.[22] This legitimates the continued violation of rights within groups espousing such doctrines and endangers the state's ability to maintain over time a just society of free and equal citizens.[23]

I would further argue that Rawls's expectation that illiberal comprehensive doctrines which are based on deeply held illiberal ideologies would be willing to accept, not merely as a modus vivendi but as an affirmative commitment, a liberal political conception of justice committed to citizens as free and equal is unfounded. Rawls himself is at least

[20] ibid 126.

[21] ibid 60–6, 170, 196.

[22] According to Rawls the political conception of justice views society as a fair system of cooperation over time between free and equal citizens. The political conception of justice is a freestanding view, or a module, that can and should be endorsed by all reasonable comprehensive doctrines. ibid 12–15.

[23] For a critique of Rawls's assessment of religious comprehensive doctrines that discriminate against women as reasonable comprehensive doctrines, see Susan Moller Okin, 'Justice and Gender: An Unfinished Debate' (2004) 72 Fordham Law Review 1537, 1555–8.

partly aware of this. He acknowledges that if the initial acquiescence to a liberal political conception as a modus vivendi is to turn, over generations, into a stable and enduring overlapping consensus, 'a certain looseness in our comprehensive views, as well as their being not fully, but only partially comprehensive, may be particularly significant'.[24] Such looseness would allow many citizens to first affirm the liberal political conception and later if an incompatibility is recognised 'between the political conception and their comprehensive doctrines, then they might very well adjust or revise the latter rather than reject the political conception'.[25] Rawls' expectation that illiberal doctrines would liberalise over time upon realising the advantages of liberalism over illiberalism – also known as liberal expectancy – is shared by other liberal theorists such as Kymlicka and Nancy Rosenblum and serves as a basis for their theories on the appropriate relations between the state and religious, national and cultural communities and associations.[26] Unfortunately, liberal expectancy seems overly optimistic, and there is no empirical evidence to back it.[27]

Furthermore, Rawls' reliance on the looseness and incompleteness of comprehensive doctrines ignores the fact that in many liberal democracies significant parts of the population adhere to fully comprehensive illiberal doctrines (mostly but not only religious) which are neither loose nor incomplete, and which resist any internal liberalisation and even work diligently and successfully to resist and reverse liberalisation of state laws in areas such as LGBTQ rights or women's reproductive rights.[28] Another way of phrasing this problem was suggested by Stoeckl, who argues that Rawls implicitly assumes that there are only two kinds of religious doctrines – fundamentalist doctrines, which are the minority and are unreasonable and therefore shunned, and all remaining religious doctrines, which he designates as reasonable and implicitly assumes that they are all liberal doctrines (at least in the sense that they willingly adopt

[24] Rawls (n 9) 193.

[25] ibid.

[26] Will Kymlicka, *Multicultural Odysseys: Navigating The New International Politics of Diversity* (Oxford University Press 2007) 94; Nancy L. Rosenblum, *Membership and Morals: The Personal Uses of Pluralism in America* (Princeton University Press 1998) 55–8.

[27] See Rosenblum (n 26) 57.

[28] On attempts by traditional religions to prevent liberalisation of state laws in areas such as gay rights and women's reproductive rights, see Kristina Stoeckl, 'Political Liberalism and Religious Claims: Four Blind Spots' (2017) 43(1) Philosophy and Social Criticism 34, 37.

a liberal political conception of justice which treats all citizens as free and equal).[29] Stoeckl argues that the empirical study of religious actors reveals that there is a third group of religious actors which she calls 'traditionalists'.[30] Traditionalists are not fundamentalists, and therefore they are not shunned either by Political Liberalism or by society.[31] However, at the same time traditionalists are unwilling to adopt a liberal political conception of justice which treats all citizens as free and equal, and they use their extensive political power, both internally within states and internationally, in order to change the consensus over the appropriate conception of justice in society.[32] Importantly, the religious resurgence across the world in recent decades has been characterised by increased support for such traditionalist religious groups with a parallel decline in the more moderate religious groups.[33] I would argue that Political Liberalism's designation of almost all comprehensive doctrines as reasonable and its failure to take into account the many religious traditionalist groups, as well as many non-religious illiberal groups, that are all committed to shifting the overlapping consensus towards non-liberal conceptions of justice, make it far too optimistic with regard to the ability to maintain over time a stable and just society of free and equal citizens. As Yael Tamir has rightly argued in the context of debates around multiculturalism, the most that can be expected from illiberal communities is to agree strategically to maintain a modus vivendi within a liberal political structure in order to protect their own status and rights.[34] However, once illiberal communities obtain enough power to challenge and change the liberal political structure to their own advantage they will

[29] ibid 34–5.

[30] Her own empirical work revealed such a group within Russian Orthodox Christianity, but other works have revealed similar traditionalists in other religions. ibid 35.

[31] Stoeckl defines traditionalists as being neither religious liberals nor religious fundamentalists. They share with religious fundamentalists their rejection of egalitarian individualism and universalism. However, unlike fundamentalists they do not retreat from society and they reject violent means of reversal. Instead, they use their significant political power and the conservative political and religious establishment strategically in order to implement their illiberal ideology. ibid 35–8.

[32] ibid 37.

[33] Peter L. Berger, 'The Desecularization of the World: A Global Overview' in Peter L. Berger (ed), *The Desecularization of the World: Resurgent Religion and World Politics* (1999) 6; John L. Esposito, 'Religious Fundamentalisms and the Global Resurgence' in Marci A. Hamilton and Mark J. Rozell (eds), *Fundamentalism, Politics, and the Law* (Palgrave Macmillamn 2011) vii–viii.

[34] Yael Tamir, 'Two Concepts of Multiculturalism' (1995) 29 Journal of Philosophy of Education 161, 170–1.

do so, since '[t]he compromise from the point of view of the illiberal community is not even a principled *modus vivendi*, based on a "live and let live", but a conditional one which is based on fear rather than respect.'[35] This important insight is all the more true for traditionalists from mainstream religions and members of other powerful illiberal groups who have no incentive to accept a liberal modus vivendi to begin with, since their own rights are never in any serious danger, and by strategically using their aggregate political power they have the ability to restrict the rights of others.

An additional reason why Political Liberalism cannot adequately protect individual rights against the influence of illiberal and especially religious illiberal groups is the idea of public reason and its corollary idea of impartiality. Rawls explains that the idea of public reason is required because where the state, through its political system, coerces citizens it must justify this coercion by using reasons that these citizens, as free and equal persons, can reasonably accept. Consequently, decisions regarding constitutional essentials and questions of basic justice need to be justified through the use of political values expressed by a political conception of justice, and cannot be derived solely from comprehensive religious and philosophical doctrines.[36] At first glance this idea seems to advance the protection of the rights of free and equal citizens. For example, it can justify the exclusion of a whole host of patriarchal religious arguments from the public debate over constitutional essentials, thereby allegedly making the task of opposing state action that discriminates against vulnerable groups such as women easier. However, a more careful analysis of the operation of the idea of public reason will show that there are two reasons why it does not serve to protect rights and can even harm them. The first reason is that the rejection of religious ideas as a basis of justification for restrictions on rights is exceedingly easy to sidestep. Any religious reason can be couched in terms that disguise its religious origins and presented in terms compatible with public reason. A classic example is the American Supreme Court case of *Harris* v. *McRae* in which the Court affirmed the Hyde Amendment, which prevented federal funding for abortions. Appellants argued that the amendment was motivated by the Roman Catholic religious objection to abortion and was therefore contrary to the American constitution's Establishment Clause, which prohibits the use of religious reasons to

35 ibid 170.
36 Rawls (n 9) 90–1.

justify state action. The Court, in a move reminiscent of Habermas's institutional translation proviso, rejected that argument, holding that: 'The Hyde Amendment, as the District Court noted, is as much a reflection of "traditionalist" values towards abortion as it is an embodiment of the views of any particular religion.'[37] The Court's reasoning is a good example for the way in which the idea of public reason can be used to whitewash religious arguments, translating them into innocuous public reasons without truly changing their religious and particularistic nature.

Furthermore, this leads to the second reason why the idea of public reason may harm rights rather than protect them. This reason is connected to the idea of impartiality, which is the corollary to the idea of public reason. The impartiality of political liberalism and its refusal to confront illiberal comprehensive doctrines (especially religious ones) on their merits and to challenge their rights-infringing aspects result in their uncritical adoption as non-public justifications for the infringement of rights. Thus, the absolute Catholic ban on abortion is not questioned or measured against the harm that it causes to the rights of women since, according to Rawls, it originates in a reasonable religious comprehensive doctrine that can only be evaluated from within its own conception of justice and not from within the public liberal political conception of justice. Hence, after eluding criticism on the grounds of impartiality, the Catholic religious ban is then whitewashed and translated into publicly acceptable 'traditionalist values' that are used to validate the denial of abortion funding for women and to justify the treatment of women by the state as less than free and equal citizens.

Moreover, a third motivation behind the proviso allowing only public reasons to participate in the decision-making process is to enable all participants in the process to understand the different and opposing views, and be open to persuasion and to changing their mind in the course of the debate. Such willingness is a precondition for reaching a reasonable overlapping consensus over a liberal political conception of the good. Accordingly, Habermas argues that the discursive and deliberative character of the public discussion is essential to its success, and that 'fair arrangements can only be found if the parties involved learn to take the perspectives of the others'.[38] However, scholars researching traditionalists/conservative religious actors, such as the Catholic Church and traditionalists within Russian Orthodox Christianity, have argued

[37] *Harris v McRae* 448 US 297, 319 (1980).
[38] Habermans (n 11) 4, 9, 12.

that while these religious actors translate religious arguments into secular arguments, they do so only strategically in order to influence the public debate and push forward a thoroughly anti-liberal agenda, while at the same time remaining closed to any possibility of change in their own positions.[39] For example, in order to advance laws that prohibit blasphemy, these traditionalists will refrain from invoking the Fourth Commandment that prohibits taking the name of the lord in vain. Instead, they will offer the harm to the integrity of individual religious believers as a secular justification that may restrict blasphemous speech within a liberal political conception.[40] However, their use of this argument will be purely strategic and will not indicate any genuine willingness to be open to other perspectives on the matter.

To conclude, Political Liberalism envisions and defends a political framework that does not offer enough protection to citizens' rights and cannot promise to maintain over time a just society of free and equal citizens. The designation of a wide range of deeply illiberal comprehensive doctrines as reasonable legitimates their internal violations of individual rights. The expectation that these doctrines would liberalise over time upon realising the advantages of liberalism over illiberalism is overly optimistic, as is the expectation that a reasonable overlapping consensus will form around a liberal political conception of justice. Further, the idea of public reason does not prevent the penetration of discriminatory religious or otherwise dogmatic ideas into public decision-making, while the idea of impartiality shields the doctrines that generate these ideas from public criticism and thereby strengthens their hold over society. It seems plausible that as long as groups supporting illiberal reasonable comprehensive doctrines in a given state are neither powerful nor determined to change the liberal political conception of justice guiding the state, Political Liberalism may offer an appropriate framework for maintaining in that state a constitutional democratic regime that enables citizens to live together and maintain over time a stable and just society of free and equal citizens. However, once such illiberal groups, whether religious or not, have more than negligible power and are determined to use it to challenge the liberal nature of the state, Political Liberalism offers no protection against such attempts and to some extent even

[39] Stoeckl (n 28) 39–40; Anja Hennig, 'Habermas's Translation Proviso and Conservative Religious Actors in the Public Sphere' in Aurelia Bardon et al. (eds), *Religious Pluralism: A Resource Book* (European University Institute 2015) 99–100.

[40] Stoeckl (n 28) 39.

facilitates them. The democratic backsliding that liberal democracies such as Poland and Hungary are experiencing may support this conclusion and indicates that a constitutional regime based on principles drawn from Political Liberalism cannot ensure maintaining over time a just society of free and equal citizens when it is faced with considerable illiberal groups determined to change its liberal character.[41] I will now turn to discuss the incompatibility of Political Liberalism in the context of Israel where such powerful illiberal groups indeed exist, and where the state from its inception has not been fully liberal.

3 Is Political Liberalism Suitable for Israel?

In this section I will claim that contrary to Mautner's suggestion, Political Liberalism is not a suitable political conception of justice for Israel because applying it in the Israeli context is impracticable, unless it is applied in a distorted manner that cannot ensure that Israel's constitutional regime will maintain over time a stable and just society of free and equal citizens. This is so for two reasons. First, because within Israeli society there are significant illiberal groups with extensive political power that are determined to undermine the liberal elements of the Israeli constitutional regime.[42] Their political power puts into question Israel's

[41] See, e.g., David Ost, 'Grappling with the Hungarian and Polish New Right in Power' NewsNet: News of the Association for Slavic, East European, and Eurasian Studies, August 2016, 1–4, www.aseees.org/sites/default/files/downloads/august%202016_2.pdf; James Dawson and Seán Hanley, 'The Fading Mirage of the "Liberal Consensus"' (2016) 27 Journal of Democracy 20–34; Ivan Krastev, 'Liberalism's Failure to Deliver' (2016) 27 Journal of Democracy 35–8. As Ost summarises: 'Eviscerating the Constitutional Court and purging the judiciary, complete politicization of the civil service, turning public media into a government mouthpiece, restricting opposition prerogatives in parliament, unilateral wholesale change of the Constitution or plain violation of it, official tolerance and even promotion of racism and bigotry, administrative assertion of old gender norms, cultural resurrection of authoritarian traditions, placing loyalty over competence in awarding state posts, surveillance without check – right-wing governments in Hungary and Poland have been directly attacking the institutions protecting the pluralism of democracy. The ruling parties, Fidesz and Law and Justice (PiS) respectively, do not even claim to adhere to "liberal" democracy anymore. Are they committed to democracy at all? Both accept it now that it has brought one-party rule by the party representing "the nation." Otherwise, "democracy" appears to be a curtsy to the political correctness they otherwise abhor' (1).

[42] The two most significant and organised groups are those of the Ultra-Orthodox Jews (OU) and the more conservative segments of the Religious Zionist Jews (RZ). For a more detailed description of these groups and their impact in Israeli politics, see below (nn 55–6) and accompanying text.

ability to maintain over time a just society of free and equal citizens. Rawls is not entirely clear on the extent of the compatibility of his theory to societies that are only partly liberal. On the one hand the purpose of Political Liberalism seems to be to offer a political framework for the consensual liberalisation of societies. As Müller explains, the question for Political Liberalism is: 'How can societies move from various forms of illiberalism to a more or less liberal, stable and self-sustaining form of political life?'[43] However, on the other hand, Rawls acknowledges and even insists that Political Liberalism cannot guarantee a successful transition from illiberalism to liberalism. Thus he explains, 'given the actual comprehensive views existing in society, no matter what their content, there is plainly no guarantee that justice as fairness, or any reasonable conception for a democratic regime, can gain the support of an overlapping consensus and in that way underwrite the stability of its political institutions'.[44] Thus, liberals who advocate the adoption of Political Liberalism in a society that is only partly liberal do so at their own risk and Rawls offers no guidance as to how to evaluate such a risk. Political Liberalism as a political conception of justice may or may not lead to the creation of a constitutional regime that will maintain over time a stable and just society of free and equal citizens, and it may even be that the application of Political Liberalism would end up undermining the cause of achieving a stable and just society of free and equal citizens, by facilitating a process in which a society that was partly liberal becomes less liberal over time. I would argue that due to the problems identified in the previous section with the concepts of reasonable comprehensive doctrines, reasonable overlapping consensus, public reason and impartiality, there is substantial danger of this happening in many societies and especially where illiberal groups have more than negligible power. As I will discuss in more detail below, this is the case in Israel.

The second reason Political Liberalism is unsuitable for Israel is that from its inception the Israeli constitutional regime has not been a liberal constitutional regime but rather a semi-liberal constitutional regime that incorporates both liberal and illiberal aspects. The application of Political

43 Jan-Werner Müller, 'Rawls, Historian: Remarks on Political Liberalism's "Historicism"' (2006) 237 Revue internationale de philosophie, 327, 329.

44 Rawls (n 9) 37; similarly: 'Views that would suppress altogether the basic rights and liberties affirmed in the political conception, or suppress them in part, say its liberty of conscience, may indeed exist, as there will always be such views. But they may not be strong enough to undermine the substantive justice of the regime. That is the hope; there can be no guarantee.' Rawls (n 1) 65.

Liberalism to a state in which the political framework includes illiberal elements embedded in its constitutional regime seems to be a case that Rawls does not discuss in his theory. While he envisions the liberalisation of societies that include illiberal groups, his scheme of Political Liberalism entails applying to the political framework in such societies a liberal political conception of justice that is expressed through a liberal constitutional regime. The hope is that applying a liberal political conception of justice as the political framework of the state will in time facilitate an overlapping consensus on this liberal constitutional regime. However, in the context of states such as Israel in which the constitutional regime is not fully liberal to begin with, an unresolved hurdle would be the need to achieve a democratic agreement over the application of such a liberal political framework even as a modus vivendi. Why would illiberal groups give up on the considerable benefits accruing to them from the illiberal aspects of semi-liberal constitutionalism?

In order to clarify the difficulty I will explain my claim that Israel's constitutionalism is semi-liberal and describe how it differs from liberal constitutionalism. Under my definition a semi-liberal constitutional system is a system that meets two conditions: first, it exhibits a simultaneous dual normative commitment to liberal rights and principles and to other values or interests that result in enduring and significant restrictions on some of these rights (*the dual normativity condition*); second, this dual normative commitment is constitutive and is expressed in the basic elements of the system (*the basic elements condition*).

The dual normativity condition: one of the fundamental ideas of Political Liberalism is that all individuals are free and equal and must be treated as such.[45] A second and related fundamental principle is the priority of the right over the good, which, according to Rawls, entails that institutions that form a part of the basic structure of a constitutional democratic regime may not impose ideas of the good on unwilling free and equal persons.[46] While a liberal constitutional system must be fully committed to these two principles, in a semi-liberal constitutional system these principles are adhered to only partially and only by some state institutions and in some areas of law. At the same time, a semi-liberal constitutional system will be committed to

[45] Rawls (n 9) 18–26.

[46] Rawls (n 1) 174–6. Rawls defines the basic structure as society's main political, social and economic institutions, and how they fit together into one unified system of social cooperation from one generation to the next.

one or more values or interests, such as a religious, communitarian or socialist dogma, or pressing economic or security needs, in a manner that rejects the liberal commitments to persons as free and equal and the priority of the right over the good in the areas in which these values and needs take precedence.

The basic elements condition: The basic elements of the system are the elements that are part of the structure of government (in each of its three branches) and that hold coercive authority over individuals. The evaluation of these basic elements is conducted not only on the basis of their express legal authority but also on the basis of their concrete functioning. If some institutions that form part of the basic elements of the system are committed to liberal values while others are committed to non-liberal values, the system will be a semi-liberal constitutional system.[47]

Why should Israel be considered a semi-liberal constitutional system under this scheme? By international standards, such as the Freedom House Report, Israel is considered a free liberal democratic country with an aggregate score of 76 out of 100.[48] However, my claim is that defining Israel as a liberal democracy is misleading. A closer look at the Israeli constitutional system reveals that there are three significant aspects in which this system is marked with illiberality in ways that are embedded in the basic elements of its constitutional system. The first deeply illiberal aspect is the continued belligerent occupation of the territories occupied in the 1967 war. Since Israel has not claimed sovereignty over most of this territory, it may still passably be argued that this aspect should not be considered part of Israel's constitutional system. Nevertheless, the belligerent occupation significantly increases the power and the impact of illiberal nationalist and religious Jewish groups in Israel, thereby affecting the possibility of achieving an overlapping consensus around a liberal political conception of justice. The second illiberal aspect of Israeli constitutionalism has to do with some Israeli laws, such as laws pertaining to land appropriation that have different effects along ethnic lines and disparately impact the rights of the Arab citizens of Israel. These laws are the illiberal practical result of the precedence given

[47] Another way to express the same idea is by saying that within the ambit of what Rawls calls the constitutional essentials a semi-liberal constitutional system is not committed to operating solely on the basis of liberal principles, as is expected from a liberal constitutional system, but blends them with some non-liberal values in specific areas. ibid 227.

[48] 'Freedom in the World 2020' Freedom House, 2020, https://freedomhouse.org/country/israel/freedom-world/2020. It should be noted that Israel's score of 76 is at the low end of the countries rated free, whose score in 2020 ranges between 70 and 100.

to the Jewish component in Israel's definition as a 'Jewish and Democratic state' over the democratic component.[49] The third aspect of illiberality, which is also a manifestation of the precedence given to Israel's Jewish character, is expressed in the nature of the relations between religion and the state in Israel and the coercive powers of its large (mostly Jewish) religious establishment that are entrenched in the basic elements of the constitutional system.[50] In particular, the exclusive jurisdiction given to religious courts in matters of marriage and divorce, and the lack of a civil marriage, result in extensive violations of women's rights as well as in violations of religious freedom.[51] While the three aforementioned aspects differ from each other in the extent and mode of their illiberality, they all contribute to the semi-liberal nature of Israeli constitutionalism. Furthermore, all these aspects contribute directly to the increase in both the symbolic and the practical political power of nationalist and religious illiberal Jewish groups in Israel. It is important to stress that in my view none of these aspects is a necessary corollary to Israel's definition as a Jewish and democratic state, and they even contradict this definition. Nevertheless, they do exist and they are justified by many on those grounds. Moreover, the recent passage of Basic Law: Israel – the Nation State of the Jewish People (Nation-State Basic Law) arguably marks a significant shift in the balance between the Jewish and

[49] Israel is defined in its Basic Laws as a Jewish and Democratic state. This definition is relatively new, and was adopted along with the two Basic Laws on human rights, Basic Law: Human Dignity and Basic Law: Freedom of Occupation: see www.knesset.gov.il/laws/special/eng/basic3_eng.htm (Human Dignity) and www.knesset.gov.il/laws/special/eng/basic4_eng.htm (Freedom of Occupation). However, the origins of this definition can be traced to the Israeli declaration of Establishment. This declaration states that Israel is to be a 'Jewish state', but at the same time that it will 'ensure complete equality of social and political rights to all its inhabitants irrespective of religion, race or sex; it will guarantee freedom of religion, conscience, language, education and culture'. 'The Declaration of Establishment of the State of Israel', 14 May 1948, www.knesset.gov.il/docs/eng/megilat_eng.htm.

[50] The authority of the various religious communities was established through legislation from the period of the British Mandate that was later incorporated into Israeli law. See Palestine Order in Council, 10 August 1922, para 51. The authority of the Muslim religious courts can still be found in Sign 52 of the King's Order in Council (1922), and that of the various Christian denominations in Sign 54 of the Order (ibid paras 52, 54). The authority of the Jewish Rabbinical Courts is set out in the Jurisdiction of Rabbinical Courts (Marriage and Divorce) Act, 1953. Rabbinical Courts Jurisdiction (Marriage and Divorce) Law, 1953 (Israel). The authority of the Druze religious courts can be found in the Druze Religious Courts Law, 1962 (Israel).

[51] See, e.g., Frances Raday, 'On Equality' in Raday et al. (eds), *Women's Status in Israeli Law and Society* (Schocken 1995) 19.

the democratic components of Israel's constitutional structure in favour of the Jewish component.[52] Proponents of the Basic Law, which was promoted by the government and passed by a narrow margin of 61 (of 120), see it as a constitutional instrument that would give Jewish interests constitutional precedence over liberal democratic principles such as equality in certain cases.[53] If used in this manner, the Nation-State Basic Law could dramatically expand and deepen the illiberal aspects of Israel's constitutional system.[54]

The two reasons for the incompatibility of Political Liberalism to Israel (the power of illiberal groups and Israel's semi-liberal constitutional system) are intertwined. The significant illiberal groups that hold extensive political power and that are determined to prevent the regime from liberalising and to undermine its existing liberal elements, are powerful not only because of their size in the population but also due to the semi-liberal nature of the regime. The semi-liberal political structure allows these illiberal groups control over coercive state power, and especially over the Jewish religious establishment, and legitimates their illiberal comprehensive doctrines. While there are important secular nationalist groups, the two most significant illiberal groups whose leaders have much to lose from the liberalisation of Israel's semi-liberal constitutionalism are the religious ultra-Orthodox community (UO) and the religious Zionist Orthodox community (RZ) who together comprise 18 per cent of the population in Israel, or 22 per cent of its Jewish population.[55] While

52 Basic Law: Israel – The Nation State of the Jewish People, 2018 (Israel).

53 The Minister of Justice at the time of the Basic Law's passage, Ayelet Shaked, has stated repeatedly that the purpose of the Nation-State Law is to change the balance between Jewish and liberal democratic in Israeli constitutionalism in favor of the Jewish. Shaked announced in one of her speeches prior to the passage of the law, that it will be a 'moral and political revolution' that will ensure that Zionism 'will not continue to bow down to the system of individual rights interpreted in a universal way'. Revital Hovel, 'Justice Minister Slams Israel's Top Court, Says It Disregards Zionism and Upholding Jewish Majority', *Haaretz*, August 2017, www.haaretz.com/israel-news/israel-s-top-court-disregards-zionism-justice-minister-says-1.5446684.

54 The clear precedence that the Nation-State Basic Law grants the Jewishness of the state over its democratic nature is evidenced among other things in the setting of the development of Jewish settlement as a national value that must be encouraged and promoted, in the demotion of the Arabic language from a second official language to a language that merely holds a special status in the State, and in the declaration that the Jewish people realises its religious right to self-determination in the State of Israel that was established in the Land of Israel (biblical Israel). Sections 7, 4, 1 respectively of Basic Law: Israel – the Nation State of the Jewish People.

55 Pew Research Center, 'Israel's Religiously Divided Society', 8 March 2016, www.pewforum.org/2016/03/08/israels-religiously-divided-society. Ultra-orthodox comprise

both communities belong to the Orthodox stream of Judaism, they differ in important respects. The RZ community is well integrated into Israeli society in terms of places of residence, of work and of army service, and its subgroups are varied in their interpretations of Orthodox Jewish religion. Nevertheless, it would be accurate to say that most of the RZ community lean towards the more conservative side of the spectrum of Orthodox Judaism, and an increasingly influential minority among them espouse the UO's ultra-conservative religious views and practices. Unlike the RZ community, the UO community is an enclave community that insists on leading its life separately from the rest of Israeli society, does not serve in the army and teaches its boys only religious studies. At the same time, just like RZ leaders, UO leaders hold key positions in Israeli politics and in the Israeli Jewish religious establishment. Furthermore, the UO community subscribes to a fairly unitary and ultra-conservative interpretation of Judaism which enables its leaders to maintain tight control over community members.[56] Because Rawls' definition of the type of fundamentalism which he will not regard as a reasonable comprehensive doctrine is ambiguous, it is not clear whether he would consider the UO to be fundamentalists for the purposes of Political Liberalism. Either way, within the Israeli context, although the UO's ultra-Orthodox version of Judaism is rejected by most non-UO on the personal level, it is, at the same time, considered a legitimate comprehensive doctrine, and not only are the UO not shunned, but many of their practices are accommodated by the state and their political leaders hold key positions in government, Parliament and in the Jewish religious establishment. Because UO and especially RZ religiosity is intertwined with a nationalist Jewish ideology, they are natural partners and close political allies of secular nationalist groups, and all these groups together have jointly been dominating Israeli politics for the past two decades. The passage of the Nation-State Basic Law, which combines religious and nationalist Jewish elements and includes no mention of democracy or equality, is the pinnacle of the cooperation between these religious and secular nationalist groups.[57]

9 per cent of Jews, religious Zionists 13 per cent, Masorti Jews (traditional) 29 per cent and secular Jews 49 percent.

[56] Samuel Heilman and Menachem Friedman, 'Religious Fundamentalism and Religious Jews: The Case of the Haredim' in Martin E. Marty and R. Scott Appleby (eds), *Fundamentalisms Observed* (University of Chicago Press 1994) 197.

[57] Arguably Section 1 of the Basic Law, which states that the (biblical) Land of Israel is the homeland of the Jewish people and that the exercise of the right to national self-

The majority of the UO as well as the majority of the RZ should be considered 'traditionalists' in Stoeckl's sense discussed above.[58] Indeed, the political leadership of these two communities operates in ways that are strikingly similar to those of traditionalists in the Catholic Church and in the Russian Orthodox Christian community discussed by Stoeckl in order to achieve their goal. Just like Christian traditionalists, the UO and RZ make extensive use of strategic translation in public discourse. Accordingly, they translate their religious arguments into secular arguments, but do so only strategically in order to influence the public debate and push forward a thoroughly anti-liberal agenda. They make use of liberal concepts such as freedom of religion and conscience, pluralism, minority rights and multiculturalism to justify their own demands for religious accommodations while at the same time remaining closed to any possibility of change in their own positions. That their use of these liberal concepts is entirely strategic is evidenced by the fact that the UO and RZ jointly control the Jewish religious establishment, which is a theocratic coercive state institution imposed on all Jews in Israel, and the leaders of both the UO and RZ adamantly object to any curtailment in its power and work diligently on its further expansion.

Under the aforementioned conditions, the application of Political Liberalism to Israel is destined to fail. If the application of Political Liberalism entails an application of a fully liberal political conception of justice to the Israeli constitutional and political framework, then considering the current semi-liberal nature of the state, such an application would require, as an initial step, a deep change in the current constitutional structure that would make it congruent with a liberal political conception of justice. There is no likelihood of obtaining a

determination in the State of Israel is unique to the Jewish People, together with Section 7 which states that 'The State views the development of Jewish settlement as a national value, and shall act to encourage and promote its establishment and strengthening', can serve as a constitutional basis for the annexation of the Occupied Territories; a cause strongly supported by many in these religious and secular nationalist groups. See, e.g., Eyal Benvenisti and Doreen Lustig, '"We the Jewish People"–A Deep Look into Israel's New Law', *Just Security*, 24 July 2018, www.justsecurity.org/59632/israel-nationality-jewish-state-law.

[58] As explained earlier, Stoeckl defines traditionalists as being neither religious liberals nor religious fundamentalists. They share with religious fundamentalists their rejection of egalitarian individualism and universalism. However, unlike fundamentalists, they do not retreat from society and they reject violent means of reversal. Instead, they use their significant political power and the conservative political and religious establishment strategically in order to implement their illiberal ideology. Stoeckl (n 28) 35–8.

democratic majority that would agree on such deep constitutional changes even as a modus vivendi. This is so not just because illiberal Jewish groups have become very powerful in Israel in the last decade. Many liberal Jews believe that it is possible to maintain a constitutional structure that reflects Israel's nature as a Jewish and democratic state while at the same time adhering to liberal norms. Many of these liberal optimists may reject the analysis offered here of Israel's constitutional regime as being semi-liberal and will point out that numerous liberal democracies around the world are far from perfect. As Tushnet observes, within liberal constitutionalism there are big variations, some of which may be attributable to 'shortfalls' in the realisation of liberal commitments. Tushnet defines these 'shortfalls' as 'reasonably enduring "failings" of a generally liberal constitutionalism to realise some of liberal constitutionalism's normative commitments'.[59] Thus, liberal optimists may look at the Israeli constitutional system and believe that it is merely suffering from shortfalls that may be overcome over time, pretty much in the spirit of Rawls's liberal expectancy. After all, they would argue, there are many respects in which the Israeli constitutional system, including its Basic Laws on Human Rights, its human rights legislation and its activist Supreme Court, protects the rights of all citizens as free and equal just as a liberal political framework is expected to. Under such circumstances it could be hoped that applying the principles of Political Liberalism to Israel's current constitutional structure would enable over time the formation of an overlapping consensus around a liberal political conception of justice that would make it possible to maintain in Israel a stable and just society of free and equal citizens.

Unfortunately, I think that the chances of achieving an overlapping consensus around a liberal political conception of justice under such circumstances are very slim. Quite to the contrary, by incorporating into the political conception of justice and the political structure elements such as a coercive religious establishment or a political concept recognising an inherent preference to Jews in the allocation of some state resources, the state legitimates coercive and discriminatory religious

[59] Mark Tushnet, 'Varieties of Constitutionalism' (2016) 14(1) International Journal of Constitutional Law 1, 2. However Tushnet also observes that shortfalls may be self-stabilising and enduring in a way that 'ought to lead us to identify the system as neither liberal nor illiberal nor authoritarian'. Since the illiberal aspects of Israel's constitutional regime which I described above are self-stabilising and enduring, it seems that even under Tushnet's analysis Israel cannot count as liberal.

and nationalist ideologies and makes them a legitimate part of public reason and of the reasonable overlapping consensus. The development of such consensus will only serve to consolidate a constitutional regime which is not fully liberal and which does not treat all its citizens as free and equal. Thus, these discriminatory and coercive aspects of religious and nationalist illiberal ideologies will no longer be tolerated only due to the need for impartiality towards reasonable, albeit illiberal and unjust, comprehensive doctrines, but would gain legitimacy as part of the political structure of an allegedly just society of free and equal citizens. Rather than facilitating the liberalisation of Israeli society, this would facilitate its further illiberalisation and would allow already powerful illiberal nationalist and religious groups to strengthen their hold over Israeli society. Unfortunately, the passage of the Nation-State Basic Law is an important step in this direction, on both the symbolic and the practical levels.

4 Conclusion

This chapter has critiqued the assumption that Political Liberalism is a suitable political theory for current Israel. In Section 2 of the chapter I critiqued the theory of Political Liberalism itself. I claimed that through the use of concepts such as reasonable comprehensive doctrines, reasonable overlapping consensus, impartiality and the idea of public reason, Political Liberalism enables and countenances restrictions on individual rights which should not be tolerated. Thus, Political Liberalism finds comprehensive doctrines that violate rights to be reasonable and shields illiberal doctrines, especially religious ones, from criticism, thereby providing insufficient protection for human rights. Furthermore, Political Liberalism's reliance on the willingness of illiberal groups to embrace it renders it ineffective in settings in which such illiberal groups wield anything more than negligible political power. Israel is such a setting.

In Section 3 I examined the possible application of Political Liberalism to the Israeli context. Political liberalism is based on a liberal constitutional structure that serves both as a basis for the constitutional protection of human rights and as an ideational basis from which the reasonableness of comprehensive doctrines and the overlapping consensus, as well as public reason, are derived. I claimed that Political Liberalism cannot be applied in Israel because Israel's constitutional structure is not liberal but semi-liberal, and includes fundamental deviations from liberal constitutional principles, both in the area of religion–state relations and in the area of ethnic (Jewish–Arab) relations. Consequently, an application of political liberalism in Israel must be preceded by a fundamental change in Israel's constitutional structure and principles, the likelihood of which is slim. Without such change the application of a form of Political Liberalism adjusted to Israel's semi-liberal constitutionalism would result in the continued violation of the rights of ethnic and religious minorities and of women, and further jeopardise Israeli democracy. Thus, when applied in the Israeli semi-liberal context the internal defects of Political Liberalism and its inability to properly protect the rights of free and equal citizens are intensified for two reasons: first, because of the significant political power of illiberal religious and nationalist groups in Israel; and second, because the constitutional understanding of the reasonable overlapping consensus expands to include clear violations of rights that become part of the accepted political conception of justice.

10

Law and Identity

An Unwieldy Dance

JOSEPH E. DAVID

The chapter addresses the complex relationships between law and identity as a jurisprudential problem and as a constitutional concern. It examines several conceptual aspects of identity right claims without taking a stance in the identarian–dignitarian moral and political debate. It sheds light on a neglected facet of identity right claims: the feasibility of the notion of identity as a foundation for constitutional rights. The conceptual feasibility of identity right claims is independent of and unconcerned with the validity and accuracy of moral ideologies. The chapter discusses whether identity right claims are conceptually defensible on the basis of constitutional reasoning. It argues that the notion of identity not only is definitionally vague, but also is a metamorphic concept that suffers from unsteadiness.

human dignity, rule of law, dignitarian constitutionalism, identity right claims, social fact, true inner self, digitized identity, impartiality, justice

1 Introduction

In recent years, the pages of law reviews have become increasingly populated with literature on identity and its central role in our contemporary moral, legal and political discourse. Yet in spite of this voluminous literature, there is no consensus defining the law's commitment towards the identity of its subjects and what duties identity imposes on lawmakers and adjudicators.

The demand that law address citizens' identities and be responsive to identity right claims has been extensively discussed in various contexts. It has been a central theme in moral debates and in the confrontation between the multiculturalist politics of difference and the politics of equal dignity that is foundational to liberalism. Identarian politics stresses the intrinsic connection between social recognition and personal identity as an utmost condition for a respectable human existence. In contrast, dignitarian politics insists that human dignity is the basic feature of a human being to which all are equally and universally entitled, and therefore the most solid source for human rights and liberties.[1]

Against the background of the CLS movement, the identarian–dignitarian controversy emerged from the moral and political discourse and made its way into legal theory, where it allied with compatible jurisprudential approaches. Multiculturalist proponents of identarian morality, such as feminist legal theorists, critical race theorists and postmodernists, came together bearing various versions of outsider jurisprudence.[2] Meanwhile, dignitarian morality preserved, energised and provided further theoretical grounds for right-based jurisprudence.

Nonetheless, endeavours to articulate the two as mutually exclusive worldviews have encountered limits. In legal practice, the fundamental distinction between the identarian and dignitarian visions has become blurred, and interfaces, even overlaps, have been disclosed. While legislation is inclined to avoid formal acknowledgment of identity rights (and references to identity altogether),[3] some adjudicators and commentators do read the identarian logic into existing constitutional principles of human dignity and freedom.[4] Thus in many cases identity right claims tend to take a similar shape to dignity right claims, ranging from protection claims (abstaining from interfering, harming or

[1] See Amy Gutmann, 'Introduction' in Gutmann (ed), *Multiculturalism: Examining the Politics of Recognition* (Princeton University Press 1994) 25–73.

[2] Richard Delgado and Jean Stefancic, 'Outsider Jurisprudence and the Electronic Revolution: Will Technology Help or Hinder the Cause of Law Reform?' (1991) 52 Ohio State Law Journal 847.

[3] Identity claims usually appear in law as exemptions (doctrines, policies or enacted arrangements), rather than main legislation.

[4] An example from European law: 'the very essence of the Convention [the International Covenant on Civil and Political Rights] is respect for human dignity and human freedom. Under Article 8 of the Convention in particular … protection is given to the personal sphere of each individual, including their right to establish details of their identity as individual human beings' (ECtHR, *Goodwin* v. *UK*, App no 28957/95, 11 July 2002, para 90). With regard to US law, Eskridge argues at length that 'most twentieth-century changes in the constitutional protection of individual rights were driven by or in response to the great identity-based social movements of the twentieth century'. See William N. Eskridge Jr, 'Some Effects of Identity-Based Social Movements on Constitutional Law in the Twentieth Century' (2002) 100 Michigan Law Review 2062.

threatening a person's identity[5]) to recognition claims (acknowledging the existence of discrimination, exclusion or oppression and acting to remedy it[6]) to claims for provision of the conditions for identity to survive and flourish.[7]

Advocacy for and against identity right claims typically relies on the ideologies that generate the moral and political discourse, and the all-encompassing nature of ideologies is such that they tend to skip across the different realms of normativity. Nonetheless, jurisprudential sensitivity obliges us to acknowledge that the move from moral to constitutional discourse is neither instant nor trivial.[8] An embrace of both identarian morality and dignitarian constitutionalism need not be an inconsistent position. This is so not only because the two perspectives can be bridged or overlap in some sense, but also because there may be reason to subscribe to dignitarian constitutionalism regardless of the availability of support from identarian morality. One way to distinguish between identarian morality and identarian constitutionalism is to conceptually examine identity right claims and the extent to which they can conform to existing constitutional settings.

2 The Aptness of Identity Right Claims

I wish to examine several conceptual aspects of identity right claims, while doing the utmost to avoid taking a stance in the identarian–dignitarian moral and political debate. I shall do so by shedding light on a neglected facet of identity right claims: the feasibility of the notion of identity as a foundation for constitutional rights. The conceptual feasibility of identity right claims is independent of and unconcerned with the validity and accuracy of the above moral ideologies and the relationship between them. This being the case, the following discussion will explore whether identity right claims are conceptually defensible on the basis of constitutional reasoning.

5 Among the most commonly invoked rights are privacy, self-determination and freedom of expression.

6 Demands for equal treatment are most common (based in the US, for example, on the Equal Protection Clause of the Constitution).

7 On the liberal doctrines used as bases for such claims, see Martha C. Nussbaum, 'Perfectionist Liberalism and Political Liberalism' (2011) 39 Philosophy & Public Affairs 3.

8 Sound argumentation for the distinct validity of moral rights, legal rights and constitutional rights has been offered by Jeremy Waldron, 'A Right-Based Critique of Constitutional Rights' (1993) 13 Oxford Journal of Legal Studies 18.

There are two strands of conceptual analysis used in argumentation against identity right claims. One stresses that identity right claims are incompatible with the foundations of democratic constitutionalism. The other focuses on the very notion of identity and its capacity to serve as grounds for right claims. I shall briefly outline these approaches and then contribute to the second by arguing that the notion of identity not only is definitionally vague, but also is a metamorphic concept that suffers from unsteadiness.

3 Identity Right Claims and Democracy

The rejection of identity right claims due to incongruency with fundamental pillars of democratic constitutionalism has two foci: dissonance with institutionalised dignitarian constitutionalism, and discordance with the pillars of the rule of law in its democratic version.

3.1 Identity and Dignitarian Constitutionalism

Dignitarian constitutionalism predominates in most modern democracies, irrespective of whether the constitutional supremacy of human dignity is explicit in a constitutional document or read into the law. In international law and the law of some states, human dignity is officially declared a supreme value or principle. In other legal systems, it appears as an implied idea that directs the interpretation and application of the law.

The trend of dignitarian constitutionalism developed on the national and the international level during the twentieth century. Nonetheless, it would be incorrect to view the constitutionalisation of human dignity merely as a product of that era.[9] Dignitarian constitutionalism cannot be understood in the absence of the recent history of political changes,

[9] Modern dignitarian morality is not a uniform idea. Some versions, significantly, do not insist on universalised and egalitarian application. Rosen articulates three meanings of dignity in modern times: dignity as moral and aesthetic category (an expression of the human ability to overcome natural inclination), dignity as intrinsic value (an inalienable 'inner, transcendental kernel' that all human beings carry inside them), and dignity as status. See Michael Rosen, *Dignity: Its History and Meaning* (Harvard University Press 2018) 1–62. Nonetheless, the institutionalisation of the value as a constitutional principle clearly stresses its universality and egalitarianism: 'All human beings are born free and equal in dignity and rights' – Universal Declaration of Human Rights, UNGA Res 217A (III), 10 December 1948, UN Doc A/810 (1948) Art 1.

intellectualism and religious morality.[10] Yet it also is an age-old tradition that can be traced to Stoic ethics, Judeo-Christian symbolism of Creation, medieval philosophy, Renaissance humanist culture, Enlightenment rationalism, Protestant individualism and modern Catholicism. Its constitutionalisation in the twentieth century resulted from the cumulative political experiences of civil revolutions,[11] massively bloody global wars, and endeavours to crystalise religious visions as modern statist politics.[12]

From the standpoint of legal and political theory, the emergence of dignitarian constitutionalism did far more than espouse human dignity as a supreme constitutional principle. Also entailed were significant changes in jurisprudence and in the relationship between the state and its citizens. Dignitarian constitutionalism reclaims human dignity as a source of rights that is external and superior to the law. Thus an analogy between the constitutional notion of human dignity and earlier conceptions of natural law and natural rights is telling. In all cases, the validity of the law and the political order is conditioned on a certain morality, and in all cases, law and politics are claimed to be constrained by extralegal or prepolitical norms as the sources of rights. Nonetheless, the differences between revered nature and the dignified human being also come into relief. Naturalist theories claim to contextualise law and politics in a higher ontology and a broader normative, but not necessarily humanistic, framework. Dignitarian constitutionalism meanwhile portrays law and politics as subservient to the dignity of human beings as such, refocusing the state–citizen relationship on the principle of human dignity. Citizens as human beings thus are not only under the law, but also objects of the law's perpetual responsibilities, commitments, duties and concern. In this sense, dignitarian constitutionalism is a version of liberal theory that

[10] Dignitarian constitutionalism is reflected at the international level in post-Second World War institutions, human rights treaties and the emerging field of human rights international law.

[11] On the US and French Revolutions as historical moments through which dignitarian morality turned into a principled political setting, see Francis Fukuyama, *The Origins of Political Order: From Prehuman Times to the French Revolution* (Farrar, Straus and Giroux 2011).

[12] Sam Moyn counters the conventional narrative that dignitarian constitutionalism is a post-Second World War secular reaction to horrific violations of human rights. He highlights its first appearance, in the Irish Constitution (1937), as a reaction to Catholic 'dignitarian corporatism'. See Moyn, *Christian Human Rights* (University of Pennsylvania Press 2015).

combines the ideas of human dignity and human liberty.[13] It vanishes the ancient exclusivity of *dignitas* and *libertas* as privileges,[14] and presents human dignity and human liberty as intrinsically interlaced.[15] Various contemporary authors argue that the modern institutionalisation of human dignity did not modify the core meaning of the notion of 'dignity' as rank. Rather, it levelled up the concept's application 'by an extension of formerly high-status treatment to all sectors of the population',[16] or generalising its application 'upwards'.[17] Nonetheless, dignitarian constitutionalism does more than merely extend and generalise the ancient *dignitas*. It also plays a role in a modification of how the first half of the phrase 'human dignity' is conceptualised and approached.

Dignitarian constitutionalism embraces, whether explicitly or tacitly, the autonomous ethos of the human being as a free rational and moral agent. This is evident in the overall association of human dignity and the right of self-determination, perhaps signifying a crossroads between the notions of human dignity and identity where the latter is understood as a combination of social recognition and self-realisation. Identity right claims thus need not be alien to dignitarian constitutionalism. On the

[13] An illustrative expression of international dignitarian constitutionalism is the Universal Declaration of Human Rights (n 9), which describes human dignity as intrinsically tied to human liberty. The preamble begins by stating that 'recognition of the inherent dignity and of the equal and inalienable rights of all members of the human family is the foundation of freedom, justice and peace', and Art 1 with the statement that 'All human beings are born free and equal in dignity.'

[14] The ancient *libertas*, like the *dignitas*, served in an exclusionary capacity, and in fact as a basic principle, as evidenced in the *Institutes* of Gaius (1.9): 'The great divide in the law of persons is into either freemen (*liberi*) or slaves (*serui*).' The significance of the shift from the ancient to the modern notion of dignity is discussed by Peter Berger in his 'On the Obsolescence of the Concept of Honour' in Stanley Hauerwas and Alasdair MacIntyre (eds), *Revisions: Changing Perspectives in Moral Philosophy* (University of Notre Dame Press 1983) 172–81.

[15] On the theoretical and practical connection between human dignity and human liberty, see Guy E. Carmi, 'Dignity versus Liberty: The Two Western Cultures of Free Speech' (2008) 26 Boston University International Law Journal 277. See also the analysis of equal protection in US law in light of liberty-based dignity in Kenji Yoshino, 'The New Equal Protection' (2011) 124 Harvard Law Review 747.

[16] James Q. Whitman, '"Human Dignity" in Europe and the US: The Social Foundations' in Georg Nolte (ed), *European and US Constitutionalism* (Cambridge University Press 2005) 110.

[17] '[T]he modern notion of human dignity involves an upwards equalization of rank, so that we now try to accord to every human being something of the dignity, rank, and expectation of respect that was formerly accorded to nobility.' Jeremy Waldron, 'How Law Protects Dignity' (2012) 71 Cambridge Law Journal 213.

contrary, such claims can be interpreted as expressions of the dignitarian vision of human beings as inherently capable of and entitled to make free choices. Indeed, some adjudicators and commentators base identity right claims on precisely this foundation.[18] Yet doubts about the soundness of this argument can be raised. I am not convinced that a simultaneous embrace of the autonomous ethos and the right of self-determination is sufficient to justify identity right claims.

All in all, the dignitarian vision is not restricted to the view of human beings as free rational and moral agents, and the identarian vision is not necessarily reliant on voluntarism. However, a dignitarian scope does seem to have a crucial need to insist on a distinction between the essentials and the contingencies of human nature, and on providing constitutional protections only for the essential parts of human dignity. Justifying identity right claims within a dignitarian framework requires confronting the distinction between the essential and the contingent, and accounting for the essentiality of this distinction. What components of the abstract idea of 'identity' are essential to one's dignity, and how are these components to be identified? Are the essential components common to all human beings regardless of their differences, particular choices, affiliations, backgrounds? Should essentiality be appraised concretely, without excluding any of the above? This is not to say that the contingencies of human existence do not deserve respect and protection, but perhaps not as constitutional rights. It seems that identity right claims are not sensitive enough to address this distinction.

More disturbing and striking is the gap between the dignitarian moral vision and the vision on which identity right claims rely. The dignitarian focus on the inherent worth of all human beings regardless of social belonging, deeds and achievements reflects a deliberate determination to overlook particularities and differences, and thus an insistence on generic, universal and egalitarian scope. The dignitarian vision seeks to be ahistorical, acultural and acontextual, transcending provisionality, partiality and particularity.[19]

[18] Jill Marshall, *Personal Freedom through Human Rights Law? Autonomy, Identity, and Integrity under the European Convention on Human Rights* (Martinus Nijhoff 2009).

[19] For an identarian rejection of identity right claims for their disregard of the universal inherent worth of human beings, see Steven C. Rockefeller, 'Comment' in Gutmann (n 1) 88: 'from the liberal democratic point of view a person has a right to claim equal recognition first and foremost on the basis of his or her universal human identity and potential, not primarily on the basis of an ethnic identity. Our universal identity as

3.2 Identity and the Rule of Law

> When I say that the object of the laws is always general, I mean that the law considers subjects collectively, and actions as abstract, never a man as an individual nor a particular action. Thus, the law may indeed decree that there shall be privileges but cannot confer them on any person by name … in a word, no function which has reference to an individual object appertains to the legislative power.[20]

The confrontation between identity right claims and the principles of the rule of law is seemingly less bearable and bridgeable than the above. Two areas of conflict between the identarian vision and the rule of law are worthy of mention here: the generality of the law, and its impartiality.

As early as ancient times, the idea of law was inherently associated with generality, an association that was stressed in various conjunctural moments throughout the history of Western legal and political theory. The association of law and generality is given various grounds, some of which concern the efficiency of the general format of law as a vehicle of certainty and stability,[21] the idea of law as rules,[22] and the fact that only the generality of the law can guarantee equality and freedom.[23]

Identity right claims contest not only modern humanistic universalism, but even some of the most fundamental assertions of the Western tradition of the rule of law. The stress on identity right claims seems an endeavour to

human beings is our primary identity and is more fundamental than any particular identity, whether it be a matter of citizenship, gender, race, or ethnic origin.'

20 Jean-Jacques Rousseau, *The Social Contract and The First and Second Discourses* (Yale University Press 2002) 179.

21 'The conception of freedom under the law … rests on the contention that when we obey laws, in the sense of general abstract rules laid down irrespective of their application to us, we are not subject to another man's will and are therefore free. It is because the lawgiver does not know the particular cases to which his rules will apply, and it is because the judge who applies them has no choice in drawing the conclusions that follow from the existing body of rules and the particular facts of the case, that it can be said that laws and not men rule. Because the rule is laid down in ignorance of the particular case and no man's will decides the coercion used to enforce it, the law is not arbitrary. This, however, is true only if by "law" we mean the general rules that apply equally to everybody. … As a true law should not name any particulars, so it should especially not single out any specific persons or group of persons.' Friedrich A. von Hayek, *The Constitution of Liberty* (Chicago University Press 2011) 221–2.

22 Frederick Schauer, 'The Generality of Law' (2004) 107 West Virginia Law Review 217.

23 Gregor Kirchhof, 'The Generality of the Law' in Klaus Meßerschmidt and A. Daniel Oliver-Lalana (eds), *Studies on the Theory and Practice of Legislation, Vol III: Rational Lawmaking under Review* (Springer 2006) 89–127.

demystify the ideals of the law's generality and equality before the law without offering an alternative. Furthermore, identity right claims advocate a deconstruction of the deep-seated concept of justice as associated with impartiality, without suggesting a grounded alternative conception of justice.[24]

These above tensions and contradictions are broadly discussed in the scholarly literature, and there is no need to summarise them here. Much less attention has been paid by legal theorists to the conceptual aspects of the notion of identity that is claimed. Now I wish to shift the focus from the congruity of identity right claims with dignitarian constitutionalism and the rule of law to the very notion of identity and its compatibility as an object of right claims.

4 Identity Right Claims: Conceptual Aspects

There is scholarly scrutiny of whether identity has the conceptual capacity to serve as a basis of right claims. This scepticism is tied to a broader jurisprudential question about the nature of the notions, or the conceptual conditions, that make constitutional right claims feasible at all. That such notions be sound and viable is of course desirable, but in practice this is not always the case. Though such a lack of definitional consensus certainly is troublesome, it is not in and of itself a sufficient reason to repudiate nonconsensual notions or terminology as grounds for constitutional protections. Thus the question of when conceptual vagueness becomes an impediment to legislation and adoption of a constitutional right is an open one, and it will not be resolved here. However, I would argue that in the case of identity right claims, the problem of definitional ambiguity is such as to deserve consideration. Accordingly, I shall outline three aspects of the notion of identity that I believe should be given attention in theoretical justifications for identity right claims. I shall not argue that these considerations make the entire idea of identity right claims unbearable, but they should give rise to further consideration and second thoughts.

4.1 Definitional Perplexity

Social scientists have conceded in various contexts that identity is a vague notion, as well as that ordinary and scholarly usages of identity are

[24] The expectation of impartial justice is rooted in ancient Greek ideas as well as the biblical vision of justice. It is also a leitmotiv of some of the most comprehensive theories of justice in our day. See Brian M. Barry, *Justice as Impartiality* (Clarendon Press 2004).

unsystematic to the point of definitional anarchy. So vague, elusive, slippery and amorphous are the conventional usages of identity that some commentators have argued that it is at best a meaningless or unhelpful notion.[25] In their provocative piece 'Beyond Identity',[26] Rogers Brubaker and Frederick Cooper criticised the category of identity as analytically lame and inappropriate, 'riddled with ambiguity, riven with contradictory meanings, and encumbered by reifying connotations'.[27] They suggested that social scientists let go of the notion altogether and move beyond scholarly language of identity that is hopelessly vague and opaque. An attempt to reconceptualise identity within a tightened analytical framework subsequently suggested viewing identity as a variable, rather than a substantive, concept.[28] Therein lies the perplexity. If identity is a contentless social variable, how can it be a basis for right claims? If identity is found to be a suspicious category for descriptive purposes, how can it be useful in the context of constitutional right claims?

The conceptual looseness of identity, the failures to conceptualise it, and the unresolved definitional problem are not irrelevant to a discussion of justifications for identity right claims. Instead, they overshadow the arguments in favour of embracing identity as the object of an enforceable constitutional norm.

4.2 *Ideological Baggage*

This conceptual perplexity may owe something to the fact that social scientists of a previous era expected to theorise and conceptualise identity as a notion independent of historical and cultural setting. Yet contrary to their assumptions, the conceptual genealogy of identity reveals a concept heavily charged with ideological baggage.

A variety of critics, proponents and opponents of identarian politics alike, counter the argument that identity is a poor analytical category

[25] See the pioneering argument of Philip Gleason, 'Identifying Identity: A Semantic History' (1983) 6 Journal of American History 910.

[26] Rogers Brubaker, 'Beyond Identity' (2002) 29 Theory and Society 1.

[27] James D. Fearon attributes this perplexity to the lack of integration among social history, literature, cultural studies and the multiculturalism debates. See 'What Is Identity (As We Now Use the Word)?' 3 November 1999, https://web.stanford.edu/group/fearon-research/cgi-bin/wordpress/wp-content/uploads/2013/10/What-is-Identity-as-we-now-use-the-word-.pdf.

[28] Rawi Abdelal et al., 'Identity as a Variable' (2006) 4 Perspectives on Politics 695.

with the argument that identity cannot be comprehended as a metahistorical and universal notion, but only as part of an accumulative network of modern ideas and Western ideologies. Not only is anxiety about identity a modern Western phenomenon, they argue, but the very notion of identity is a product of modern experiences and Western values and interests.

Commentators have given various accounts of the notion of identity against the backdrop of the modern Western world. Gerald Izenberg designates political events and intellectual interests as the causes behind the emergence of identity in modern times. In particular, he specifies the collapse of the European international order due to the First World War, which challenged the traditional essentialised, objective and stable conceptualisation of identity, and the emergence of identity psychology (through the fifties, under the influence of Erik Erikson), which impacted social, political and moral theories for the remainder of the twentieth century.[29]

Meanwhile, cultural critics and thinkers emphasise that the modern notion of identity is based on a variety of expressions and understandings of the true inner self, an idea that is foundational to Western modernity. Charles Taylor thus traces the idea of identity to the eighteenth-century Romantic movement and the idea of authenticity. Identity, in this analysis, reflects the individual's attachment to moral feelings, rather than reasoning, and the individual's inner voice is viewed as the ultimate source of morality, which can be individualised.[30] Fukuyama similarly traces the origins of modern identity to the theological grounds of Luther's articulation of the inner self, which Luther valorised over external social existence. This theological construction, argues Fukuyama, took a secular form through the eighteenth century and corresponded with socioeconomic changes in industrial society.[31]

Avoiding the secular turn, Zygmunt Bauman explicated the emergence of the modern notion of identity against the backdrop of premodern Christian imagination of spatial existential experience. He suggested that while premodern identity was designed through the metaphoric imagination of a pilgrimage journey across dichotomic distances (geographical

[29] Gerald Izenberg, *Identity: The Necessity of a Modern Idea* (University of Pennsylvania Press 2016).

[30] Charles Taylor, 'The Politics of Recognition' in Gutmann (n 1).

[31] Francis Fukuyama, *Identity: The Demand for Dignity and the Politics of Resentment* (Farrar, Straus and Giroux 2018).

and chronological, sentimental and normative), modern identity is imagined as inward tourism across a destabilised and fragmented spectrum, with no commitments, destinations or consistency.[32] On the basis of Bauman's conceptual typology, some stressed the affinity of the current notion of identity with postmodernist ideas and tendencies. The major conceptual shift, then, is from an identity comprehended in naturalist and essentialist terms as a fixed and sustainable category to an identity that is fluid, contingent and described as a discursive construction that is mutable and multiple. The latter notion of identity is one of a process – '*becoming*, rather than *being*';[33] a 'positioning'; and a 'resource of meaning'.[34]

Brubaker and Cooper described the failure of conceptualisation as a reason to proceed beyond identity to more accurate and more efficient categories. Looking 'behind identity', at its deep ideological connotations, might explain the failure to define and conceptualise identity as an analytical category. It is an inescapable truth that the identity of our current usages is an epitome of modern and Western ideas and ideologies – and therefore cannot but fall short of comprising a general analytical category and a universal concern.

Here again, the fact that the notion of identity is not neutral and independent of particular perceptions of the modern West is not sufficient reason to deny identity right claims. However, it is a reminder that identarian morality is not merely a call for inclusiveness of differences and against particularism. The notion of identity and its surrounding discourse, like that of human dignity, is a reflection of certain cultural and ideological values of modern Western society. It is a part of the modern Western narrative that emerged from the theological currents of European Christendom.

4.3 *Conceptual Surrogacy*

The preceding features are highlighted when identity right claims appear in court, where the performance of such claims can teach us about the conceptual nature of identity. This aspect of the identity right claim is

[32] Zygmunt Bauman, 'From Pilgrim to Tourist – or a Short History of Identity' in Stuart Hall and Paul Du Gay (eds), *Questions of Cultural Identity* (Sage 1996).

[33] Stuart Hall, 'Who Needs "Identity"?' (1996) 16 Questions of Cultural Identity 1.

[34] Mustafa Koç, 'Cultural Identity Crisis in the Age of Globalization and Technology' (2006) 1 Turkish Online Journal of Educational Technology 37.

related to the pragmatics of identity in claims for constitutional protection or interference. In a detailed analysis of the American equal protection doctrine that pertains to identarian jurisprudence, Lauren Lucas examined the mediating character of identity right claims.[35] She observed that in practice, such claims indirectly appeal to existing constitutional protections, values and principles, and that such an indirect appeal is not only unwieldy but also unavailing. She concluded by advocating a 'value-based jurisprudence', which she describes as more effective than 'identity-based jurisprudence'. Most relevant to our discussion is the phenomenology of identity right claims that she observed within 'identity-as-proxy jurisprudence', noting that the notion of identity in the common discourse of identity right claims serves as a proxy that signifies social differences yet fails to efficiently treat inequality.

Identity, as it appears in the above analysis, is not a self-sufficient notion, but a mediating category that appeals to related principles and values. Considering the above phenomenology, I would like to suggest that identity be viewed as a surrogate concept. Identity not only invokes other ideas and values, but *hosts* distinct interests and concerns. In other words, another reason for the unsteadiness of identity as a basis for right claims is its surrogative nature. This surrogacy is demonstrated by the fact that identity, within the legal discourse, is used to designate three distinct ideas, each pertaining to different legal, or constitutional, interests and concerns: identity as social fact, identity as true inner self and identity as information.

4.3.1 Identity as Social Fact

Identity as social fact is an attribute comparable to physical traits. It can be described in terms of belonging, or group membership – as an attribute that is ascribed to the group and shared by its members. Identity in this sense corresponds to some of the differences between human beings, as individuals and as groups, and can fairly be considered as mapping social differences according to conventional markers such as ethnicity, gender, territory, history, language, culture, religious belief and experience, ideology, vocation and political views. Thus understood, identity operates in a relatively steady sociopolitical universe in which differences between individuals and groups are discernible, stable and representative of social status and rank. Identity as social fact invites

[35] Lauren Sudeall Lucas, 'Identity as Proxy' (2015) 115 Columbia Law Review 1605.

description in quasi-essentialist terminology as 'natural', 'given' or 'begotten', though it is not unamenable to mobility of identities or identity transference.[36] Identity thus functions inside and outside the group. It facilitates social cohesiveness of the group and its members, and it provides meanings to intergroup differences between 'us' and 'them' and to intragroup differences between individuals.

The involvement of the law with identity in this sense is group-oriented and basically regulative. The law's interest is to enable, preserve and stabilise differences of identity within the social order, and to monitor and normalise the interactions and interplay between social groups, including mobility between groups.[37] This interest extends to the rectification of past and present discrimination and of inequality between groups and sectors.

4.3.2 Identity as True Inner Self

Identity as true inner self, as described above, is a fairly modern perspective that is reliant on ideas of inwardness, individuality and selfness. As opposed to identity as social fact, this idea focuses on individuals and their agency. Here, the actualisation of the individual is perceived as crucial to that person's being and therefore an existential and necessary condition for a meaningful life and for social interactions that are functional and healthy.

There are multiple descriptions and definitions of identity as true inner self, among them both essentialist and constructivist approaches. Many are inspired by psychological theories of development, and many others by postmodernist views. At one end of the spectrum are views of identity as an 'inner kernel' that is formed and structured through a process of crystallisation. Thus identity is a thing to be discovered, achieved and given coherency, stability and integrity, but also a thing that can be diffused, become confused, fall into crisis and moratorium. At the other end are views of identity as more fluid and elastic, and susceptible to changes and adaptations. Identity in this sense is a product

[36] The nature of identity and the legitimacy of identity change are separate and independent matters: whether identity is perceived as essentially given or voluntarily chosen is independent of the question of the legitimacy of changes in identity.

[37] An example of such a law–identity interaction is the commonplace exemption in various postcolonial countries of 'personal status' from state law and jurisdiction and the placement of such matters under the jurisdiction of the religious laws of those involved. This arrangement is of course a legacy of premodern imperial arrangements, such as the Ottoman *millet* system, and colonialist compromises with local traditional societies.

of discursive mechanisms, and it is therefore a sort of narrative that is told, by us and by others, about who and what we are.

The involvement of the law with this sense of identity is individually oriented and an expression of responsibility for personal autonomy and integrity. The law is committed to protecting individuals' identities against preventable harm, to ensuring the necessary conditions for undisturbed development of healthy identities. Some go so far as to argue, with a perfectionist enthusiasm, that the law must provide the conditions for identities to flourish.

4.3.3 Identity as Data

The earth-shattering scientific discoveries and rapid technological development of our age have dramatically changed most of our social and economic conduct. They also herald crucial modifications of the very notion of identity and concerns about who we are. The medical capacity to intervene and manipulate the human endocrine system and to modify biological markers of gender differences has had an undeniable impact on the practical, as well as the discursive, aspects of gender identity. The voluntary aspect of identity has been accordingly and greatly intensified.

The ability to reconstruct genetic information about our ancestries is not only enriching our knowledge of heredity and lineages, but also changing how we comprehend ourselves, our ethnic affinities and our national and racial identities. The linguistic representations of our identities use not only the nouns and adjectives of yesteryear, such as 'female', 'Christian' or 'Caucasian', but also quantitative measures, such as '4 per cent Afro-American' or '21 per cent West-European'.

The reduction of identity to data is probably most apparent in the phenomenon of digitised identity – a format of identity that we so often practise, both consciously and unwittingly. We pay and travel using cards or numbers that represent our financial capabilities. Our deeds and interests, observed online and off, are documented, collected and processed into repositories and databases that include basic identifying details (such as birth date and ID number), wide-ranging information about our behaviour (where we go, what we do, with whom we have dined), preferences and dispositions. Our data identity contains much more than we know, more than we can remember or even grasp.

Identity in this sense reflects a cardinal shift from the preceding notions of identity. It consists not of the conscious feelings and inwardness of any individual human being, but of something external and objective, based not on the conception of the self, but on the idea of *persona*. Identity in this sense is detachable from the person with whom it is affiliated. Therefore, 'identity as data' introduces differently, and more severely, the questions of who owns an identity and to whom one's identity belongs.[38] Such an identity usually is not a self-determined or self-governed choice, but rather information that is controlled by third parties – governments, actors in the markets, media owners and the like. While identity in the previous sense is crucially important to individuals, identity as data is valuable mainly to others who can use this information for endless purposes, including the manipulation of duly profiled persons and organisations.

This sense of identity confronts the law with a different set of concerns and challenges. Protection from fraud and identity theft, and with them confidentiality, privacy and protection from undesired uses and manipulations of 'identity as data', are at stake, and they are obviously different from traditional concerns. Thus three distinct meanings of identity represent three distinct sets of concerns, commitments and expectations of the law.

5 Conclusion

I'm nobody! Who are you?
Are you nobody, too?
Then there's a pair of us – don't tell!
They'd banish us, you know.

How dreary to be somebody!
How public, like a frog
To tell your name the livelong day
To an admiring bog!

In the sparse words of this brilliant poem,[39] Emily Dickinson seeks to challenge the obsession with identity. She suggests a view of identity as compulsory, imposed on us from outside: a communicative necessity of living in a public habitus, but nevertheless a constraint, not a choice or a true essence. Dickinson invites us to think about ourselves and about our very existence without identity. She encourages us to think not merely

[38] Some argue that this sense introduces a distinction between ownership and management of identity, claiming that even nowadays identity is owned by individuals despite the fact that they have little control over it and it is managed by third parties.

[39] *The Complete Poems of Emily Dickinson* (Little, Brown 2015) No. 288.

'beyond identity' or 'behind identity', but rather 'without identity'. Her association of identity with social necessity resonates with Nietzsche's insight about the epistemological costs of socialisation.[40] The departure to a social contract from a solipsistic world in which an individual has a 'unique and entirely individual experience' is the moment when language is legislated (*Gesetzgebung der Sprache*[41]), 'a word becomes a concept',[42] images are dissolved into concepts,[43] and so impressions and ideas are universalised and become 'fixed, canonical, and binding'.

Identity is a crucial notion in our moral and political life, and we neither can nor should give up on it or seek to ignore it. We should, however, acknowledge that the notion of identity has become a source of changing ideas and a nominal representation of views on the fundamental conditions of human existence. As a term, it has distinct denotations, and as a concept it surrogates different ideas, concerns and interests. Wouldn't it be more efficient to give up on the surrogating intermediation of identity and approach these interests directly?

[40] Fredrich Nietzsche, 'On Truth and Lies in a Nonmoral Sense' in *Philosophy and Truth: Selections from Nietzsche's Notebooks of the Early 1870's* (trans D. Breazeale, Humanities Press 1979).

[41] ibid 83.

[42] ibid 81.

[43] ibid 84.

11

David Kretzmer

An Academic Biographical Portrait

PNINA LAHAV

Interview with Professor David Kretzmer: his journey from South Africa to Israel, what triggered his life-long passion for human rights and steps in his academic career.

human rights, international law, political and civil liberties

I met David Kretzmer in the fall of 1967 as we Israelis were slowly digesting the meaning of that earth-shattering event known as the Six Day War. David had just graduated at the top of his class from the law faculty of the Hebrew University and was known as one of the best and brightest recent law graduates. The spring of 1967 brought the law school to a halt. Israel declared a state of emergency and mobilised its reserves. As a result, only women and a handful of men – Israeli Arabs and Jews who were not eligible for military service – remained in the classroom. The professors tried, heroically, to continue the lectures as usual but after a short while gave up and the law school closed down.

During the 1967 war, I was a second-year law student. In the fall of that year, as we prepared to return to school we heard that some fundamental changes would be introduced into the curriculum. The law school was breaking with its Continentalist/German tradition and embracing the American model of legal education. In that stressful spring of 1967 we were studying a mandatory course called 'obligations' made of a mix of contracts and torts. This was a part of the heritage of German legal education. Because of the impending war, we did not get to study the section on torts. It was announced that from now on the course called 'obligations' would be formally split into torts and contracts and that we would be the first class to study torts as an independent course. Moreover, we would be taught by a brilliant young professor who had just returned from a year at Harvard Law School, Aharon Barak (later Israel's Chief Justice, who served on the Supreme Court in the years

1978–2006). Barak, known for his extraordinary persuasive skills, convinced the faculty to shift to the American model, teach contracts and torts separately and let him teach the course on torts. The plan was that he would give lectures to the entire class, but the class would also be divided into sections and a teaching assistant would meet us once a week to clarify and deepen our understanding of the subject matter. That teaching assistant was David Kretzmer.

Dave, as everyone called him, had an ambitious plan. Barak gave him a free hand to develop his pedagogic ideas and he took full advantage of his freedom. Instead of rehearsing the details of assigned cases as other research assistants had done, he created a series of legal problems. Students received the problems in advance and were expected to read relevant cases and come to class ready to analyse the legal issues they identified. This felt like a revolution. We had never encountered such a teaching method before and while we agreed that it was quite demanding, we also found it electrifying. Dave proved to be a very gifted teacher and confidently opened before the class a vast window into the intricacies of the common law, its doctrines and the interplay between *stare decisis*, *ratio decidendi*, *obiter dicta* and holding. He did not lecture but rather asked penetrating questions, engaging the students, challenging us and inviting us to challenge him in return. It was all novel and very exciting and somehow fit into the revolutionary atmosphere of the post-67 Israel. In hindsight we realised that we were experiencing the famous Socratic Method developed by Christopher Columbus Langdell, in practice at Harvard Law School.

I was a student in one of Dave's sections. He was closer to us in age and very friendly and we soon found ourselves discussing with him many issues unrelated to tort law. Dave was spending at the time a few years with a law firm in Tel Aviv. He then decided that legal practice was not for him and in 1972 he received a stipend to pursue doctoral studies at Osgood Hall in Toronto, Canada. I later understood that had he been interested, he could have been admitted to Harvard or Yale Law School, but he was modest and perhaps not too versed in the academic hierarchy, and in any event Osgood Hall was a very good school and was offering him a stipend.[1]

[1] Osgood Hall was also willing to accept Dave's LLM degree and let him proceed straight to the doctorate. 'I had aging parents and did not want to be away from Israel for more than two years.' DK in this interview.

Dave specialised in tort law, and when he returned to Jerusalem after a few years as a young lecturer, he started teaching the main course in torts. By then I had returned from my studies at Yale Law School where I specialised in constitutional law and in particular in political and civil liberties. We remained in touch when he was in Canada and I in the United States, and when we both returned to Jerusalem our friendship deepened.

I sat with Dave to discuss his academic and intellectual history in order to add a personal touch to the articles collected in this volume.[2]

PL Tell me about the early stages of your legal career.

DK I graduated in 1967 and was admitted to the Israeli bar at the end of 1968. During the Six Day War, I served as an articled clerk ('stajer') at the Supreme Court in the chambers of Justice Zvi Berinson[3]. After that I trained in the office of Yigal Arnon who had just opened his law firm.[4] Arnon suggested that I join him in opening a branch of his firm in Tel Aviv, but I decided to remain in academia. At that time, I was pursuing an LLM degree at the Hebrew University and during 1969 I worked as a researcher at the Institute for Legislative Studies and Comparative Law at the Faculty of Law. In 1970 I began work with a law firm in Tel Aviv and remained there for two and a half years.

I have always been interested in human rights. Already as a young attorney, I represented left-wing Israelis who were accused of participating in illegal demonstrations. I was also interested in politics. In the 1969 elections to the seventh Knesset I was active in the 'Peace Party' ('Reshimat Hashalom'). It was a group of mostly academics from the Hebrew University[5] but it failed to get public support. At that time I became close to Professor Yehoshua Arieli and joined progressive circles that opposed any annexation of the Occupied Territories.[6]

PL You also founded the Association for Civil Rights and Civil Liberties (ACRI).

DK We founded ACRI in 1972 just before I was to leave for Osgood Hall. The founders were mainly academics from various fields, including the

[2] Ramat Hasharon, 30 October 2019.

[3] Before taking the bar exams, a student had to complete two years of staj.

[4] Yigal Arnon LLP, one of the leading law firms in Israel.

[5] A Google search shows that Dave was number 11 on their list, not likely to have won a Knesset seat but still pretty well respected by the group: www.idi.org.il/media/7009/%D7%9B%D7%A0%D7%A1%D7%AA-7-%D7%A8%D7%A9%D7%99%D7%9E%D7%AA-%D7%94%D7%A9%D7%9C%D7%95%D7%9D.pdf. Other members of that circle were Gadi Yatziv, Nathan Yellin-Mor, Shaul Fogel, Reuven Kaminer, Yossi Levy and Snait Gissis.

[6] Arieli was a distinguished professor of American history, best known for his book *Individualism and Nationalism in American Ideology* (Harvard University Press 1964).

late Professor Daniel Amit (physics), Arnold Enker (law), Ernest Stock (political science) and the journalist Nissim Rejwan. We received assistance from the branch of the American Jewish Committee in Israel, whose director, Bernard Reznikov, was very supportive.

PL When you joined the law faculty, after completing your dissertation, you taught torts but you were drawn to public law.

DK I always liked administrative law, which I studied with Yitzhak Zamir. It fit my interests in human rights and the idea of the necessary limitations on government. Administrative law offered a framework to check if the government imposed excessive limitations on the person. At the time, the Israeli conception of human rights was very limited and there was no constitution. The only way to defend human rights was through administrative law. This law offered a way to challenge the legitimacy of the discretion exercised by the government. I should add that I like the common law, I like its dynamic much better than statutory law or statutory interpretation.

I started teaching administrative law because the faculty was looking for a person to teach the subject when Zamir left.[7] Later I started teaching constitutional law and my focus was on human rights.

PL How did you get to international law?

DK I was interested in the legal status of the Occupied Territories. For this purpose, I had to understand the international law that applied to them. My first article on this topic addressed house demolitions. I examined the sanction of house demolition as it appears in the Defense (Emergency) Regulations of 1945, through the lens of international law. I also addressed the issue of freedom of expression.[8]

In 1995 the Ministry of Foreign Affairs asked me to submit my candidacy for the Human Rights Committee that monitors implementation of the International Covenant on Civil and Political Rights. These were the days of the Rabin government; David Libai who was the Minister of Justice and Yossi Beilin who was at the Ministry of Foreign Affairs were both interested in human rights and supported my candidacy. I was elected as a member and began serving on that treaty body. In 1993 the Hebrew University's Faculty of Law founded the Center for Human Rights, in cooperation with the Truman Institute. I was the director of the Center and we managed to get support from the German Minerva Foundation. This was a grant awarded to the Hebrew University and Tel Aviv University jointly. In 1997 the Center for Human Rights became the Minerva Center for Human Rights. I served as academic director for the first three years.

PL What areas of international law interest you in particular?

[7] Itzhak Zamir served as Israel's Attorney General between 1978 and 1986. In 1994 he was appointed as a justice on Israel's Supreme Court.

[8] Dave Kretzmer, 'Racism and Freedom of Speech' (1987) 8 Cardozo Law Review 445.

DK I am interested in three aspects of international law: human rights, humanitarian law and the use of force. In Jerusalem I did not teach the introductory course on international law. However, I did teach a seminar on international human rights law. I taught an introduction to an international law course in the College of Law and Business at Ramat Gan and afterwards at Sapir College.

PL Tell us about your membership in the Human Rights Committee.

DK Members are nominated by their own states but once elected they serve as independent experts and not as representatives of their states. They are excluded from dealing with issues connected to their own states. Membership enabled me to familiarise myself with the various mechanisms of international law and deepened my understanding of international law, and I gained expertise.

PL Tell us about your personal background

DK I was born in South Africa and grew up in a very liberal milieu. I was a member of Habonim – a socialist-Zionist youth movement. We objected to apartheid. I studied at a Jewish High School and the principal hired teachers who could not find teaching jobs in other schools because of their political activities. They were good teachers. When emergency rule was declared in South Africa, my history teacher disappeared. It turned out that she was placed under administrative detention. The reason was her membership as a student many years earlier in a communist group. She simply disappeared and the authorities did not allow the press to report that she had been detained. She returned to teach us after three months in detention. After I had left for Israel, my English teacher was sentenced to two and a half years in prison. I therefore did my military service and left soon thereafter. I came to Israel in 1963 and did not return to South Africa for forty years. When I arrived in Israel, I was a young man with a very high political consciousness.

PL These traumatic experiences must have influenced your commitment to human rights. Did they give you a different standard by which to evaluate the emerging Israeli practice of occupation, is this correct?

DK It is difficult to know what the connection was. Today I see the parallels in the West Bank between the apartheid regime and government policies and practices there. The constant efforts to delegitimise opposition as 'extreme left' also remind me of the way the apartheid regime labelled anyone who opposed it as a 'communist'.

PL Do you think that this is a particular sensibility of persons who come from South Africa, because of their experience with the practice of apartheid? I note that the late Leon Shellef (a member of the Tel Aviv Law Faculty) and Dan Simon (a member of the USC law faculty who worked for several years at the Israeli Association for Civil Rights and Liberties) grew up in South Africa. Maybe it is easier to see the injustice when you have had such experiences? Perhaps your sensitivity is heightened?

DK Perhaps. But Leon and Dan were the exceptions. Most of my colleagues in the human rights field were not former South Africans, and very few former South Africans with a similar background to my own were active. At the end of the 1967 war I was already four years in Israel, and I understood that we are in trouble. I remember the public advertisements 'we liberated, not occupied'. Arieli told me that he cried when the IDF conquered the West Bank because 'it is easy to enter and hard to exit'.

Today I see the situation in Israel in an even more radical way. The South Africans tolerated apartheid because it was wrapped in religious ideology. The Dutch Reformed Church provided the ideological justification. There were a few priests who criticised apartheid and the link between religion and racism but they were few and far between.

When I see the effort to justify the control of the Occupied Territories through religion – I cannot help but see the similarities. I find it outrageous because it undermines my own understanding of the Jewish religion and Jewish values and because from the political perspective it puts us on the road to catastrophe.

PL I remember that when we were young lecturers at the Hebrew University we had many arguments about judicial review.

DK I believed then, as I do now, that judicial review for protection of human rights is essential. You and I wrote a joint article about this way back in the late 1970s. But I do not have illusions that judicial review is the panacea for all political problems, and I have been critical of the extension of judicial review beyond issues of human rights. The Court cannot solve major political issues (such as the conscription of *Yeshiva* students). Its attempts to do so harm its legitimacy and thereby weaken its ability to protect human rights.

I am in favour of judicial review whenever individuals claim that the government violated their rights. I wrote in favour of judicial review in my article on the *Bank Hamizrahi* case.[9] My concern is about matters other than rights. I have always been worried that the Court would pay a price for becoming involved in parliamentary proceedings and coalition agreements; I feared that by considering these matters it was wasting the ammunition it had as a High Court of Justice. For example, I was against judicial intervention when it comes to drafting *Yeshiva* (ultra-Orthodox) students. I do not see the decision to exempt them from military service as a violation of human dignity. If the majority wishes to give them a privilege, I do not see why the Court should intervene.

[9] 'The Path to Judicial Review in Human Rights Cases: From *Bergman* and *Kol Ha'am* to *Mizrahi Bank*' (1997) 28 *Mishpatim* 359 (Hebrew). Civil Administration 6821/93, *United Mizrahi Bank v Migdal*, https://versa.cardozo.yu.edu/opinions/united-mizrahi-bank-v-migdal-cooperative-village. Israel's Supreme Court held that Basic Law: Human Dignity and Freedom recognised the judicial power to review statutes alleged to violate the Basic Law and, if necessary, invalidate them.

When it comes to corruption, I think that the Court did make an important contribution and solidified norms of public ethics. On the other hand, it may well be that the legislature felt encouraged to do nothing because it expected the Court to do the job. It worries me that when the Court declines to intervene the public sees it as a legitimation of the practice under consideration.

PL With respect to the Occupied Territories, what do you think the Court's role should have been?

DK The most important aspect of judicial review in Israel is that the High Court of Justice does not discriminate between citizens and non-citizens, residents and non-residents. The Court hears every petitioner who claims that the Israeli government violated their rights. The Court is open to everyone and this is also very important. All of this began in the very first years of the occupation. The Government did not object and this is also important. The 'justice' of the occupying state is the 'justice' of the occupant. This is universal. It cannot be otherwise. But, even under these circumstances, the Court could have done more.

The Court has provided remedies (partial or full) to a fair number of individuals. At the same time, it has legitimised virtually all government policies and practices, even when they are clearly incompatible with international law. Furthermore, even if some of these actions were legal, they were not legitimate. In my book *The Occupation of Justice*[10] I did not ask the question whether it would have been desirable or not for the Court to exercise judicial review over the Occupied Territories. It could hardly have avoided doing so. Clearly, a judicial distancing from the practices under occupation could not have lasted for such a long time. In the new edition of my book I write about this. When I look at Palestinians in the Occupied Territories, there is no doubt that there are many whose situation would have been much worse without judicial review. Without the High Court of Justice there would have been much more governmental arbitrariness and many people would have been denied relief. On the other hand, when I look at the general picture, it is quite clear that the decisions of the High Court of Justice lent legitimacy to the policies and practices of Israeli occupation. This is especially true when it comes to the settlements and use of public lands.

With regard to the policy of house demolition, I think that if early on the High Court of Justice had ruled that house demolitions were illegal the government would have accepted its judgment and ordered the military to discontinue with the practice. We would not be in the situation we are in today.

This is a complex matter. I can offer a legal analysis of how they did and how they should have decided. I could demand that they do more in

[10] *The Occupation of Justice: The Supreme Court of Israel and the Occupied Territories* (State University of New York Press 2002).

terms of the injustice of the occupation. On the other hand the Court is a political institution. I would have liked to see it do more but realistically it is hard to say that a court in any other country would have functioned differently.

PL Tell us about your books. In keeping with your intense interest in human rights, you wrote a book about the status of Israeli Arabs and then a book about the legal situation obtaining in the West Bank.

DK In 1990 I published *The Legal Status of the Arabs in Israel* (Westview Press 1990). The book was revised and translated into Arabic as a second edition (Institute for Israeli Arab Studies 2002) (Arabic). A second edition of my book *The Occupation of Justice* (with Yaël Ronen) on judicial review over the government's actions in the Occupied Territories will soon be published by Oxford University Press.

PL And which of your many articles do you think best reflect Dave Kretzmer, the person and the scholar?

DK 'Transformation of Tort Liability in the Nineteenth Century: The Visible Hand' (1984) 4 *Oxford Journal of Legal Studies* 46.

'Racism and Freedom of Speech' (1987) 8 *Cardozo Law Review* 445

'Targeted Killings of Suspected Terrorists: Extra-Judicial Executions or Legitimate Means of Self-Defence?' (2005) 16 *European Journal of International Law* 171.

'Politics, Law and the Legal Process: The Case of the High Court of Justice and the Occupied Territories' (together with Gerson Gorenberg) (2016) 17 *Law and Government* 249 (in Hebrew).

PL Before we say goodbye, could you tell us what you are presently working on and what are you looking forward to?

DK Together with my colleague, Yaël Ronen, we have completed a second and expanded version of *The Occupation of Justice* (Oxford University Press 2021). I look forward to more years of research in human rights and related issues and teaching an occasional course.

12

David Kretzmer

A Role Model*

MORDECHAI KREMNITZER

The chapter describes David Kretzmer as a role model for a world-renowned expert: the exceptional breadth of his expertise, the razor-sharpness of his inquiries, his ability to differentiate between law and politics in sensitive issues, his courage to deal critically with 'the embarrassing', his exemplary teaching, his impeccable intellectual integrity, his activism in protecting human rights and his modesty. The article briefly describes Kretzmer's contributions on several issues: the legal status of the Israeli Arab-Palestinian citizens, the Israeli belligerent occupation and counter-terrorism measures like deportations, house demolitions and targeted killings, judicial activism and other trends (both transparent and hidden) in the Israeli case law, and racial incitement as a criminal offense. It exemplifies Kretzmer's impact on the Israeli Supreme Court.

Israeli Arabs, belligerent occupation, terrorism, human rights, judicial activism, racial incitement, targeted killings, demolitions, deportation, confiscation, judicial activism, Supreme Court

There are very few researchers (and I say this only out of caution) whose legal expertise is as varied as Professor David Kretzmer's, spanning civil law as well as public and international law. Kretzmer has always excelled in razor-sharp, accurate legal inquiry and has the incredible ability to perfectly analyse any legal subject, taking into consideration every relevant aspect. He has the extraordinary aptitude to look 'outside the box', pinpoint key trends, evaluate legal occurrences as they really are, and recognise the deep meaning behind the Court's rulings. It is possible to assume that mastery in different legal disciplines – their principles, doctrines and concepts – strengthens the 'muscles' for legal analysis and contributes to the highest level of legal proficiency indicative of

* I am grateful to Ms Hen Ben Eliezer for her devoted research assistance.

Professor Kretzmer's skills. His exceptional abilities as a researcher were also reflected in his excellent teaching, known for its uncompromising quality. His students who chose to invest in their required studies acquired priceless tools and assets that will be of use to them for the rest of their professional lives.

Kretzmer's path as a researcher is unique due to his choice to focus on the most difficult and sensitive issues. One major challenge in Kretzmer's work is the separation between law and politics, which Kretzmer has maintained diligently, as illustrated in his groundbreaking writing on the Arab minority in Israel, the Israeli occupation of the West Bank and Gaza Strip, targeted killings and house demolition. Choosing these subjects and analysing them using clear-cut legal standards, without embellishment, is a testimony to Professor Kretzmer's courage, unfortunately not a very common trait. Other guiding criteria for Kretzmer's academic choices were their importance and relevance.

1 The Legal Status of the Arabs in Israel

In light of the common tendency to blur the distinction between Arab-Israeli citizens and Palestinians residing in the Occupied Territories, Kretzmer's research on the Israeli Arabs, published in the book *The Legal Status of the Arabs in Israel*, is of paramount importance. Kretzmer dives into a discussion of land policy issues, a topic he considered as one of utmost importance, 'possibly the most painful in the relationship between the Arabs and the Jewish State', being shaped by and shaping the attitude towards the Arab-Israeli minority.[1] He examines the entire Israeli and early British Mandate legislation later adopted by the state of Israel, used as a tool to construct a discriminating policy towards the Arab-Israeli minority and to allow the expropriation of its land.[2] Kretzmer also identifies the Court's stance as making use of Israel's Jewish identity as a justification for violation of human rights.[3] Inter alia, Kretzmer elaborates on the 'special historical reasons' – an argument adopted by the Court, leading it to rule against the restitution of property to its rightful Palestinian owner due to the need to preserve the Jewish nature of the Jewish quarter of Jerusalem. Hence, the Court approved a governmental policy to restrict the sale of

[1] David Kretzmer, *The Legal Status of the Arabs in Israel* 50–1 (Westview Press 1990).
[2] Ibid 176–7.
[3] Ibid 140.

local properties there solely to army veterans and new immigrants, i.e. those who are not Arabs. Kretzmer notes that this argument is used as a judicial tool for justifying religious or ethnic-based discrimination against Arabs.[4]

Kretzmer describes and analyses the existence of discrimination in various fields and criticises the poor enforcement of the state's obligation to uphold and grant complete equality to all its citizens. For example, he criticises the national institutions, whose activities are openly aimed at promoting the Jewish majority. These institutions are granted full governmental support and inclusion in decision-making processes of utmost importance – for instance, agriculture and land development – and are even granted exclusive authority over specific issues, such as the planning of rural settlements.[5] Kretzmer argues that this structural formation is an expression of discrimination towards the Arab minority, which is left excluded from partaking in such processes. He adds that the transfer of governmental authorities to the national institutions results in the Arab minority being denied equal rights.[6]

Kretzmer also criticises the Court's lack of authority – which has not changed after the legislation of Basic Law: Human Dignity and Liberty – to conduct judicial review of previous legislation such as the Defence (Emergency) Regulations 1945, even if its application violates human rights.[7]

His inclination to address 'the bigger picture' is reflected in his writing on the Israeli Basic Laws on human rights. His comprehensive analyses of the Supreme Court's rulings are always made from a broad and developmental perspective. In this context, he pointed out the Court's tendency to interpret Article 7a of Basic Law: The Knesset narrowly with regard to the state's Jewish identity, in a way that expands its protection of the right to participate in political activities. For instance, he mentioned the Court's ruling against the suspension of a member of the Knesset who was convicted of a criminal offence, while waiting for his appeal.[8] This approach has remained relevant long after the article's

[4] Ibid 80–1; Professor Kretzmer based his argument on HCJ 114/78 *Bourkan* v. *Minister of Finance* (1978) 32 PD 800.

[5] Ibid 94–6.

[6] Ibid 96–7.

[7] Ibid 8; David Kretzmer, 'The Path to Judicial Review in Human Rights Cases: From Bergman and Kol Ha'am to Mizrahi Bank' (1997) 28 Mishpatim 359, 381 (in Hebrew) .

[8] David Kretzmer, 'Judicial Review of Knesset Decisions' (1988) 8 Tel Aviv University Studies in Law 95, 120. He also refers to the annulment by the Court of the Knesset

publication and is considered a positive change compared to the precedent set in the Yardor case. This approach is highly different from the abovementioned ruling, in which the Court revoked the right of a political party that rejected the existence of the state of Israel as a Jewish state to take part in the elections, in the absence of legal authorisation to do so, at that time. Kretzmer presents the rule-of-law approach of the Court, demanding a specific authorisation by law as a prerequisite to justify infringements upon rights and the Yardor case as a deviation from it.[9]

2 Belligerent Occupation and Counter-Terrorism Measures

Another important field of Kretzmer's study is the law of belligerent occupation. Kretzmer recognises the court's contribution to the international law of belligerent occupation, such as granting the residents of the Occupied Territories direct access to Israeli courts, specifically to the High Court of Justice, unlike any other occupying state.[10] This novelty in Israel's jurisprudence is a mixed bag.

On one hand, this opening of judicial review shapes a restraining impact on the use of powers by the occupation authorities; on the other hand, it endows Israel's ongoing control over the Occupied Territories with unique legitimacy. To this mix, one should add the question of the application and compatibility of international law norms *vis-à-vis* an occupation lasting five decades, with no end in sight. Even more so: the increasingly likely possibility that what might have started as a temporary control in good faith may have, over time, become a takeover whose real purpose is permanent control, and which focuses on strengthening Israel's interests while dispossessing and harming the interests of the occupied population, both individually and collectively. The danger set in this field of study, especially in ongoing conflicts, is the temptation to construct the reality in a way that makes the state's deeds just and justified. The first 'victims' who are likely to succumb to such a temptation are the decision-makers themselves, including legal and judicial

decision to remove parliamentary immunity. See David Kretzmer, 'Hamishim Shana Shel Mishpat Tzibury BeBeit HaMishpat HaEliyon' / 'Fifty Years of Public Law in the Supreme Court – Human Rights' (1999) 5 Mishpat Umimshal 297, 323.

[9] Kretmer, 'Fifty years' (n 8) 303.

[10] Kretzmer (n 1) 11; David Kretzmer, The Law of Belligerent Occupation in the Supreme Court of Israel, (2012) 94 International Review of the Red Cross 207, 236.

decision-makers but academic researchers, and sons and daughters of society, are also susceptible to this bias. Three qualities make Professor Kretzmer suitable to handle such difficult subjects: his impressive control of international law and its varied layers; the ability to comprehend reality in its fullest; and his impeccable intellectual integrity.

Kretzmer singled out a consistent gap in the Court's jurisprudence, between the application of human rights in the Occupied Territories and their application within Israel. He did so by examining the Court's approach while shedding light on internal contradictions in its rulings. For example, he convincingly proves that house demolitions are inconsistent with international law, particularly Article 53 of the Geneva Convention, Article 23 of the Hague Regulations, and basic principles of criminal law.[11] Kretzmer presented the questionable basis of the Court's rulings and unveiled the true nature of demolitions, by citing different *obiter dicta* within the Court's rulings – indicating the punitive character of house demolitions – in contrast to the Court's denying the punitive character of this measure. He scrutinised the erroneous comparison made by the Court between the suffering of a family whose member is incarcerated and the suffering of a family whose house has been demolished due to one of its member's involvement in terrorism, as justification for the demolition order.[12] Kretzmer refines the comparison, explaining that in the first case the family's anguish is an unwanted, incidental result, while in the second case the family's suffering is a direct and intended consequence, the rationale of the demolition that makes it a forbidden collective punishment of those who are not involved in terroristic activities.[13]

He also points out that the Court's support of the IDF's actions is far greater than its tendency to rule in favour of military restraint and forbid military actions.[14] He describes the jurisprudence of these decisions as 'blatantly government-minded'. For example, Kretzmer notes the Court's interpretation of Article 49 of the Fourth Geneva Convention: permitting deportation of Palestinian individuals from their living areas is inconsistent with the common interpretation of the Article, held by most

[11] David Kretzmer, *The Occupation of Justice: The Supreme Court of Israel and the Occupied Territories* (State University of New York Press 2002) 147.

[12] Ibid 150.

[13] Ibid 151. Kretzmer supports his argument using the words of Justice Dorner in HCJ 1730/96 *Sabich v Commander of IDF Forces in Judea and Samaria*, 353(1) PD (1996).

[14] Kretzmer (n 11) 188.

if not all commentators, prohibiting forcible transfer from occupied territories – mass deportation as well as deportation of individuals.[15] With regards to the issue of the settlements as a violation of Article 49, the Court has so far avoided directly ruling on the matter but has *de facto* justified the settlements by applying to them the concept of military necessity, thus permitting numerous military and civilian actions in the Occupied Territories. Kretzmer criticises the Court's jurisprudence and shows its discrepancy with international law, according to which the transfer of civilian population of the occupying power to occupied territories and the confiscation and transfer of land to this population are not recognised as military necessity.[16] He demonstrates the Court's reluctance to rule on the legality of the land policy in the Occupied Territories. Kretzmer argues that the Court evades a clear and definite ruling in land policy issues due to political reasons, using two methods: relying on the non-justiciability of the question, and lowering the level of scrutiny in security issues.[17] Kreztmer criticises the Court's approach by pointing to its methodological mistakes, such as the non-application of the least invasive measures test with regards to jurisprudence related to the Occupied Territories. Compared to the general jurisprudence of the Court, which demands additional justification for a given act (other than security considerations as its purpose), the Court does not insist at all on such justification in cases related to the Occupied Territories.[18]

Due to his utmost even-handedness and aspiration to develop a wide-scale picture of the issues at hand, Kretzmer sheds light on the important distinction between the Court's reluctant approach on substantive protection of human rights, and its willingness to strengthen the procedural aspect of their application. For example, the Court obligated the IDF to conduct hearings before the execution of a house demolition order and recommended the establishment of courts of appeal for IDF actions in the Occupied Territories.[19]

Kretzmer is not indifferent to legitimate security needs, taking into account the problematic situation in which terrorists enter the state of Israel from the Gaza Strip, an area that is not subjected to an effective and cooperative rule of law. This distress created the necessity for Israel to use

[15] Ibid 187.
[16] Ibid 77.
[17] Ibid 79–81.
[18] Ibid 81.
[19] Kretzmer (n 1) 189.

targeted killings, as a measure of self-defence. However, Kretzmer is not quick to undo the leash. He reviews the procedural and evidentiary predicaments involved, and offers a limited use of targeted killings in a narrow space, in order to resolve the difficulties he identifies. Kretzmer set the required conditions to legalise targeted killings under a mixed model that incorporates both international humanitarian law and human rights law.[20] According to this model, first, targeted killings are rendered lawful only if required in order to protect potential victims of terrorist acts in cases of an imminent attack; second, the attack must be absolutely necessary, under the requirement of necessity and proportionality, i.e the state cannot use other measures; third, there must be credible evidence indicating active involvement in terrorist action by the intended target.[21]

3 Judicial Activism and Other Trends in Case Law

Kretzmer is one of the first academics, if not the earliest, whose research focused on the Court's turn of attitude towards its role later named 'judicial activism' – examining the specific changes in the Court's approach and their common denominator.[22] A considerable part of his work is dedicated to jurisprudential analysis, especially of the Supreme Court of Israel. Some of his outstanding skills have been expressed in his analysis. Kretzmer has been able to observe what only keen-eyed researchers are able to discover: with regards to decisions ordering the termination of office of ministers and deputy ministers charged with criminal offences, he noted that underneath the reference to the prime minister's decision not to dismiss them as unreasonable, there is a definite legal rule, shaped by the Court, instructing the termination of service when the charge relates to severe offences qualified with moral turpitude.

Should one diminish the annulment of a decision due to lack of reasonableness, only when it is possible to formulate a defined legal rule? When possible, one must prefer straightforward legal rules, allowing guidance and instruction. The harder question is: should one reduce unreasonableness only to such instances or allow the use of this cause even when

[20] David Kretzmer, 'Targeted Killing of Suspected Terrorists: Extra-Judicial Executions or Legitimate Means of Defence?' (2005) 16 European Journal of International Law 171, 202.

[21] Ibid 203–4.

[22] Ibid 323; Kretzmer, 'Judicial Review' (n 8) 120.

it is not based on the infringement of a specific rule? This is not the place to resolve these challenging questions, yet it seems that the answer depends on another inquiry: is the judiciary trustworthy enough to use the cause of unreasonableness (beyond violation of clear rules) in a restrained manner?

Kretzmer's analytical abilities are remarkable in disclosing and pointing out what is *not* said but still has a profound influence on Court rulings, even if it is hard to prove. These factors require an astute understanding and skill, which Kretzmer possesses. Kretzmer's suggested distinction between cases in which the Court tacitly considered the plaintiff to be an 'alien enemy' and cases in which the petitioner is perceived as a legitimate member of the community, can serve as an example. The Court's willingness to protect alien enemies is minimal, if not entirely absent. This is explained by a lack of a universal approach in these cases. Though Kretzmer states that it is a mere conjecture, it has been proven by him to be very telling.[23]

4 Kretzmer's Impact on the Court

Kretzmer's contribution is not only noticeable in academia; it has been widely used in the Supreme Court's jurisprudence.

The Court used Professor Kretzmer's view regarding the legality of the Israel–West Bank barrier, stating that the military commander's obligation to protect the lives of the civilian population continues to apply even if they are located inside Occupied Territories, and even if the approval of the creation of settlements is illegal. Former Chief Justice Barak based his opinion on Kretzmer's article 'The Advisory Opinion: The Light Treatment of International Humanitarian Law', where he analysed the opinion of the International Court of Justice.[24] In this article, Kretzmer criticises the narrowness of the Court's ruling that focuses only on two topics,[25] arguing it should have used this opportunity to state its opinion on other legal aspects of the Israeli-Palestinian conflict, which were, until this point, dealt with only domestically (for example,

23 Kretzmer, 'Fifty Years' (n 8) 325–6.

24 David Kretzmer, 'The Advisory Opinion: The Light Treatment of International Humanitarian Law' (2005) 99 American Journal of International Law 88, 93; HCJ 7957/04 *Mara'abe* v. *The Prime Minister of Israel* (2005) 60(2) PD 477, 15.

25 Kretzmer (n 24) 89. According to the article, the ICJ discussed two subjects: first, the Israeli settlements, and second, the seizure of land and destruction of property.

questions of IHL).[26] He points to the importance of such scrutiny, since until then it was only academia that had the opportunity to properly inspect these difficult subjects.[27] This narrowness is reflected in both the selection of topics, which Kretzmer reckons as too limited, and the superficial fashion of the review. Kretzmer finds the comprehensive conclusion of the Court, stating that IDF policy protecting the settlements does not amount to military necessity, as contradictive to 'fundamental notions of IHL'.[28] He further argues that the mere fact that citizens reside in Occupied Territories, in a seemingly contradictive manner to international law, does not affect the military commander's obligation to protect them. The Supreme Court accepted his view, ruling that the authority and obligation of the military commander to defend 'unprotected persons' in accordance with the Geneva Convention applies to all residents of the Occupied Territories, regardless of the legality of the settlements.[29]

In addition, the Court based its ruling in the Plonit case on Kretzmer's previous writing, which called for restraint in judicial review over the decisions of the Attorney General.[30] Such restraint is necessary in order to avoid establishing the Court as a 'super-prosecutor' or turning it into an appeals committee above the Attorney General and impairing in this way the separation of powers.[31] Kretzmer explained that judicial restraint is necessary since an intervention of the Court impairs the perception of due process in the eyes of defendants and negatively affects both functioning and objective appearance of 'courts of first instance'.[32]

Professor Kretzmer's opinions were of use to the Court in matters of freedom of speech and freedom of assembly, as reflected in the Wilk case, deciding on the right to protest near the home of a high-ranking police officer. In his article 'Demonstrations and the Law', Kretzmer stipulates

[26] For example, Kretzmer argues that the ICJ focus on these subjects does not explain *why* the violations committed by Israel in the West Bank result in the illegality of the entire barrier or segments of it. See ibid 100.

[27] ibid 88.

[28] ibid 93.

[29] *Mara'abe* (n 24) 12–14.

[30] HCJ 5699/07 (2008) *Plonit (A)* v. *The Attorney General* 62(3) PD 550 37; David Kretzmer, *Bikoret shiputit al hahlatot hayoetz hamishpati lamemshala* / 'Judicial Review of Attorney General's Prosecutorial Decisions' (1996) 5 Plilim 121, 136–7 (hereinafter: Kretzmer Attorney General); HCJ 2684/12 (2015) *Movement to Strengthen Tolerance in Religious Education et al.* v. *Attorney General*, 26–7.

[31] *Plonit* (n 30) 37.

[32] Kretzmer (n 30) 136.

that the right to protest is of constitutional status, regardless of the location of the demonstration – whether it is near the residence of a public figure or in front of his or her workplace – due to the affinity between its location and its effectiveness.[33] On the other hand, Kretzmer notes the right of privacy and its importance to public figures, suggesting that due to their stature, the right should be slightly less protected in relation to them. The Court adopted Kretzmer's reasoning, noting that even if freedom of speech and assembly prevail over the right of privacy, their scope of application is not unlimited. Thus, setting restrictions in the matter is permitted, according to a horizontal balance between freedom of assembly and speech and the right to privacy, resulting in the favouring of the first. However, the importance of the expressive rights cannot justify a limitless scope of application. Although the court certified the plaintiff's constitutional right, it did not rule in his favour in this specific case. In light of the plaintiff's refusal to limit the time and place of the demonstration, the Court ruled in favour of the respondent, affirming its refusal to approve the demonstration.[34]

5 Racial Incitement as a Criminal Offence

Kretzmer does not stop in front of the criminal law 'door'. In his writing on freedom of speech and incitement to racial discrimination, he dived into principles and doctrines of criminal law.[35] His article discusses these subjects in a wide yet thorough manner, with no stone left unturned. His analysis distinguished and separated substantive interests relevant to the protected values of the offence, and matters of legal policy. While the first part of the discussion concludes with a strong justification of the criminal prohibition, the second part is restrained and cautious with regards to the application of such prohibition. Kretzmer's article measures up to the best criminal law writings.

In this context, I wish to comment on a personal moment, which I consider emotional and exciting to this day, more than twenty years later. It involves a management meeting of the Association of Civil Rights in Israel (ACRI), which David was part of, not long after the

[33] David Kretzmer, 'Demonstrations and the Law' (1984) 19 Israel Law Review 47, 120.

[34] HCJ 2481/93 (1994) *Dayan* v. *Wilk* 48(2) PD 456, 25; AdminC(Jer) 4053/05 (2005) *Baruch Marzel* v. *State of Israel* 2002(2) 942, 954.

[35] David Kretzmer, 'Freedom of Speech and Racism' (1987) 8 Cardozo Law Review 445, 462.

assassination of Prime Minister Yitzhak Rabin. During the meeting, a participant spoke ill of 'religious people', classifying the group as a whole, and associated them with Yigal Amir. I will never forget David's sorrowful response, to the effect that by this generalisation all religious people were put on the same footing with the murderous Yigal Amir, who pretended to be a man of faith.

6 Kretzmer – an Activist and a World-Renowned Expert

Though Kretzmer's writing has addressed the most difficult problems of Israeli society, and by doing so contributed to the legal and public debate, David did not remain solely within the borders of academia. He took part in the establishment and development of the Minerva Center for Human Rights at the Hebrew University. Furthermore, David was a dedicated and influential participant in the public debate regarding the protection of human rights, particularly through his activity in ACRI and B'Tselem. He was active along with others in opening West Bank universities, which were closed by the military commander in the 1980s. In the early days of the First Intifada, Kretzmer collaborated with others to organize a 'sit in' that hosted students and professors, at the expense of everyday teaching, replacing it with debates over the military occupation and its consequences. It is important to mention that Kretzmer kept a strong distinction, often hard to maintain, between his academic career and public operation. In both cases, Kretzmer is known as one of the leading Israeli public scholars.

David earned his title as a globally recognised scholar and intellectual. A leading researcher in his field, he is invited to teach and work by the best academic institutions in the world. He was the first Israeli elected to the UN Human Rights Committee, which he was a member of for eight years, and served as the deputy chairman for two. If some criticism is in place, one could mention that Kretzmer is too humble. If he had not avoided public relations and self praise, he would have been granted even greater recognition and would have acquired the academic and public status he fully deserves.

We wish him good health and many more years of academic research and public activity for the protection of human rights.

DAVID KRETZMER: SELECTED PUBLICATIONS*

Books

The Law of Assault and Battery (Harry and Michael Sacher Institute for Legislative Research and Comparative Law 1981) (in Hebrew)

The Law of Nuisance (Harry and Michael Sacher Institute for Legislative Research and Comparative Law 1982) (in Hebrew)

The Legal Status of the Arabs in Israel (International Center for Peace in the Middle East 1987)

The Legal Status of the Arabs in Israel (Westview Press 1990)

The Legal Status of the Arabs in Israel (rev 2nd edn, Institute for Israeli Arab Studies 2002) (in Arabic)

The Occupation of Justice: The Supreme Court of Israel and the Occupied Territories (State University of New York Press 2002)

Books Co-Authored

David Kretzmer, Uriel Procaccia and Ariel L. Miller, *The Rights of the Disabled in Israel – Proposals for Reform* (Harry and Michael Sacher Institute for Legislative Research and Comparative Law 1979) (in Hebrew)

Avishai Benish, Mordechai Kremnitzer and David Kretzmer, *The Basic Laws as a Foundation for a Constitution* (Israel Democracy Institute 2002) (published also in Hebrew)

David Kretzmer and Yaël Ronen, *The Occupation of Justice: The Supreme Court of Israel and the Occupied Territories* (Oxford University Press 2021)

Books Edited

David Kretzmer and Eckart Klein (eds), *The Concept of Human Dignity in Human Rights Discourse* (Kluwer Law International 2002)

* The editors are grateful to Dr Yoel Kretzmer-Raziel for his assistance in compiling the list.

David Kretzmer and Francine Kershman Hazan (eds), *Freedom of Speech and Incitement against Democracy* (Martinus Nijhoff 2000)

Chapters in Books

'Manufacturer's Liability in Israel' in Stephen Goldstein (ed), *Israeli Reports to the Tenth International Congress of Comparative Law* (Harry and Michael Sacher Institute for Legislative Research and Comparative Law 1978)

'The Constitutional and Legal Status of Freedom of Speech in Israel' in Celia W. Fassberg (ed), *Israeli Reports to the XIII International Congress of Comparative Law* (Harry and Michael Sacher Institute for Legislative Research and Comparative Law 1990)

'The Influence of First Amendment Jurisprudence on Judicial Decision Making in Israel' in Shlomo Slonim (ed), *The Constitutional Bases of Political and Social Change in the United States* (Praeger 1990)

'Allocating Resources to Protect Demonstrations: The Israeli Approach' in David Schneiderman (ed), *Freedom of Expression and the Charter* (Carswell Legal Publications 1991)

'Judicial Review of Demolition and Sealing of Houses in the Occupied Territories' in Itzhak Zamir (ed), *Klinghoffer Book on Public Law* (Harry and Michael Sacher Institute for Legislative Research and Comparative Law 1993) (in Hebrew)

'Constitutional Law' in Amos Shapira and Keren C. DeWitt-Arar (eds), *Introduction to the Law of Israel* (Kluwer Law International 1995)

'Racial Incitement in Israel' in Monroe H. Freedman and Eric M. Freedman (eds), *Group Defamation and Freedom of Speech: The Relationship between Language and Violence* (Greenwood Press 1995)

'Domestic Politics, Law and the Peace Process: A View From Israel' in Eugene Cotran and Chibli Mallat (eds), *The Arab–Israeli Accords: Legal Perspectives* (Kluwer Law International 1996)

'Basic Laws as a Surrogate Bill of Rights: The Case of Israel' in Philip Alston (ed), *Promoting Human Rights through Bills of Rights: Comparative Perspectives* (Oxford University Press 1999)

'Israel's Basic Laws on Human Rights' in Alfredo Mordechai Raballo (ed), *Israeli Reports to the XV International Congress of Comparative Law* (Harry and Michael Sacher Institute for Legislative Research and Comparative Law 1999)

'The Duty to Protect and to Ensure Human Rights According to the Law of Israel' in Eckart Klein (ed), *The Duty to Protect and to Ensure Human Rights* (Berliner Wissenschafts-Verlag 2000)

'Foreword' in David Kretzmer and Francine Kershman Hazan (eds), *Freedom of Speech and Incitement against Democracy* (Kluwer Law International 2000)

Eckart Klein and David Kretzmer, 'Foreword' in David Kretzmer and Eckart Klein (eds), *The Concept of Human Dignity in Human Rights Discourse* (Kluwer Law International 2002)

'Human Dignity in Israeli Jurisprudence' in David Kretzmer and Eckart Klein (eds), *The Concept of Human Dignity in Human Rights Discourse* (Kluwer Law International 2002)

'A Jewish and Democratic State: Paradox and Harmony' in Eliezer Schweid and Naftali Rothenberg (eds), *Jewish Identity in Modern Israel* (Urim 2002)

'The Torture Debate: Israel and Beyond' in David Downes, Paul Rock, Christine Chinkin and Conor Gearty (eds), *Crime, Social Control and Human Rights: From Moral Panics to States of Denial: Essays in Honour of Stanley Cohen* (Willan 2007)

'Civilian Immunity in War: Legal Aspects' in Igor Primoratz (ed), *Civilian Immunity in War* (Oxford University Press 2007)

'International Law in Domestic Courts: Israel' in David Sloss (ed), *The Role of Domestic Courts in Treaty Enforcement: A Comparative Study* (Cambridge University Press 2009)

'Jurisprudence of Justice Barak Relating to the Occupied Territories' in Celia W. Fassberg, Barak Medina and Eyal Zamir (eds), *The Judicial Legacy of Aharon Barak* (Nevo 2009) (in Hebrew)

'International Law and the "War on Terror"' in Clemens N. Nathan (ed), *Current Issues in Human Rights and International Relations: Papers from the Clemens Nathan Research Centre* (Martinus Nijhoff 2010)

'Il caso Scalk e Kopf c. Austria in tema di unioni omosessuali' in Marta Cartabia (ed), *Dieci casi sui diritii in Europa* (il Mulino Itinerari 2011) 59.

'Use of Lethal Force against Suspected Terrorists' in Ana Maria Salinas De Friás, Katja L. H. Samuel and Nigel D. White (eds), *Counter-Terrorism: International Law and Practice* (Oxford University Press 2012)

'The Law of Belligerent Occupation as a System of Control: Dressing up Exploitation in Respectable Garb' in Daniel Bar-Tal and Izhak Schnell (eds), *The Impacts of Lasting Occupation: Lessons from Israeli Society* (Oxford University Press 2013)

'The Law of Belligerent Occupation as a System of Control: Dressing up Exploitation in Respectable Garb' in Daniel Bar-Tal and Izhak Schnell (eds), *The Impacts of Lasting Occupation: Lessons from Israeli Society* (Israeli Association for Political Science 2013)

'The Legal Regime Governing the Use of Lethal Force in the Fight against Terrorism' in Larissa van den Herik and Nico Schrijver (eds), *Counter-Terrorism Strategies in a Fragmented International Legal Order: Meeting the Challenges* (Cambridge University Press 2013)

'Terrorism and the International Law of Occupation' in Ben Saul (ed), *Research Handbook on International Law and Terrorism* (Edward Elgar 2014)

David Kretzmer and Micheline Ishay, 'Reclaiming Human Rights: An Alternative Approach to the Israel-Palestine Conflict' in John Ehrenberg and Yoav Peled (eds), *Israel and Palestine: Alternative Perspectives on Statehood* (Rowman & Littlefield 2016)

David Kretzmer and Yaniv Lushinsky, 'LGBTQ Rights in International Law' in Einav H. Morgenstern, Yaniv Lushinsky and Alon Harel (eds), *LGBTQ Rights in Israel: Gender Identity, Sexual Orientation and the Law* (Nevo 2016)

'The Right to Life in the Eyes of the Human Rights Committee' in Gabriela Pacheco, Oscar Parra Vera and Romina Sijniensky (eds), *La lucha por los derechos humanos hoy / The Battle for Human Rights Today: Essays in Honour of Cecilia Medina Quiroga* (2017) 81.

'US Extra-Territorial Actions against Individuals: Bin Laden, Al Awlaki, and Abu Khattalah – 2011 and 2014' in Tom Ruys, Olivier Corten and Alexandra Hofer (eds), *The Use of Force in International Law: A Case-Based Approach* (Oxford University Press 2018)

'Terrorism and the International Law of Occupation' in Ben Saul (ed), *Research Handbook on International Law and Terrorism* (2nd edn, Edward Elgar 2020)

Journal Articles

'The Acquiring of Equitable Title' (1969) 4 Israel Law Review 452

'The Standard Contracts Law, 1964, in Light of Its Amendment' (1969) 3 Mishpatim 414 (in Hebrew)

'The Malpractice Suit: Is It Needed?' (1973) 11 Osgoode Hall Law Journal 55

'No-Fault Comes to Israel: The Compensation for Victims of Road-Accidents Law' (1976) 11 Israel Law Review 288

'Judicial Discretion and the Consequences of Breach of Contract' (1977) 8 Mishpatim 138 (in Hebrew)

David Kretzmer and Pnina Lahav, 'Who's Afraid of Absolute Rights? A Reply to Dr Shilo' (1977) 7 Mishpatim 541 (in Hebrew)

'Judicial Conservatism v. Economic Liberalism: Anatomy of a Nuisance Case' (1978) 13 Israel Law Review 298

'Rescission for Delay in Performance' (1978) 13 Israel Law Review 264

David Kretzmer and E. D. Richter, 'Prevention through Pre-Review in Occupational Health and Safety' (1980) 70 American Journal of Public Health 157

'Demonstrations and the Law' (1984) 19 Israel Law Review 47

'Transformation of Tort Liability in the Nineteenth Century: The Visible Hand' (1984) 4 Oxford Journal of Legal Studies 46

'Intent in Criminal Libel: Statutory Interpretation or Judicial Imagination?' (1986) 21 Israel Law Review 591

'Freedom of Speech and Racism' (1987) 8 Cardozo Law Review 445
'Judicial Review of Knesset Decisions' (1988) 8 Tel Aviv University Studies in Law 95
'The Constitutional Debate in Israel' (1990) 1 Constitutional Forum 13
'Forty Years of Public Law' (1990) 24 Israel Law Review 341
David Kretzmer and Itzhak Zamir, '40 Years of Law in the State of Israel: Public Law' (1990) 19 Mishpatim 551
'The New Basic Laws on Human Rights: A Mini-Revolution in Israeli Constitutional Law?' (1992) 26 Israel Law Review 238
'Political Agreements – A Critical Introduction' (1992) 26 Israel Law Review 407
'Racial Incitement in Israel' (1993) 22 Israel Yearbook on Human Rights 243
'The Application and Interpretation of Geneva Convention IV – Domestic Enforcement and Interpretation' (1995) 26 Mishpatim 49
'Les Droits de L'Homme en Israel' (1995) 72 Pouvoirs 35
'The Supreme Court and the Fourth Geneva Convention: Domestic Enforcement and Interpretation' (1995) 26 Mishpatim 49 (in Hebrew)
'Democracy in the Jurisprudence of the Supreme Court of Israel' (1996) 26 Israel Yearbook on Human Rights 267
'Judicial Review of Attorney General's Prosecutorial Decisions' (1996) 5 Plilim 121
'The New Basic Laws on Human Rights: A Mini-Revolution in Israeli Constitutional Law?' (1996) 14 Netherlands Quarterly of Human Rights 173
'The Path to Judicial Review in Human Rights Cases: From Bergman and Kol Ha'am to Mizrahi Bank' (1997) 28 Mishpatim 359 (in Hebrew)
'Fifty Years of Public Law in the Supreme Court – Human Rights' (1999) 5 Mishpat Umimshal 297
'The Supreme Court of Israel: Judicial Review over Hostilities during Armed Conflict' (2004) 47 German Yearbook of International Law 392
'The Advisory Opinion: The Light Treatment of International Humanitarian Law' (2005) 99 American Journal of International Law 88
'Introduction: Special Double Issue: Domestic and International Judicial Review of the Construction of the Separation Barrier' (2005) 38 Israel Law Review 6
'Targeted Killing of Suspected Terrorists: Extra-Judicial Executions or Legitimate Means of Defence?' (2005) 16 European Journal of International Law 171
'Presidential Elements in Government Experimenting with Constitutional Change: Direct Election of the Prime Minister in Israel' (2006) 2 European Constitutional Law Review 60
David Kretzmer, Rotem Giladi and Yuval Shany, 'International Humanitarian Law and International Human Rights Law: Exploring Parallel Application' (2007) 40 Israel Law Review 306
'Rethinking the Application of International Humanitarian Law in Non-International Armed Conflicts' (2009) 42 Israel Law Review 8

'The Law of Belligerent Occupation in the Supreme Court of Israel' (2012) 94 International Review of the Red Cross 207

'The Inherent Right to Self-Defence and Proportionality in *Jus ad Bellum*' (2013) 24 European Journal of International Law 235

David Kretzmer, Aviad Ben-Yehuda and Meirav Furth, '"Thou Shall Not Kill": The Use of Lethal Force in Non-International Armed Conflicts' (2014) 47 Israel Law Review 191

David Kretzmer and Eckart Klein, 'The Human Rights Committee: Monitoring States Parties' Reports' (2015) 45 Israel Yearbook on Human Rights 133

David Kretzmer and Eckart Klein, 'The UN Human Rights Committee: The General Comments – The Evolution of an Autonomous Monitoring Instrument' (2015) 58 German Yearbook of International Law 189

David Kretzmer and Gershom Gorenberg, 'Politics, Law and the Judicial Process: The Case of the High Court of Justice and the Territories' (2016) 17 Mishpat Umimshal 249

David Kretzmer, 'Symposium on Revisiting Israel's Settlements: Settlements in the Supreme Court of Israel' (2017) 111 American Journal of International Law Unbound 41

Encyclopedia Entries

'States of Emergency', *Max Planck Institute Encyclopedia of Public International Law* (Oxford University Press, last updated 1 February 2008)

'Human Rights: States' Reports', *Max Planck Institute Encyclopedia of Public International Law* (Oxford University Press, last updated 1 October 2008)

'West Bank and Gaza' in David P. Forsythe (ed), *Encyclopedia of Human Rights* (Oxford University Press 2009)

'Israeli Supreme Court and the Occupation', *Encyclopedia of the Israeli-Palestinian Conflict* vol 2 (Lynn Rienner 2010)

'Torture, Prohibition of', *Max Planck Institute Encyclopedia of Public International Law* 880 (Oxford University Press, last updated December 2010)

'Unlawful Combatants', *Encyclopedia of War* (Wiley-Blackwell, last updated 13 November 2011)

Book Reviews

'Book Review of *The Costs of Accidents: A Legal and Economic Analysis*, by Guido Calabresi' (1974) 9 Israel Law Review 148

'Book Review of *Autonomy: Flexible Solutions to Ethnic Conflicts*, by Ruth Lapidot' (2000) 34 Israel Law Review 134

INDEX